Slackware Linux
Installation and Getting Started

Version 2.2.2, 11 February 1995.
Version 3.0 by Walnut Creek CDROM based on Version 2.2.2 by Matt Welsh
Updated November 1996
This book is an installation and new-user guide for the Slackware Linux system, meant for UNIX novices and gurus alike. Contained herein is information on how to obtain Linux, installation of the software, a beginning tutorial for new UNIX users, and an introduction to system administration. It is meant to be general enough to be applicable to any distribution of the Linux software.

Quick Start your Slackware Linux installation with the included CD-ROM by jumping directly to chapter 2 to get started.

Contents

Preface   **xiii**

    Audience xiv

    Organization xiv

    Acknowledgments xv

    Acknowledgments for Version 3.0 xvi

    Credits and Legalese xvi

    Documentation Conventions xix

1   Introduction to Slackware Linux   **1**

    1.1   About This Book 2

    1.2   A Brief History of Linux 3

    1.3   System Features 5

    1.4   Software Features 7

          1.4.1   Basic commands and utilities 7

          1.4.2   Text processing and word processing 9

          1.4.3   Programming languages and utilities 12

          1.4.4   The X Window System 13

          1.4.5   Networking 15

          1.4.6   Telecommunications and BBS software 16

          1.4.7   Interfacing with MS-DOS 18

1.4.8 Other applications 19

1.5 About Linux's Copyright 20

1.6 The Design and Philosophy of Linux 22

    1.6.1 Hints for UNIX novices 24

    1.6.2 Hints for UNIX gurus 25

1.7 Differences Between Linux and Other Operating Systems 26

    1.7.1 Why use Linux? 26

    1.7.2 Linux vs. MS-DOS 27

    1.7.3 Linux vs. The Other Guys 28

    1.7.4 Other implementations of UNIX 29

1.8 Hardware Requirements 31

    1.8.1 Motherboard and CPU requirements 32

    1.8.2 Memory requirements 32

    1.8.3 Hard drive and SCSI controller requirements 32

    1.8.4 Hard drive space requirements 34

    1.8.5 Monitor and video adaptor requirements 34

    1.8.6 Miscellaneous hardware 35

    1.8.7 Ethernet cards 38

    1.8.8 Sound cards 39

    1.8.9 ISDN support 40

    1.8.10 Non-intelligent multiport serial cards 40

    1.8.11 Intelligent multiport serial cards 41

1.9 Sources of Linux Information 41

    1.9.1 Online documents 41

    1.9.2 Linux on the World Wide Web 42

    1.9.3 Books and other published works 43

    1.9.4 USENET newsgroups 43

    1.9.5 Internet mailing lists 46

1.10 Getting Help 46

2 Installing Slackware Linux   **51**

2.1 Sources of documentation 51

2.2 Hardware requirements 52

2.3 Slackware space requirements 53

    2.3.1 Creating the installation floppies 55

    2.3.2 Boot disc description 56

2.4 Preparing a partition for Slackware 63

2.5 Using Linux fdisk to create a Linux partition 64

    2.5.1 Floppyless Installation 65

    2.5.2 Creating Linux partitions 65

2.6 Installing the Slackware distribution 68

    2.6.1 Setup was not successful accessing your CDROM drive. . . . 71

    2.6.2 Installing Slackware from MS-DOS 73

    2.6.3 LILO - Linux loader 76

    2.6.4 Networking 78

2.7 Booting the installed Slackware system 78

2.8 Post-installation configuration 79

    2.8.1 User accounts 79

    2.8.2 Securing your machine 80

2.9 Installing Slackware Linux with other operating systems. 81

    2.9.1 Installing Linux with OS/2 and DOS on the same disk. . . . 81

    2.9.2 Installing Linux with Windows 95 and Windows 3.1 on the same disk. 87

3 Slackware Linux Tutorial   **95**

3.1 Introduction 95

3.2 Basic UNIX Concepts 96

3.2.1	Creating an account	96
3.2.2	Logging in	97
3.2.3	Virtual consoles	97
3.2.4	Shells and commands	98
3.2.5	Logging out	99
3.2.6	Changing your password	100
3.2.7	Files and directories	100
3.2.8	The directory tree	101
3.2.9	The current working directory	101
3.2.10	Referring to home directories	102
3.3	First Steps into UNIX	103
3.3.1	Moving around	103
3.3.2	Looking at the contents of directories	104
3.3.3	Creating new directories	106
3.3.4	Copying files	107
3.3.5	Moving files	107
3.3.6	Deleting files and directories	108
3.3.7	Looking at files	108
3.3.8	Getting online help	109
3.4	Summary of Basic Commands	109
3.5	Exploring the File System	112
3.6	Types of shells	117
3.7	Wildcards	118
3.8	UNIX Plumbing	121
3.8.1	Standard input and output	121
3.8.2	Redirecting input and output	122
3.8.3	Using pipes	123
3.8.4	Non-destructive redirection	125

3.9   File Permissions 125

    3.9.1   Concepts of file permissions 125

    3.9.2   Interpreting file permissions 126

    3.9.3   Dependencies 128

    3.9.4   Changing permissions 128

3.10 Managing file links 129

    3.10.1 Hard links 129

    3.10.2 Symbolic links 130

3.11 Job Control 131

    3.11.1 Jobs and processes 131

    3.11.2 Foreground and background 132

    3.11.3 Backgrounding and killing jobs 133

    3.11.4 Stopping and restarting jobs 135

3.12 Using the vi Editor 138

    3.12.1 Concepts 138

    3.12.2 Starting vi 139

    3.12.3 Inserting text 139

    3.12.4 Deleting text 141

    3.12.5 Changing text 142

    3.12.6 Moving commands 143

    3.12.7 Saving files and quitting vi 144

    3.12.8 Editing another file 144

    3.12.9 Including other files 145

    3.12.10 Running shell commands 145

    3.12.11 Getting help 146

3.13 Customizing your Environment 146

    3.13.1 Shell scripts 147

    3.13.2 Shell variables and the environment 148

3.13.3 Shell initialization scripts 152

3.14 So You Want to Strike Out on Your Own? 153

4 System Administration   **155**

4.1 About Root, Hats, and the Feeling of Power 155

    4.1.1 The `root` account 156

    4.1.2 Abusing the system 157

    4.1.3 Dealing with users 158

    4.1.4 Setting the rules 159

    4.1.5 What it all means 159

4.2 Booting the System 160

    4.2.1 Using a boot floppy 160

    4.2.2 Using LILO 161

4.3 Shutting Down 162

4.4 Managing Users 163

    4.4.1 User management concepts 163

    4.4.2 Adding users 165

    4.4.3 Disabling users 165

    4.4.4 Setting user attributes 165

    4.4.5 Groups 166

4.5 Archiving and Compressing Files 167

    4.5.1 Using `tar` 167

    4.5.2 `gzip` and `compress` 168

    4.5.3 Putting them together 169

4.6 Using Floppies and Making Backups 170

    4.6.1 Using floppies for backups 171

    4.6.2 Using floppies as filesystems 171

4.7 Upgrading and Installing New Software 172

    4.7.1 Upgrading the kernel 173

4.7.2   Upgrading the libraries 175

4.7.3   Upgrading gcc 176

4.7.4   Upgrading other software 176

4.8   Managing Filesystems 177

4.8.1   Mounting filesystems 177

4.8.2   Checking filesystems 179

4.9   Using a swap file 180

4.10 Miscellaneous Tasks 182

4.10.1 System startup files 182

4.10.2 Setting the hostname 182

4.11 What To Do In An Emergency 184

4.11.1 Recovering using a maintenance diskette 184

4.11.2 Fixing the root password 185

4.11.3 Fixing trashed filesystems 185

4.11.4 Recovering lost files 186

4.11.5 Fixing trashed libraries 186

5 Advanced Features   187

5.1   The X Window System 187

5.1.1   Hardware requirements 188

5.1.2   Installing XFree86 191

5.1.3   Configuring XFree86 193

5.1.4   Filling in video card information 202

5.1.5   Running XFree86 207

5.1.6   Running into trouble 208

5.2   Accessing MS-DOS Files 209

5.3   Networking with TCP/IP 210

5.3.1   Hardware Requirements 211

5.3.2   Configuring TCP/IP on your system 211

	5.3.3	SLIP Configuration	220
	5.3.4	Using `dip`	223
5.4	Networking with UUCP		226
5.5	Electronic Mail		227
5.6	News and USENET		227

6 Installing Linux PPP   **231**

6.1	Introduction		231
	6.1.1	Clients and Servers	232
	6.1.2	Differences between Linux distributions	233
6.2	IP Numbers		234
6.3	Aim of this Document		236
	6.3.1	Setting up a PPP Client	236
	6.3.2	Setting up a PPP server	236
	6.3.3	Linking two LANs or a LAN to the Internet using PPP	237
	6.3.4	This document at present does NOT cover...	237
6.4	Software versions covered		237
6.5	Other Useful/Important Documents		238
	6.5.1	Useful Linux Mailing Lists	239
6.6	Configuring your Linux Kernel		239
	6.6.1	Installing the Linux Kernel source	239
	6.6.2	Knowing your hardware	240
	6.6.3	Kernel compilation - the Linux 1.2.13 kernel	240
	6.6.4	Kernel compilation - the Linux 1.3.x and 2.0.x kernels	241
	6.6.5	General kernel config considerations	242
6.7	Getting the Information you need about the PPP service		243
	6.7.1	Testing your Modem Connection for outgoing calls	243
6.8	A note about serial ports and speed capabilities		245
6.9	Configuring your modem		245

    6.9.1   Note on Serial Flow Control 247

6.10 Using PPP and root privileges 247

6.11 Setting up the PPP connection files 248

    6.11.1 The supplied options.tpl file 250

    6.11.2 What options should I use? 257

6.12 Setting up your /etc/resolv.conf file 259

6.13 The PAP/CHAP secrets file 260

    6.13.1 The PAP secrets file 261

    6.13.2 The CHAP secrets file 262

6.14 Setting up the PPP connection manually 262

6.15 Automating your connections - Creating the connection scripts . . . 266

    6.15.1 Connection scripts for Username/Password Authentication . 266

    6.15.2 The ppp-on script 267

    6.15.3 Editing the supplied PPP startup scripts 268

    6.15.4 What a Chat script means... 271

    6.15.5 A chat script for PAP/CHAP authenticated connections . . . 272

    6.15.6 The pppd debug and -f option_ file options 273

6.16 Testing your connection script 273

6.17 Shutting down the PPP link 277

6.18 Debugging 278

    6.18.1 I compiled in PPP but Linux says I don't have it! 278

    6.18.2 I cannot set up a default route 279

6.19 Linking two networks using PPP 279

    6.19.1 Setting up IP numbers 280

    6.19.2 Setting up the routing 280

    6.19.3 Network security 280

6.20 After the link comes up... 281

    6.20.1 Special routing 281

6.20.2 Handling email 283

6.21 Shutting down the link 284

6.22 Routing issues on a LAN 285

6.22.1 Note on Security 286

6.23 Getting Help when totally stuck 287

6.24 Common Problems once the link is working 287

6.24.1 I can't see beyond the PPP server I connect to 287

6.24.2 I can send email, but not receive it 288

6.24.3 Why can't people finger, WWW, gopher, talk etc to my machine? 288

6.25 Using Internet services with Dynamic IP numbers 289

6.25.1 Setting up email 289

6.25.2 Setting Up a local Name server 290

6.26 Setting up a PPP server 291

6.26.1 Kernel compilation 291

6.26.2 Overview of the server system 291

6.26.3 Getting the software together 292

6.26.4 Setting up standard (shell access) dialup. 293

6.26.5 Setting up the PPP options files 293

6.26.6 Setting pppd up to allow users to (successfully) run it 294

6.26.7 Setting up the global alias for pppd 294

6.27 Using PPP across a null modem (direct serial) connection 295

A Sources of Linux Information   297

A.1 Online Documents 297

A.2 Linux Documentation Project Manuals 300

A.3 Books and Other Published Works 301

A.3.1 Using UNIX 301

A.3.2 Systems Administration 302

A.3.3 The X Window System 303

A.3.4 Programming 304

A.3.5 Kernel Hacking 304

B FTP Tutorial and Site List   **307**

B.1 Starting `ftp` 308

B.2 Logging In 308

B.3 Poking Around 309

B.4 Downloading files 311

B.5 Quitting FTP 313

B.6 Using `ftpmail` 313

B.7 Linux FTP Site List 314

C Linux BBS List   **317**

C.1 United States 317

C.2 Outside of the United States 320

D The GNU General Public License   **323**

D.1 Preamble 323

D.2 Terms and Conditions for Copying, Distribution, and Modification . 325

D.3 Appendix: How to Apply These Terms to Your New Programs . . . 330

Preface

"You are in a maze of twisty little passages, all alike."

Before you looms one of the most complex and utterly intimidating systems ever written. Linux, the free UNIX clone for the personal computer, produced by a mishmash team of UNIX gurus, hackers, and the occasional loon. The system itself reflects this complex heritage, and although the development of Linux may appear to be a disorganized volunteer effort, the system is powerful, fast, and free. It is a true 32-bit operating system solution.

My own experiences with Linux began several years ago, when I sat down to figure out how to install the only "distribution" available at the time—a couple of diskettes made available by H.J. Lu. I downloaded a slew of files and read pages upon pages of loosely-organized installation notes. Somehow, I managed to install this basic system and get everything working together. This was long before you could buy the Linux software on CD-ROM from worldwide distributors; before, in fact, Linux even knew how to access a CD-ROM drive. This was before XFree86, before Emacs, before commercial software support, and before Linux became a true rival to MS-DOS, Microsoft Windows, and OS/2 in the personal computer market.

You hold in your very hands the map and guidebook to the world of Linux. It is my hope that this book will help you to get rolling with what I consider to be the fastest, most powerful operating system for the personal computer. Setting up your own Linux system can be a great deal of fun—so grab a cup of coffee, sit back, and read on.

Grab a cup for me, too, while you're at it. I've been up hacking Linux for days.

Audience

This book is for any personal computer user who wants to install and use Slackware Linux on their system. We assume that you have basic knowledge about personal computers and operating systems such as MS-DOS. No previous knowledge about Linux or UNIX is assumed.

Despite this, we strongly suggest that UNIX novices invest in one of the many good UNIX books out there. Several of them are listed in Appendix A.

Organization

This book contains the following chapters.

Chapter 1, *Introduction to Slackware Linux*, gives a general introduction to what Linux is, what it can do for you, and what is required to run it on your system. It also provides helpful hints for getting help and reducing overall stress.

Chapter 2, *Obtaining and Installing Slackware Linux*, explains how to obtain the Slackware Linux software, as well as how to install it—from repartitioning your drive, creating filesystems, and loading the software on the system. It contains instructions meant to be general for any distribution of Linux, and relies on the documentation provided for your particular release to fill in any gaps.

Chapter 3, *Slackware Linux Tutorial*, is a complete introduction to using the Slackware Linux system for UNIX novices. If you have previous UNIX experience, most of this material should be familiar.

Chapter 4, *System Administration*, introduces many of the important concepts of system administration under Slackware Linux. This will also be of interest to UNIX system administrators who want to know about the Slackware Linux-specific issues of running a system.

Chapter 5, *Advanced Features*, introduces the reader to a number of advanced features supported by Slackware Linux, such as the X Window System and TCP/IP networking. A complete guide to configuring XFree86-3.1 is included.

Chapter 6, *Installing Linux PPP*, a guide to helping you install PPP under Linux. Special thanks to Robert Hart for this chapter.

Appendix A, *Sources of Linux Information*, is a listing of other sources of information about Slackware Linux, including newsgroups, mailing lists, online documents, and books.

Appendix B, *FTP Tutorial and Site List*, is a tutorial for downloading files from the Internet with FTP. This appendix also includes a listing of FTP archive sites which carry Linux software.

Appendix C, *Linux BBS List*, is a listing of bulletin board systems worldwide which carry Linux software. Because most Linux users are do not have access to the Internet, it is important that information on BBS systems becomes available.

Appendix D, *The GNU General Public License*, contains a copy of the GNU GPL, the license agreement under which Linux is distributed. It is very important that Linux users understand the GPL; many disagreements over the terms of the GPL have been raised in recent months.

Acknowledgments

This book has been long in the making, and many people are responsible for the outcome. In particular, I would like to thank Larry Greenfield and Karl Fogel for their work on the first version of Chapter 3, and to Lars Wirzenius for his work on Chapter 4. Thanks to Michael K. Johnson for his assistance with the LDP and the LaTeX conventions used in this manual, and to Ed Chi, who sent me a printed copy of the book for edition.

Thanks to Melinda A. McBride at SSC, Inc., who did an excellent job completing the index for Chapters 3, 4, and 5. I would also like to thank Andy Oram, Lar Kaufman, and Bill Hahn at O'Reilly and Associates for their assistance with the Linux Documentation Project.

Thanks to Linux Systems Labs, Morse Telecommunications, Yggdrasil Computing, and others for their support of the Linux Documentation Project through sales of this book and other works.

Much thanks to the many activists, including (in no particular order) Linus Torvalds, Donald Becker, Alan Cox, Remy Card, Ted T'so, H.J. Lu, Ross Biro, Drew Eckhardt, Ed Carp, Eric Youngdale, Fred van Kempen, Steven Tweedie, and a score of others, for devoting so much time and energy to this project, and without whom there wouldn't be anything to write a book about.

Special thanks to the myriad of readers who have sent their helpful comments and corrections. There are far too many to list here. Who needs a spell checker, when you have an audience?

Matt Welsh

13 January 1994

Acknowledgments for Version 3.0

Published in September 1996 by Walnut Creek CDROM
4041 Pike Lane Suite D
Concord, California
94520
Orders Toll-free: 1-800-786-9907
Orders: 510 674-0783
Fax: 510 674-0821
Electronic Mail: info@cdrom.com
WWW: http://www.cdrom.com

Executive Editor: Jack Velte
Assistant Editor: Jamil Weatherbee, David Chen
Additional Editing and LATEX layout: Eric "E.T." Tremblay
(ericet@cam.org, eric@cdrom.com)
Published Cover Design: Ellen Hsu

Special Thanks to:

Matt Welsh for the original version of this book.
Robert Hart for the Linux PPP HOWTO
Hamish Moffatt for the Linux + OS/2 (+DOS) mini-HOWTO
Robert Goodwin for the Windows 95 + Windows 3.x + Linux HOWTO

Credits and Legalese

The Linux Documentation Project is a loose team of writers, proofreaders, and editors who are working on a set of definitive Linux manuals. The overall coordinator of the project is Matt Welsh, aided by Lars Wirzenius and Michael K. Johnson.

This manual is but one in a set of several being distributed by the Linux Documentation Project, including a Linux User's Guide, System Administrator's Guide, and Kernel Hacker's Guide. These manuals are all available in LATEX source format

and Postscript output for anonymous FTP from `sunsite.unc.edu`, in the directory
`/pub/Linux/docs/LDP`.

We encourage anyone with a penchant for writing or editing to join us in improving Linux documentation. If you have Internet e-mail access, you can join the
`DOC` channel of the `Linux-Activists` mailing list by sending mail to

```
linux-activists-request@niksula.hut.fi
```

with the line

```
X-Mn-Admin:   join DOC
```

as the first line of the message body.

Feel free to get in touch with the author and coordinator of this manual if you
have questions, postcards, money, or ideas. Matt Welsh can be reached via Internet
e-mail at `mdw@sunsite.unc.edu`.

UNIX is a trademark of X/Open.

Linux is not a trademark, and has no connection to UNIX™ or X/Open.

The X Window System is a trademark of the Massachusetts Institute of Technology.

MS-DOS and Microsoft Windows are trademarks of Microsoft, Inc.

Exceptions to these rules may be granted for academic purposes: Write to Matt Welsh, at the above address, or email `mdw@sunsite.unc.edu`, and ask. These restrictions are here to protect us as authors, not to restrict you as educators and learners.

The author encourages distributors of Linux software in any medium to use the book as an installation and new user guide. Given the copyright above, you are free to print and distribute copies of this book with your software. You may either distribute this book free of charge, or for profit. If doing so, you may wish to include a short "installation supplement" for your release.

The author would like to know of any plans to publish and distribute this book commercially. In this way, we can ensure that you are kept up-to-date with new revisions. And, should a new version be right around the corner, you might wish to delay your publication of the book until it is available.

If you are distributing this book commercially, donations, royalties, and/or printed copies are greatly appreciated by the author. Contributing in this way shows your support for free software and the Linux Documentation Project.

All source code in *Linux Installation and Getting Started* is placed under the GNU General Public License. See Appendix D for a copy of the GNU "GPL."

Documentation Conventions

These conventions should be obvious, but we'll include them here for the pedantic.

Bold   Used to mark **new concepts**, **WARNINGS**, and **keywords** in a language.

italics   Used for *emphasis* in text, and occasionally for quotes or introductions at the beginning of a section. Also used to indicate commands for the user to type when showing screen interaction (see below).

⟨*slanted*⟩   Used to mark **meta-variables** in the text, especially in representations of the command line. For example,

ls -l ⟨*foo*⟩

where ⟨*foo*⟩ would "stand for" a filename, such as `/bin/cp`.

Typewriter   Used to represent screen interaction, as in

```
$ ls -l /bin/cp

-rwxr-xr-x  1 root     wheel     12104 Sep 25 15:53 /bin/cp
```

Also used for code examples, whether it is C code, a shell script, or
something else, and to display general files, such as configuration
files. When necessary for clarity's sake, these examples or figures
will be enclosed in thin boxes.

Key   Represents a key to press. You will often see it in this form:

Press return to continue.

◇   A diamond in the margin, like a black diamond on a ski hill, marks
"danger" or "caution." Read paragraphs marked this way carefully.

Chapter 1

Introduction to Slackware Linux

Linux is quite possibly the most important achievement of free software since the original *Space War*, or, more recently, Emacs. It has developed into the operating system for businesses, education, and personal productivity. Linux is no longer just for UNIX wizards who sit for hours in front of the glowing console (although we assure you that quite a number of users fall into this category). This book will help you get the most out of it.

Linux (pronounced with a short *i*, as in *LIH-nucks*) is a clone of the UNIX operating system that runs on Intel 80x86 and compatible, SPARC, m68k, PowerPC and DEC Alpha computers. It supports a wide range of software, from TeX to X Windows to the GNU C/C++ compiler to TCP/IP. It's a versatile, bona fide implementation of UNIX, freely distributed by the terms of the GNU General Public License (see Appendix D).

Linux can turn any PC into a workstation. It will give you the full power of UNIX at your fingertips. Businesses are installing Linux on entire networks of machines, using the operating system to manage financial and hospital records, a distributed user computing environment, telecommunications, and more. Universities worldwide are using Linux for teaching courses on operating systems programming and design. And, of course, computing enthusiasts everywhere are using Linux at home, for programming, productivity, and all-around hacking.

What makes Linux so different is that it is a *free* implementation of UNIX. It was

1

and still is developed by a group of volunteers, primarily on the Internet, exchanging code, reporting bugs, and fixing problems in an open-ended environment. Anyone is welcome to join in the Linux development effort: all it takes is interest in hacking a free UNIX clone and some kind of programming know-how. The book that you hold in your hands is your tour guide.

1.1   About This Book

This book is an installation and entry-level guide to the Linux system. The purpose is to get new users up and running with the system by consolidating as much important material as possible into one book. Instead of covering many of the volatile technical details, those things which tend to change with rapid development, we give you enough background to find out more on your own.

Linux is not difficult to install and use. However, as with any implementation of UNIX, there is often some black magic involved to get everything working correctly. We hope that this book will get you on the Linux tour bus and show you how groovy this operating system can be.

In this book, we cover the following topics.

- What is Linux? The design and philosophy of this unique operating system, and what it can do for you.

- All of the details of what is needed to run Linux, including suggestions on what kind of hardware configuration is recommended for a complete system.

  This edition also contains specific instructions for the Slackware distribution of Linux.

- A brief introductory UNIX tutorial, for those users who have never had experience with UNIX before. This tutorial should, hopefully, provide enough material for complete novices to have enough basic know-how to find their way around the system.

- An introduction to systems administration with Linux. This covers the most important tasks that new Linux administrators will need to be familiar with, such as creating users, managing filesystems, and so forth.

- Information on configuring more advanced aspects of Linux, such as the X Window System, networking with TCP/IP and SLIP, and the setup of electronic mail and news systems.

This book is for the personal computer user wishing to get started with Linux. We don't assume previous UNIX experience, but do expect novices to refer to other materials along the way. For those unfamiliar with UNIX, a list of useful sources of information is given in Appendix A. In general, this book is meant to be read along with another book on basic UNIX concepts.

1.2   A Brief History of Linux

UNIX is one of the most popular operating systems worldwide because of its large support base and distribution. It was originally developed as a multitasking system for minicomputers and mainframes in the mid-1970's, but has since grown to become one of the most widely used operating systems anywhere, despite its sometimes confusing interface and lack of central standardization.

The real reason for UNIX's popularity? Many hackers feel that UNIX is the Right Thing—the One True Operating System. Hence, the development of Linux by an expanding group of UNIX hackers who want to get their hands dirty with their own system.

Versions of UNIX exist for many systems—ranging from personal computers to supercomputers such as the Cray Y-MP. Most versions of UNIX for personal computers are quite expensive and cumbersome. At the time of this writing, a one-machine version of AT&T's System V for the 386 runs at about US$1500.

Linux is a freely distributable version of UNIX developed primarily by Linus Torvalds at the University of Helsinki in Finland. Linux was developed with the help of many UNIX programmers and wizards across the Internet, allowing anyone with enough know-how and gumption the ability to develop and change the system. The Linux kernel uses no code from AT&T or any other proprietary source, and much of the software available for Linux is developed by the GNU project at the Free Software Foundation in Cambridge, Massachusetts. However, programmers all over the world have contributed to the growing pool of Linux software.

Linux was originally developed as a hobby project by Linus Torvalds. It was inspired by Minix, a small UNIX system developed by Andy Tanenbaum, and the first discussions about Linux were on the USENET newsgroup `comp.os.minix`. These discussions were concerned mostly with the development of a small, academic UNIX system for Minix users who wanted more.

The very early development of Linux was mostly dealing with the task-switching features of the 80386 protected-mode interface, all written in assembly code. Linus writes,

> "After that it was plain sailing: hairy coding still, but I had some
> devices, and debugging was easier. I started using C at this stage, and it
> certainly speeds up development. This is also when I start to get serious
> about my megalomaniac ideas to make 'a better Minix than Minix'. I
> was hoping I'd be able to recompile `gcc` under Linux some day. . .
>
> "Two months for basic setup, but then only slightly longer until I had
> a disk-driver (seriously buggy, but it happened to work on my machine)
> and a small filesystem. That was about when I made 0.01 available
> [around late August of 1991]: it wasn't pretty, it had no floppy driver,
> and it couldn't do much anything. I don't think anybody ever compiled
> that version. But by then I was hooked, and didn't want to stop until I
> could chuck out Minix."

No announcement was ever made for Linux version 0.01. The 0.01 sources
weren't even executable: they contained only the bare rudiments of the kernel
source, and assumed that you had access to a Minix machine to compile and play
with them.

On 5 October 1991, Linus announced the first "official" version of Linux, version
0.02. At this point, Linus was able to run `bash` (the GNU Bourne Again Shell) and
`gcc` (the GNU C compiler), but not very much else was working. Again, this was
intended as a hacker's system. The primary focus was kernel development—none
of the issues of user support, documentation, distribution, and so on had even been
addressed. Today, the Linux community still seems to treat these ergonomics issues
as secondary to the "real programming"—kernel development.

Linus wrote in `comp.os.minix`,

> "Do you pine for the nice days of Minix-1.1, when men were men
> and wrote their own device drivers? Are you without a nice project and
> just dying to cut your teeth on a OS you can try to modify for your
> needs? Are you finding it frustrating when everything works on Minix?
> No more all-nighters to get a nifty program working? Then this post
> might be just for you.
>
> "As I mentioned a month ago, I'm working on a free version of a
> Minix-look-alike for AT-386 computers. It has finally reached the stage
> where it's even usable (though may not be depending on what you want),
> and I am willing to put out the sources for wider distribution. It is just

version 0.02...but I've successfully run `bash`, `gcc`, `gnu-make`, `gnu-sed`, `compress`, etc. under it."

After version 0.03, Linus bumped the version number up to 0.10, as more people started to work on the system. After several further revisions, Linus increased the version number to 0.95, to reflect his expectation that the system was ready for an "official" release very soon. (Generally, software is not assigned the version number 1.0 until it is theoretically complete or bug-free.) This was in March of 1992. Almost a year and a half later, in late December of 1993, the Linux kernel was still at version 0.99.pl14—asymptotically approaching 1.0. As of the time of this writing, the current kernel version is 2.0.7

Today, Linux is a complete UNIX clone, capable of running X Windows, TCP/IP, Emacs, UUCP, mail and news software, you name it. Almost all of the major free software packages have been ported to Linux, and commercial software is becoming available. Much more hardware is supported than in original versions of the kernel. Many people have executed benchmarks on 80586 Linux systems and found them comparable with mid-range workstations from Sun Microsystems and Digital Equipment Corporation. Who would have ever guessed that this "little" UNIX clone would have grown up to take on the entire world of personal computing?

1.3 System Features

Linux supports most of the features found in other implementations of UNIX, plus quite a few that aren't found elsewhere. This section is a nickel tour of the Linux kernel features.

Linux is a complete multitasking, multiuser operating system (just like all other versions of UNIX). This means that many users can be logged into the same machine at once, running multiple programs simultaneously.

The Linux system is mostly compatible with a number of UNIX standards (inasmuch as UNIX has standards) on the source level, including IEEE POSIX.1, System V, and BSD features. It was developed with source portability in mind: therefore, you are most likely to find commonly-used features in the Linux system which are shared across multiple implementations. A great deal of free UNIX software available on the Internet and elsewhere compiles on Linux out of the box. In addition, all source code for the Linux system, including the kernel, device drivers, libraries, user programs, and development tools, is freely distributable.

Other specific internal features of Linux include POSIX job control (used by shells such as `csh` and `bash`), pseudoterminals (`pty` devices), and support for national or customized keyboards using dynamically-loadable keyboard drivers. Linux also supports **virtual consoles**, which allow you to switch between multiple login sessions from the system console in text mode. Users of the "`screen`" program will find the Linux virtual console implementation familiar.

The kernel is able to emulate 387-FPU instructions itself, so that systems without a math coprocessor can run programs that require floating-point math instructions.

Linux supports various filesystem types for storing data. Various filesystems. such as the *ext2fs* filesystem, have been developed specifically for Linux. Other filesystem types, such as the Minix-1 and Xenix filesystems, are also supported. The MS-DOS filesystem has been implemented as well, allowing you to access MS-DOS files on hard drive or floppy directly. The ISO 9660 CD-ROM filesystem type, which reads all standard formats of CD-ROMs, is also supported. We'll talk more about filesystems in Chapters 2 and 4.

Linux provides a complete implementation of TCP/IP networking. This includes device drivers for many popular Ethernet cards, SLIP/CSLIP (Serial Line Internet Protocol, allowing you to access a TCP/IP network via a serial connection), PLIP (Parallel Line Internet Protocol), PPP (Point-to-Point Protocol), NFS (Network File System), and so on. The complete range of TCP/IP clients and services is supported, such as FTP, `telnet`, NNTP, and ESMTP. We'll talk more about networking in Chapter 5.

The Linux kernel is developed to use the special protected-mode features of the Intel 80386 and 80486 processors. In particular, Linux makes use of the protected-mode descriptor-based memory management paradigm and many of the other advanced features of these processors. Anyone familiar with 80386 protected-mode programming knows that this chip was designed for a multitasking system such as UNIX (or, actually, Multics). Linux exploits this functionality.

The Linux kernel supports demand-paged loaded executables. That is, only those segments of a program which are actually used are read into memory from disk. Also, copy-on-write pages are shared among executables, meaning that if several instances of a program are running at once, they will share pages in physical memory, reducing overall memory usage.

In order to increase the amount of available memory, Linux also implements disk paging: that is, up to 256 megabytes of "swap space"[1] can be allocated on disk. When the system requires more physical memory, it will swap out inactive pages to disk, thus allowing you to run larger applications and support more users at once. However, swap is no substitute for physical RAM—it is much slower due to drive access latency times.

The kernel also implements a unified memory pool for user programs and disk cache. In this way, all free memory is used for caching, and the cache is reduced when running large programs.

Executables use dynamically linked shared libraries, meaning that executables share common library code in a single library file found on disk, not unlike the SunOS shared library mechanism. This allows executable files to occupy much less space on disk, especially those that use many library functions. There are also statically-linked libraries for those who wish to use object debugging or maintain "complete" executables without the need for shared libraries to be in place. Linux shared libraries are dynamically linked at run-time, allowing the programmer to replace modules of the libraries with their own routines.

To facilitate debugging, the Linux kernel does core dumps for post-mortem analysis. Using a core dump and an executable linked with debugging support, it is possible to determine what caused a program to crash.

1.4 Software Features

In this section, we'll introduce you to many of the software applications available for Linux, and talk about a number of common computing tasks. After all, the most important part of the system is the wide range of software available for it. The fact that most of this software is freely distributable is even more impressive.

1.4.1 Basic commands and utilities

Virtually every utility that you would expect to find on standard implementations of UNIX has been ported to Linux. This includes basic commands such as `ls`, `awk`, `tr`, `sed`, `bc`, `more`, and so on. You name it, Linux has it. Therefore, you can expect your familiar working environment on other UNIX systems to be duplicated on

---

[1]Swap space is inappropriately named: entire processes are not swapped, but rather individual pages. Of course, in many cases entire processes will be swapped out, but this is not necessarily always the case.

Linux. All of the standard commands and utilities are there. (Novice Linux users should see Chapter 3 for an introduction to these basic UNIX commands.)

Many text editors are available, including vi, ex, pico, jove, as well as GNU Emacs and variants such as Lucid Emacs (which incorporates extensions for use under X Windows) and joe. Whatever text editor you're accustomed to using has more than likely been ported to Linux.

The choice of a text editor is an interesting one. Many UNIX users still use "simple" editors such as vi (in fact, the author wrote this book using vi under Linux). However, vi has many limitations, due to its age, and more modern (and complex) editors such as Emacs are gaining popularity. Emacs supports a complete LISP-based macro language and interpreter, a powerful command syntax, and other fun-filled extensions. Emacs macro packages exist to allow you to read electronic mail and news, edit the contents of directories, and even engage in an artificially intelligent psychotherapy session (indispensible for stressed-out Linux hackers).

One interesting note is that most of the basic Linux utilities are GNU software. These GNU utilities support advanced features not found in the standard versions from BSD or AT&T. For example, GNU's version of the vi editor, elvis, includes a structured macro language which differs from the original AT&T implementation. However, the GNU utilities strive to remain compatible with their BSD and System V counterparts. Many people consider the GNU versions of these programs superior to the originals.

The most important utility to many users is the **shell**. The shell is a program which reads and executes commands from the user. In addition, many shells provide features such as **job control** (allowing the user to manage several running processes at once—not as Orwellian as it sounds), input and output redirection, and a command language for writing **shell scripts**. A shell script is a file containing a program in the shell command language, analogous to a "batch file" under MS-DOS.

There are many types of shells available for Linux. The most important difference between shells is the command language. For example, the **C Shell** (csh) uses a command language somewhat like the C programming language. The classic **Bourne Shell** uses a different command language. One's choice of a shell is often based on the command language that it provides. The shell that you use defines, to some extent, your working environment under Linux.

No matter what shell you're accustomed to, some version of it has probably been ported to Linux. The most popular shell is the GNU Bourne Again Shell (`bash`), a Bourne shell variant which includes many advanced features, such as job control, command history, command and filename completion, an Emacs-like interface for editing the command line, and powerful extensions to the standard Bourne shell language. Another popular shell is `tcsh`, a version of the C Shell with advanced functionality similar to that found in `bash`. Other shells include `zsh`, a small Bourne-like shell; the Korn shell (`ksh`); BSD's `ash`; and `rc`, the Plan 9 shell.

What's so important about these basic utilities? Linux gives you the unique opportunity to tailor a custom system to your needs. For example, if you're the only person who uses your system, and you prefer to exclusively use the `vi` editor, and `bash` as your shell, there's no reason to install other editors or shells. The "do it yourself" attitude is prevalent among Linux hackers and users.

1.4.2 Text processing and word processing

Almost every computer user has a need for some kind of document preparation system. (How many computer enthusiasts do you know who still use pen and paper? Not many, we'll wager.) In the PC world, *word processing* is the norm: it involves editing and manipulating text (often in a "What-You-See-Is-What-You-Get" environment) and producing printed copies of the text, complete with figures, tables, and other garnishes.

In the UNIX world, *text processing* is much more common, which is quite different than the classical concept of word processing. With a text processing system, text is entered by the author using a "typesetting language", which describes how the text should be formatted. Instead of entering the text within a special word processing environment, the source may be modified with any text editor such as `vi` or Emacs. Once the source text (in the typesetting language) is complete, the user formats the text with a separate program, which converts the source to a format suitable for printing. This is somewhat analogous to programming in a language such as C, and "compiling" the document into a printable form.

There are many text processing systems available for Linux. One is `groff`, the GNU version of the classic `nroff` text formatter originally developed by Bell Labs and still used on many UNIX systems worldwide. Another modern text processing system is TeX, developed by Donald Knuth of computer science fame. Dialects of TeX, such as LaTeX, are also available.

Text processors such as TeX and `groff` differ mostly in the syntax of their formatting languages. The choice of one formatting system over another is also based upon what utilities are available to satisfy your needs, as well as personal taste.

For example, some people consider the `groff` formatting language to be a bit obscure, so they use TeX, which is more readable by humans. However, `groff` is capable of producing plain ASCII output, viewable on a terminal, while TeX is intended primarily for output to a printing device. However, various programs exist to produce plain ASCII from TeX-formatted documents, or to convert TeX to `groff`, for example.

Another text processing system is `texinfo`, an extension to TeX used for software documentation by the Free Software Foundation. `texinfo` is capable of producing a printed document, or an online-browsable hypertext "Info" document from a single source file. Info files are the main format of documentation used by GNU software such as Emacs.

Text processors are used widely in the computing community for producing papers, theses, magazine articles, and books (in fact, this book was produced using LaTeX). The ability to process the source language as a plain text file opens the door to many extensions to the text processor itself. Because source documents are not stored in an obscure format, readable only by a particular word processor, programmers are able to write parsers and translators for the formatting language, extending the system.

What does such a formatting language look like? In general, the formatting language source consists mostly of the text itself, along with "control codes" to produce a particular effect, such as changing fonts, setting margins, creating lists, and so on.

As an example, take the following text:

Mr. Torvalds:

We are very upset with your current plans to implement *post - hypnotic suggestion* in the **Linux** terminal driver code. We feel this way for three reasons:

1. Planting subliminal messages in the terminal driver is not only immoral, it is a waste of time;

2. It has been proven that "post-hypnotic suggestions" are totally ineffective when used upon unsuspecting UNIX hackers;

3. We have already implemented high-voltage electric shocks, as a security measure, in the code for `login`.

We hope you will reconsider.

This text would appear in the LaTeX formatting language as the following:

```
\begin{quote}
Mr. Torvalds:

We are very upset with your current plans to implement
{\em post-hypnotic suggestion\/} in the {\bf Linux} terminal
driver code. We feel this way for three reasons:
\begin{enumerate}
\item Planting subliminal messages in the kernel driver is not only
        immoral, it is a waste of time;
\item It has been proven that ''post-hypnotic suggestions'' are
        ineffective when used upon unsuspecting UNIX hackers;
\item We have already implemented high-voltage electric shocks,
        as a security measure, in the code for {\tt login}.
\end{enumerate}
We hope you will reconsider.
\end{quote}
```

The author enters the above "source" text using any text editor, and generates the formatted output by processing the source with LaTeX. At first glance, the typesetting language may appear to be obscure, but it's actually quite easy to learn. Using a text processing system enforces typographical standards when writing. For example, all enumerated lists within a document will look the same, unless the author modifies the definition of the enumerated list "environment". The primary goal is to allow the author to concentrate on writing the actual text, instead of worrying about typesetting conventions.

WYSIWYG word processors are attractive for many reasons; they provide a powerful (and sometimes complex) visual interface for editing the document. However, this interface is inherently limited to those aspects of text layout which are accessible to the user. For example, many word processors provide a special "format language" for producing complicated expressions such as mathematical formulae. This is identical text processing, albeit on a much smaller scale.

The subtle benefit of text processing is that the system allows you to specify exactly what you mean. Also, text processing systems allow you to edit the source text with any text editor, and the source is easily converted to other formats. The tradeoff for this flexibility and power is the lack of a WYSIWYG interface.

Many users of word processors are used to seeing the formatted text as they edit it. On the other hand, when writing with a text processor, one generally does not worry about how the text will appear when formatted. The writer learns to expect how the text should look from the formatting commands used in the source.

There are programs which allow you to view the formatted document on a graphics display before printing. For example, the `xdvi` program displays a "device independent" file generated by the TEX system under the X Windows environment. Other software applications, such as `xfig`, provide a WYSIWYG graphics interface for drawing figures and diagrams, which are subsequently converted to the text processing language for inclusion in your document.

Admittedly, text processors such as `nroff` were around long before word processing was available. However, many people still prefer to use text processing, because it is more versatile and independent of a graphics environment. In either case, the `idoc` word processor is also available for Linux, and before long we expect to see commercial word processors becoming available as well. If you absolutely don't want to give up word processing for text processing, you can always run MS-DOS, or some other operating system, in addition to Linux.

There are many other text-processing-related utilities available. The powerful METAFONT system, used for designing fonts for TEX, is included with the Linux port of TEX. Other programs include `ispell`, an interactive spell checker and corrector; `makeindex`, used for generating indicies in LATEX documents; as well as many `groff` and TEX-based macro packages for formatting many types of documents and mathematical texts. Conversion programs to translate between TEX or `groff` source to a myriad of other formats are available.

1.4.3   Programming languages and utilities

Linux provides a complete UNIX programming environment, including all of the standard libraries, programming tools, compilers, and debuggers that you would expect to find on other UNIX systems. Within the UNIX software development world, applications and systems programming is usually done in C or C++. The standard C and C++ compiler for Linux is GNU's `gcc`, which is an advanced, modern compiler supporting many options. It is also capable of compiling C++ (including AT&T 3.0 features) as well as Objective-C, another object-oriented dialect of C.

Besides C and C++, many other compiled and interpreted programming languages have been ported to Linux, such as Smalltalk, FORTRAN, Pascal, LISP, Scheme, and Ada (if you're masochistic enough to program in Ada—we're not going to stop you). In addition, various assemblers for writing protected-mode 80386 code are available, as are UNIX hacking favorites such as Perl (the script language to end all script languages) and Tcl/Tk (a shell-like command processing system including support for developing simple X Windows applications).

The advanced `gdb` debugger has been ported, which allows you to step through a program to find bugs, or examine the cause for a crash using a core dump. `gprof`, a profiling utility, will give you performance statistics for your program, letting you know where your program is spending most of its time executing. The Emacs text editor provides an interactive editing and compilation environment for various programming languages. Other tools include GNU `make` and `imake`, used to manage compilation of large applications; and RCS, a system for source locking and revision control.

Linux implements dynamically-linked shared libraries, which allow binaries to be much smaller as the subroutine code is linked at run-time. These DLL libraries also allow the applications programmer to override function definitions with their own code. For example, if a programmer wished to write her own version of the `malloc()` library routine, the linker would use the programmer's new routine instead of the one found in the libraries.

Linux is ideal for developing UNIX applications. It provides a modern programming environment with all of the bells and whistles. Various standards such as POSIX.1 are supported, allowing software written for Linux to be easily ported to other systems. Professional UNIX programmers and system administrators can use Linux to develop software at home, and then transfer the software to UNIX systems at work. This not only can save a great deal of time and money, but will also let you work in the comfort of your own home.[2] Computer Science students can use Linux to learn UNIX programming and to explore other aspects of the system, such as kernel architecture.

With Linux, not only do you have access to the complete set of libraries and programming utilities, but you also have the complete kernel and library source code at your fingertips.

1.4.4 The X Window System

The X Window System is the standard graphics interface for UNIX machines. It is a powerful environment supporting many applications. Using X Windows, the user can have multiple terminal windows on the screen at once, each one containing a

---

[2]The author uses his Linux system to develop and test X Windows applications at home, which can be directly compiled on workstations elsewhere.

different login session. A pointing device such as a mouse is often used with the X interface, although it isn't required.

Many X-specific applications have been written, such as games, graphics utilities, programming and documentation tools, and so on. With Linux and X, your system is a bona fide workstation. Coupled with TCP/IP networking, you can even display X applications running on other machines on your Linux display, as is possible with other systems running X.

The X Window System was originally developed at MIT, and is freely distributable. However, may commercial vendors have distributed proprietary enhancements to the original X Windows software. The version of X Windows available for Linux is known as XFree86, a port of X11R6 made freely distributable for 80386-based UNIX systems such as Linux. XFree86 supports a wide range of video hardware, including VGA, Super VGA, and a number of accelerated video adaptors. This is a complete distribution of the X Windows software, containing the X server itself, many applications and utilities, programming libraries, and documentation.

Standard X applications include `xterm` (a terminal emulator used for most text-based applications within an X window); `xdm` (the X Session Manager, which handles logins); `xclock` (a simple clock display); `xman` (an X-based man page reader), and more. The many X applications available for Linux are too numerous to mention here, but the base XFree86 distribution includes the "standard" applications found in the original MIT release. Many others are available separately, and theoretically any application written for X Windows should compile cleanly under Linux.

The look and feel of the X Windows interface is controlled to a large extent by the **window manager**. This friendly program is in charge of the placement of windows, the user interface for resizing, iconifying, and moving windows, the appearance of window frames, and so on. The standard XFree86 distribution includes `twm`, the classic MIT window manager, although more advanced window managers such as the Open Look Virtual Window Manager (`olvwm`) are available as well. One window manager that is popular among Linux users is `fvwm`. This is a small window manager, requiring less than half of the memory used by `twm`. It provides a 3-D appearance for windows, as well a virtual desktop—if the user moves the mouse to the edge of the screen, the entire desktop is shifted as if the display were much larger than it actually is. `fvwm` is greatly customizable, and allows all functions to be accessed from the keyboard as well as the mouse. Many Linux distributions use `fvwm` as the standard window manager.

The XFree86 distribution contains programming libraries and include files for those wily programmers who wish to develop X applications. Various widget sets, such as Athena, Open Look, and Xaw3D are supported. All of the standard fonts, bitmaps, man pages, and documentation are included. PEX (a programming interface for 3-D graphics) is also supported.

Many X applications programmers use the proprietary Motif widget set for development. Several vendors sell single and multiple-user licenses for a binary version of Motif for Linux. Because Motif itself is relatively expensive, not many Linux users own it. However, binaries statically linked with Motif routines may be freely distributed. Therefore, if you write a program using Motif and wish to distribute it freely, you may provide a binary so that users without Motif can use the program.

The only major caveats with X Windows are the hardware and memory requirements. A 386 with 4 megabytes of RAM is capable of running X, but 16 megabytes or more of physical RAM are needed to use it comfortably. A faster processor is nice to have as well, but having enough physical RAM is much more important. In addition, to achieve really slick video performance, an accelerated video card (such as a local bus S3-chipset card) is strongly recommended. Performance ratings in excess of 140,000 xstones have been acheived with Linux and XFree86. With sufficient hardware, you'll find that running X and Linux is as fast, or faster, than running X on other UNIX workstations.

In Chapter 5 we'll discuss how to install and use X on your system.

1.4.5 Networking

Interested in communicating with the world? Yes? No? Maybe? Linux supports the two primary networking protocols for UNIX systems: **TCP/IP** and **UUCP**. TCP/IP (Transmission Control Protocol/Internet Protocol, for acronym aficionados) is the set of networking paradigms that allow systems all over the world to communicate on a single network known as the Internet. With Linux, TCP/IP, and a connection to the network, you can communicate with users and machines across the Internet via electronic mail, USENET news, file transfers with FTP, and more. There are many Linux systems currently on the Internet.

Most TCP/IP networks use Ethernet as the physical network transport. Linux supports many popular Ethernet cards and interfaces for personal computers, including the D-Link pocket Ethernet adaptor for laptops.

However, because not everyone has an Ethernet drop at home, Linux also supports **SLIP/PPP** (Serial Line Internet Protocol / Point-to-Point Protocol), which allows   you to connect to the Internet via modem. In order to use SLIP/PPP, you'll need to have access to a SLIP/PPP server, a machine connected to the network which allows dial-in access. Many businesses and universities provide such SLIP/PPP servers. In fact, if your Linux system has an Ethernet connection as well as a modem, you can configure it as a SLIP/PPP server for other hosts.

NFS (Network File System) allows your system to seamlessly share files with other machines on the network. FTP (File Transfer Protocol) allows you to transfer files between other machines. Other applications include `sendmail`, a system for sending and receiving electronic mail using the SMTP protocol; NNTP-based electronic news systems such as C-News and INN; `telnet`, `rlogin`, and `rsh`, which allow you to login and execute commands on other machines on the network; and `finger`, which allows you to get information on other Internet users. There are literally tons of TCP/IP-based applications and protocols out there.

The full range of mail and news readers are available for Linux, such as `elm`, `pine`, `rn`, `nn`, and `tin`. Whatever your preference, you can configure your Linux system to send and receive electronic mail and news from all over the world.

If you have experience with TCP/IP applications on other UNIX systems, Linux will be very familiar to you. The system provides a standard socket programming interface, so virtually any program which uses TCP/IP can be ported to Linux. The Linux X server also supports TCP/IP, allowing you to display applications running on other systems on your Linux display.

In Chapter 5 we'll discuss configuration and setup of TCP/IP, including SLIP, for Linux.

UUCP (UNIX-to-UNIX Copy) is an older mechanism used to transfer files, electronic mail, and electronic news between UNIX machines. Classically, UUCP machines connected to each other over the phone lines via modem, but UUCP is able to transport over a TCP/IP network as well. If you do not have access to a TCP/IP network or a SLIP server, you can configure your system to send and receive files and electronic mail using UUCP. See Chapter 5 for more information.

1.4.6   Telecommunications and BBS software

If you have a modem, you will be able to communicate with other machines using one of the telecommunications packages available for Linux. Many people use telecommunications software to access bulletin board systems (BBSs), as well as commercial online services such as Prodigy, CompuServe, and America On-Line. Other people use their modems to connect to a UNIX system at work or school. You can even use your modem and Linux system to send and receive facsimiles.

Telecommunications software under Linux is very similar to that found under MS-DOS or other operating systems. Anyone who has ever used a telecommunications package will find the Linux equivalent familiar.

One of the most popular communications packages for Linux is Seyon, an X application providing a customizable, ergonomic interface, with built-in support for various file transfer protocols such as Kermit, ZModem, and so on. Other telecommunications programs include C-Kermit, pcomm, and minicom. These are similar to communications programs found on other operating systems, and are quite easy to use.

If you do not have access to a SLIP server (see the previous section), you can use term to multiplex your serial line. term will allow you to open multiple login sessions over the modem connection to a remote machine. term will also allow you to redirect X client connections to your local X server, through the serial line, allowing you to display remote X applications on your Linux system. Another software package, KA9Q, implements a similar SLIP-like interface.

Running a bulletin board system (BBS) is a favorite hobby (and means of income) for many people. Linux supports a wide range of BBS software, most of which is more powerful than what is available for other operating systems. With a phone line, a modem, and Linux, you can turn your system into a BBS, providing dial-in access to your system to users worldwide. BBS software for Linux includes XBBS and the UniBoard BBS packages.

Most BBS software locks the user into a menu-based system where only certain functions and applications are available. An alternative to BBS access is full UNIX access, which would allow users to dial into your system and login as a regular user. While this would require a fair amount of maintenance on the part of the system administrator, it can be done, and providing public UNIX access from your Linux system is not difficult to do. Along with a TCP/IP network, you can provide electronic mail and news access to users on your system.

If you do not have access to a TCP/IP network or UUCP feed, Linux will also allow you to communicate with a number of BBS networks, such as FidoNet, with which you can exchange electronic news and mail via the phone line. More information on telecommunications and BBS software under Linux can be found in Chapter 5.

1.4.7   Interfacing with MS-DOS

Various utilities exist to interface with the world of MS-DOS. The most well-known
application is the Linux MS-DOS Emulator, which allows you to run many MS-
DOS applications directly from Linux. Although Linux and MS-DOS are completely different operating systems, the 80386 protected-mode environment allows
certain tasks to behave as if they were running in 8086-emulation mode, as MS-DOS
applications do.

The MS-DOS emulator is still under development, yet many popular applications
run under it. Understandably, however, MS-DOS applications which use bizarre
or esoteric features of the system may never be supported, because it is only an
emulator. For example, you wouldn't expect to be able to run any programs which
use 80386 protected-mode features, such as Microsoft Windows (in 386 enhanced
mode, that is).

Applications which run successfully under the Linux MS-DOS Emulator include
4DOS (a command interpreter), Foxpro 2.0, Harvard Graphics, MathCad, Stacker
3.1, Turbo Assembler, Turbo C/C++, Turbo Pascal, Microsoft Windows 3.0 (in
real mode), and WordPerfect 5.1. Standard MS-DOS commands and utilities (such
as PKZIP, and so on) work with the emulator as well.

The MS-DOS Emulator is meant mostly as an ad hoc solution for those people
who need MS-DOS only for a few applications, but use Linux for everything else. It's
not meant to be a complete implementation of MS-DOS. Of course, if the Emulator
doesn't satisfy your needs, you can always run MS-DOS as well as Linux on the
same system. Using the LILO boot loader, you can specify at boot time which
operating system to start. Linux can coexist with other operating systems, such as
OS/2, as well.

Linux provides a seamless interface for transferring files between Linux and MS-
DOS. You can mount an MS-DOS partition or floppy under Linux, and directly
access MS-DOS files as you would any other.

Currently under development is a project known as **WINE**—a Microsoft Windows emulator for the X Window System under Linux. This is similar to the
proprietary WABI Windows emulator from Sun Microsystems.

In Chapter 5 we'll talk about the MS-DOS tools available for Linux.

1.4.8   Other applications

A host of miscellany is available for Linux, as one would expect from such a hodge-podge operating system. Linux's primary focus is currently for personal UNIX computing, but this is rapidly changing. Business and scientific software is expanding, and commercial software vendors are beginning to contribute to the growing pool of applications.

Several relational databases are available for Linux, including Postgres, Ingres, and Mbase. These are full-featured, professional client/server database applications similar to those found on other UNIX platforms. /rdb, a commercial database system, is available as well.

Scientific computing applications include FELT (a finite element analysis tool); gnuplot (a plotting and data analysis application); Octave (a symbolic mathematics package, similar to MATLAB); xspread (a spreadsheet calculator); xfractint, an X-based port of the popular Fractint fractal generator; xlispstat (a statistics package), and more. Other applications include Spice (a circuit design and analysis tool) and Khoros (an image/digital signal processing and visualization system).

Of course, there are many more such applications which have been, and can be, ported to run on Linux. Whatever your field, porting UNIX-based applications to Linux should be quite straightforward. Linux provides a complete UNIX programming interface, sufficient to serve as the base for any scientific application.

As with any operating system, Linux has its share of games. These include classic text-based dungeon games such as Nethack and Moria; MUDs (multi-user dungeons, which allow many users to interact in a text-based adventure) such as DikuMUD and TinyMUD; as well as a slew of X games such as xtetris, netrek, and Xboard (the X11 version of gnuchess). The popular shoot-em-up arcade-style *Doom* has also been ported to Linux.

For audiophiles, Linux has support for various sound cards and related software, such as CDplayer (a program which can control a CD-ROM drive as a conventional CD player, surprisingly enough), MIDI sequencers and editors (allowing you to compose music for playback through a synthesizer or other MIDI-controlled instrument), and sound editors for digitized sounds.

Can't find the application you're looking for? The Linux Software Map, described in Appendix A, contains a list of many software packages which have been written and ported to Linux. While this list is far from complete, it contains a great deal of software. Another way to find Linux applications is to look at the INDEX files found on Linux FTP sites, if you have Internet access. Just by poking around you'll find a great deal of software just waiting to be played with.

If you absolutely can't find what you need, you can always attempt to port the application from another platform to Linux. Most freely distributable UNIX-based software will compile on Linux with few problems. Or, if all else fails, you can write the application yourself. If it's a commercial application you're looking for, there may be a free "clone" available. Or, you can encourage the software company to consider releasing a Linux binary version. Several individuals have contacted software companies, asking them to port their applications to Linux, and have met with various degrees of success.

1.5   About Linux's Copyright

Linux is covered by what is known as the GNU *General Public License*, or *GPL*. The GPL was developed for the GNU project by the Free Software Foundation. It makes a number of provisions for the distribution and modification of "free software". "Free" in this sense refers to freedom, not just cost. The GPL has always been subject to misinterpretation, and we hope that this summary will help you to understand the extent and goals of the GPL and its effect on Linux. A complete copy of the GPL is included in Appendix D.

Originally, Linus Torvalds released Linux under a license more restrictive than the GPL, which allowed the software to be freely distributed and modified, but prevented any money changing hands for its distribution and use. On the other hand, the GPL allows people to sell and make profit from free software, but does not allow them to restrict the right for others to distribute the software in any way.

First, it should be explained that "free software" covered by the GPL is *not* in the public domain. Public domain software is software which is not copyrighted, and is literally owned by the public. Software covered by the GPL, on the other hand, is copyrighted to the author or authors. This means that the software is protected by standard international copyright laws, and that the author of the software is legally defined. Just because the software may be freely distributed does not mean that it is in the public domain.

GPL-licensed software is also not "shareware". Generally, "shareware" software is owned and copyrighted by the author, but the author requires users to send in money for its use after distribution. On the other hand, software covered by the GPL may be distributed and used free of charge.

The GPL also allows people to take and modify free software, and distribute their own versions of the software. However, any derived works from GPL software must also be covered by the GPL. In other words, a company could not take Linux, modify it, and sell it under a restrictive license. If any software is derived from Linux, that software must be covered by the GPL as well.

The GPL allows free software to be distributed and used free of charge. However, it also allows a person or organization to distribute GPL software for a fee, and even to make a profit from its sale and distribution. However, in selling GPL software, the distributor cannot take those rights away from the purchaser; that is, if you purchase GPL software from some source, you may distribute the software for free, or sell it yourself as well.

This might sound like a contradiction at first. Why sell software for profit when the GPL allows anyone to obtain it for free? As an example, let's say that some company decided to bundle a large amount of free software on a CD-ROM and distribute it. That company would need to charge for the overhead of producing and distributing the CD-ROM, and the company may even decide to make profit from the sales of software. This is allowed by the GPL.

Organizations which sell free software must follow certain restrictions set forth in the GPL. First, they cannot restrict the rights of users who purchase the software. This means that if you buy a CD-ROM of GPL software, you can copy and distribute that CD-ROM free of charge, or resell it yourself. Secondly, distributors must make it obvious to users that the software is indeed covered by the GPL. Thirdly, distributors must provide, free of charge, the complete source code for the software being distributed. This will allow anyone who purchases GPL software to make modifications of that software.

Allowing a company to distribute and sell free software is a very good thing. Not everyone has access to the Internet to download software, such as Linux, for free. The GPL allows companies to sell and distribute software to those people who do not have free (cost-wise) access to the software. For example, many organizations sell Linux on diskette, tape, or CD-ROM via mail order, and make profit from these sales. The developers of Linux may never see any of this profit; that is the understanding that is reached between the developer and the distributor when software is licensed by the GPL. In other words, Linus knew that companies may wish to sell Linux, and that he may not see a penny of the profits from those sales.

In the free software world, the important issue is not money. The goal of free software is always to develop and distribute fantastic software and to allow anyone to obtain and use it. In the next section, we'll discuss how this applies to the development of Linux.

1.6   The Design and Philosophy of Linux

When new users encounter Linux, they often have a few misconceptions and false
expectations of the system. Linux is a unique operating system, and it is important
to understand its philosophy and design in order to use it effectively. Time enough
for a soapbox. Even if you are an aged UNIX guru, what follows is probably of
interest to you.

In commercial UNIX development houses, the entire system is developed with
a rigorous policy of quality assurance, source and revision control systems, documentation, and bug reporting and resolution. Developers are not allowed to add
features or to change key sections of code on a whim: they must validate the change
as a response to a bug report and consequently "check in" all changes to the source
control system, so that the changes can be backed out if necessary. Each developer
is assigned one or more parts of the system code, and only that developer may alter
those sections of the code while it is "checked out".

Internally, the quality assurance department runs rigorous regression test suites
on each new pass of the operating system, and reports any bugs. It is the responsibility of the developers to fix these bugs as reported. A complicated system of
statistical analysis is employed to ensure that a certain percentage of bugs are fixed
before the next release, and that the operating system as a whole passes certain
release criteria.

In all, the process used by commercial UNIX developers to maintain and support their code is very complicated, and quite reasonably so. The company must
have quantitative proof that the next revision of the operating system is ready to
be shipped; hence, the gathering and analysis of statistics about the operating system's performance. It is a big job to develop a commercial UNIX system, often large
enough to employ hundreds (if not thousands) of programmers, testers, documen-
tors, and administrative personnel. Of course, no two commercial UNIX vendors
are alike, but you get the general picture.

With Linux, you can throw out the entire concept of organized development,
source control systems, structured bug reporting, or statistical analysis. Linux is,
and more than likely always will be, a hacker's operating system.[3]

Linux is primarily developed as a group effort by volunteers on the Internet from
all over the world. Across the Internet and beyond, anyone with enough know-

---

[3] What I mean by "hacker" is a feverishly dedicated programmer, a person who enjoys exploiting
computers and generally doing interesting things with them. This is in contrast to the common
denotation of "hacker" as a computer wrongdoer or outlaw.

how has the opportunity to aid in developing and debugging the kernel, porting new software, writing documentation, or helping new users. There is no single organization responsible for developing the system. For the most part, the Linux community communicates via various mailing lists and USENET newsgroups. A number of conventions have sprung up around the development effort: for example, anyone wishing to have their code included in the "official" kernel should mail it to Linus Torvalds, which he will test and include in the kernel (as long as it doesn't break things or go against the overall design of the system, he will more than likely include it).

The system itself is designed with a very open-ended, feature-minded approach. While recently the number of new features and critical changes to the system have diminished, the general rule is that a new version of the kernel will be released about every few months (sometimes even more frequently than this). Of course, this is a very rough figure: it depends on a several factors including the number of bugs to be fixed, the amount of feedback from users testing pre-release versions of the code, and the amount of sleep that Linus has had this week.

Let it suffice to say that not every single bug has been fixed, and not every problem ironed out between releases. As long as the system appears to be free of critical or oft-manifesting bugs, it is considered "stable" and new revisions will be released. The thrust behind Linux development is not an effort to release perfect, bug-free code: it is to develop a free implementation of UNIX. Linux is *for* the developers, more than anyone else.

Anyone who has a new feature or software application to add to the system generally makes it available in an "alpha" stage—that is, a stage for testing by those brave or unwary users who want to bash out problems with the initial code. Because the Linux community is largely based on the Internet, alpha software is usually uploaded to one or more of the various Linux FTP sites (see Appendix B) and a message posted to one of the Linux USENET newsgroups about how to get and test the code. Users who download and test alpha software can then mail results, bug fixes, or questions to the author.

After the initial problems in the alpha code have been fixed, the code enters a "beta" stage, in which it is usually considered stable but not complete (that is, it works, but not all of the features may be present). Otherwise, it may go directly to a "final" stage in which the software is considered complete and usable. For kernel code, once it is complete the developer may ask Linus to include it in the standard kernel, or as an optional add-on feature to the kernel.

Keep in mind that these are only conventions—not rules. Some people feel so confident with their software that they don't need to release an alpha or test version. It is always up to the developer to make these decisions.

You might be amazed that such a nonstructured system of volunteers, programming and debugging a complete UNIX system, could get anything done at all. As it turns out, it is one of the most efficient and motivated development efforts ever employed. The entire Linux kernel was written *from scratch*, without employing any code from proprietary sources. A great deal of work was put forth by volunteers to port all of the free software under the sun to the Linux system. Libraries were written and ported, filesystems developed, and hardware drivers written for many popular devices.

The Linux software is generally released as a *distribution*, which is a set of pre-packaged software making up an entire system. It would be quite difficult for most users to build a complete system from the ground up, starting with the kernel, adding utilities, and installing all of the necessary software by hand. Instead, there are a number of software distributions including everything that you need to install and run a complete system. One of the most popular is the Slackware distribution, which will be discussed in Chapter 2.

Despite the completeness of the Linux software, you will still need a bit of UNIX know-how to install and run a complete system. No distribution of Linux is completely bug-free, so you may be required to fix small problems by hand after installation. Running a UNIX system is not an easy task, not even for commercial versions of UNIX. If you're serious about Linux, bear in mind that it will take a considerable amount of effort and attention on your part to keep the system running and take care of things: this is true of *any* UNIX system, and Linux is no exception. Because of the diversity of the Linux community and the many needs which the software is attempting to meet, not everything can be taken care of for you all of the time.

1.6.1   Hints for UNIX novices

Installing and using your own Linux system does not require a great deal of background in UNIX. In fact, many UNIX novices successfully install Linux on their systems. This is a worthwhile learning experience, but keep in mind that it can be very frustrating to some. If you're lucky, you will be able to install and start using your Linux system without any UNIX background. However, once you are ready to delve into the more complex tasks of running Linux—installing new software, recompiling the kernel, and so forth—having background knowledge in UNIX is going to be a necessity.

Fortunately, by running your own Linux system you will be able to learn the
essentials of UNIX necessary for these tasks. This book contains a good deal of
information to help you get started—Chapter 3 is a tutorial covering UNIX basics,
and Chapter 4 contains information on Linux system administration. You may wish
to read these chapters before you attempt to install Linux at all—the information
contained therein will prove to be invaluable should you run into problems.

Nobody can expect to go from being a UNIX novice to a UNIX system administrator overnight. No implementation of UNIX is expected to run trouble- and
maintenance-free. You must be aptly prepared for the journey which lies ahead.
Otherwise, if you're new to UNIX, you may very well become overly frustrated with
the system.

1.6.2   Hints for UNIX gurus

Even those people with years of UNIX programming and systems administration
experience may need assistance before they are able to pick up and install Linux.
There are still aspects of the system that UNIX wizards will need to be familiar
with before diving in. For one thing, Linux is not a commercial UNIX system. It
does not attempt to uphold the same standards as other UNIX systems you have
may have come across. To be more specific, while stability is an important factor
in the development of Linux, it is not the *only* factor.

More important, perhaps, is functionality. In many cases, new code will make it
into the standard kernel even though it is still buggy and not functionally complete.
The assumption is that it is more important to release code which users can test
and use than delay a release until it is "complete". As an example, WINE (the
Microsoft Windows Emulator for Linux) had an "official" alpha release before it
was completely tested. In this way, the Linux community at large had a chance to
work with the code, test it, and help develop it, while those who found the alpha
code "good enough" for their needs could use it. Commercial UNIX vendors rarely,
if ever, release software in this manner.

If you have been a UNIX systems administrator for more than a decade, and
have used every commercial UNIX system under the Sun (no pun intended), Linux
may take some getting used to. The system is very modern and dynamic. A new
kernel release is made approximately every few months. New software is constantly
being released. One day your system may be completely up-to-date with the current
trend, and the next day the same system is considered to be in the Stone Age.

With all of this dynamic activity, how can you be expected to keep up with the ever-changing Linux world? For the most part, it is best to upgrade incrementally; that is, upgrade only those parts of the system that *need* upgrading, and then only when you think an upgrade is necessary. For example, if you never use Emacs, there is little reason to continuously install every new release of Emacs on your system. Furthermore, even if you are an avid Emacs user, there is usually no reason to upgrade it unless you find that some feature is missing that is in the next release. There is little or no reason to always be on top of the newest version of software.

We hope that Linux will meet or exceed your expectations of a homebrew UNIX system. At the very core of Linux is the spirit of free software, of constant development and growth. The Linux community favors expansion over stability, and that is a difficult concept to swallow for many people, especially those so steeped in the world of commercial UNIX. You cannot expect Linux to be perfect; nothing ever is in the free software world. However, we believe that Linux really is as complete and useful as any other implementation of UNIX.

1.7   Differences Between Linux and Other Operating Systems

It is important to understand the differences between Linux and other operating systems, such as MS-DOS, OS/2, and other implementations of UNIX for the personal computer. First of all, it should be made clear that Linux will coexist happily with other operating systems on the same machine: that is, you can run MS-DOS and OS/2 along with Linux on the same system without problems. There are even ways to interact between the various operating systems, as we'll see.

1.7.1   Why use Linux?

Why use Linux instead of a well-known, well-tested, and well-documented commercial operating system? We could give you a thousand reasons. One of the most important, however, is that Linux is an excellent choice for personal UNIX computing. If you're a UNIX software developer, why use MS-DOS at home? Linux will allow you to develop and test UNIX software on your PC, including database and X Windows applications. If you're a student, chances are that your university computing systems run UNIX. With Linux, you can run your own UNIX system and tailor it to your own needs. Installing and running Linux is also an excellent way to learn UNIX if you don't have access to other UNIX machines.

But let's not lose sight. Linux isn't just for personal UNIX users. It is robust and complete enough to handle large tasks, as well as distributed computing needs. Many businesses—especially small ones—are moving to Linux in lieu of other UNIX-based workstation environments. Universities are finding Linux to be perfect for teaching courses in operating systems design. Larger commercial software vendors are starting to realize the opportunities that a free operating system can provide.

The following sections should point out the most important differences between Linux and other operating systems. We hope that you'll find that Linux can meet your computing needs, or (at least) enhance your current computing environment. Keep in mind that they best way to get a taste for Linux is just to try it out—you needn't even install a complete system to get a feel for it. In Chapter 2, we'll show you how.

1.7.2   Linux vs. MS-DOS

It's not uncommon to run both Linux and MS-DOS on the same system. Many Linux users rely on MS-DOS for applications such as word processing. While Linux provides its own analogues for these applications (for example, TeX), there are various reasons why a particular user would want to run MS-DOS as well as Linux. If your entire dissertation is written using WordPerfect for MS-DOS, you may not be able to easily convert it to TeX or some other format. There are many commercial applications for MS-DOS which aren't available for Linux, and there's no reason why you can't use both.

As you might know, MS-DOS does not fully utilize the functionality of the better processors. On the other hand, Linux runs completely in the processor's protected mode, and exploits all of the features of the processor. You can directly access all of your available memory (and beyond, using virtual RAM). Linux provides a complete UNIX interface not available under MS-DOS—developing and porting UNIX applications under Linux is easily done, while under MS-DOS you are limited to a small subset of the UNIX programming functionality. Because Linux is a true UNIX system, you do not have these limitations.

We could debate the pros and cons of MS-DOS and Linux for pages on end. However, let it suffice to say that Linux and MS-DOS are completely different entities. MS-DOS is inexpensive (compared to other commercial operating systems), and has a strong foothold in the PC computing world. No other operating system for the PC has reached the level of popularity of MS-DOS—largely because the cost of these other operating systems is unapproachable to most personal computer

users. Very few PC users can imagine spending $1000 or more on the operating
system alone. Linux, however, is free, and you finally have the chance to decide.

We will allow you to make your own judgments of Linux and MS-DOS based
on your expectations and needs. Linux is not for everybody. If you have always
wanted to run a complete UNIX system at home, without the high cost of other
UNIX implementations for the PC, Linux may be what you're looking for.

There are tools available to allow you to interact between Linux and MS-DOS.
For example, it is easy to access MS-DOS files from Linux. There is also an MS-DOS
emulator available, which allows you to run many popular MS-DOS applications.

1.7.3   Linux vs. The Other Guys

A number of other advanced operating systems are on the rise in the PC world.
Specifically, IBM's OS/2 and Microsoft's Windows NT are becoming very popular
as more users move away from MS-DOS.

Both OS/2 and Windows NT are full multitasking operating systems, much like
Linux. Technically, OS/2, Windows NT, and Linux are quite similar: they support
roughly the same features in terms of user interface, networking, security, and so
forth. However, the real difference between Linux and The Other Guys is the fact
that Linux is a version of UNIX, and hence benefits from the contributions of the
UNIX community at large.

What makes UNIX so important? Not only is it the most popular operating
system for multiuser machines, it is also the foundation for the majority of the free
software world. If you have access to the Internet, nearly all of the free software
available there is written specifically for UNIX systems. (The Internet itself is
largely UNIX-based.)

There are many implementations of UNIX, from many vendors, and no single
organization is responsible for distribution. There is a large push in the UNIX
community for standardization in the form of open systems, but no single corporation controls this design. Hence, any vendor (or, as it turns out, any hacker) may
implement these standards in an implementation of UNIX.

OS/2 and Windows NT, on the other hand, are proprietary systems. The interface and design are controlled by a single corporation, and only that corporation
may implement that design. (Don't expect to see a free version of OS/2 anytime
in the near future.) In one sense, this kind of organization is beneficial: it sets a
strict standard for the programming and user interface unlike that found even in

the open systems community. OS/2 is OS/2 wherever you go—the same holds for Windows NT.

However, the UNIX interface is constantly developing and changing. Several organizations are attempting to standardize the programming model, but the task is very difficult. Linux, in particular, is compliant with the POSIX.1 standard for the UNIX programming interface. As time goes on, it is expected that the system will adhere to other such standards, but standardization is not the primary issue in the Linux development community.

1.7.4 Other implementations of UNIX

There are several other implementations of UNIX for the 80x86. The 80386 architecture lends itself to the UNIX design, and a number of vendors have taken advantage of this.

Feature-wise, other implementations of UNIX for the PC are quite similar to Linux. You will see that almost all commercial versions of UNIX support roughly the same software, programming environment, and networking features. However, there are some strong differences between Linux and commercial versions of UNIX.

First of all, Linux supports a different range of hardware from commercial implementations. In general, Linux supports most hardware devices. However, commercial UNIX vendors generally have a more controlled support base, and tend to support less hardware. We'll cover the hardware requirements for Linux in Section 1.8.

Secondly, commercial implementations of UNIX usually come bundled with a complete set of documentation as well as user support from the vendor. In contrast, most of the documentation for Linux is limited to documents available on the Internet—and books such as this one. In Section 1.9 we'll list sources of Linux documentation and other information.

The most important factor to consider for many users is price. The Linux software is free, if you have access to the Internet (or another computer network) and can download it. If you do not have access to such a network, you may need to purchase it via mail order on CD-ROM . Of course, you may copy Linux from a friend who may already have the software, or share the cost of purchasing it with someone else. If you are planning to install Linux on a large number of machines, you need only purchase a single copy of the software—Linux is not distributed on a "single machine" license.

The value of commercial UNIX implementations should not be demeaned: along with the price of the software itself, one usually pays for documentation, support, and assurance of quality. These are very important factors for large institutions, but personal computer users may not require these benefits. In any case, many businesses and universities are finding that running Linux on a lab of inexpensive personal computers is preferable to running a commercial version of UNIX in a lab of workstations. Linux can provide the functionality of a workstation on PC hardware at a fraction of the cost.

As a "real-world" example of Linux's use within the computing community, Linux systems have travelled the high seas of the North Pacific, managing telecommunications and data analysis for an oceanographic research vessel. Linux systems are being used at research stations in Antarctica. As a more mundane example, perhaps, several hospitals are using Linux to maintain patient records. It is proving to be as reliable and useful as other implementations of UNIX.

There are other free or inexpensive implementations of UNIX for the 80x86. One of the most well-known is FreeBSD, an implementation and port of BSD UNIX for the 386. FreeBSD is comparable to Linux in many ways, but which one is "better" depends on your own personal needs and expectations. The only strong distinction that we can make is that Linux is developed openly (where any volunteer can aid in the development process), while FreeBSD is developed within a closed team of programmers who maintain the system. Because of this, serious philosophical and design differences exist between the two projects. The goals of the two projects are entirely different: the goal of Linux is to develop a complete UNIX system from scratch (and have a lot of fun in the process), and the goal of FreeBSD is in part to modify the existing BSD code for use on the 386.

Another project of note is HURD, an effort by the Free Software Foundation to develop and distribute a free version of UNIX for many platforms. Contact the Free Software Foundation (the address is given in Appendix D) for more information about this project. At the time of this writing, HURD is still in early stages of development.

Other inexpensive versions of UNIX exist as well, such as Coherent (available for about $99) and Minix (an academic but useful UNIX clone upon which early development of Linux was based). Some of these implementations are of mostly academic interest, while others are full-fledged systems for real productivity. Needless to say, however, many personal UNIX users are moving to Linux.

1.8   Hardware Requirements

Updated as of July 1996

Now you must be convinced of how wonderful Linux is, and all of the great things that it can do for you. However, before you rush out and install the software, you need to be aware of the hardware requirements and limitations that Linux has.

Keep in mind that Linux was developed by its users. This means, for the most part, that the hardware which is supported by Linux is only the hardware which the users and developers actually have access to. As it turns out, most hardware and peripherals for 80x86 systems are supported (in fact, Linux supports more hardware than most commercial implementations of UNIX). However, some of the more obscure and esoteric devices aren't supported yet. As time goes on, a wider range of hardware is supported, so if your favorite devices aren't listed here, chances are that support for them is forthcoming.

Another drawback for hardware support under Linux is that many companies have decided to keep the hardware interface proprietary. The upshot of this is that volunteer Linux developers simply can't write drivers for those devices (if they could, those drivers would be owned by the company that owned the interface, which would violate the GPL). The companies that maintain proprietary interfaces write their own drivers for operating systems such as MS-DOS and Microsoft Windows; the end user (that's you) never needs to know about the interface. Unfortunately, this does not allow Linux developers to write drivers for those devices.

There is very little that can be done about the situation. In some cases, programmers have attempted to write hackish drivers based on assumptions about the interface. In other cases, developers will work with the company in question and attempt to obtain information about the device interface, with varying degrees of success.

In the following sections, we'll attempt to summarize the hardware requirements for Slackware Linux, this list has been updated as of July 1996.

Disclaimer: a good deal of hardware support for Linux is currently in the development stage. Slackware Linux may or may not support these experimental features. This section primarily lists hardware which has been supported for some time and is known to be stable.

1.8.1   Motherboard and CPU requirements

Linux currently supports systems with a 80386 (including SX, with or without a math coprocessor), 80486, Pentium, and Pentium Pro processors and compatables. Motherboards can be any ISA, EISA, VL-bus, or PCI PC motherboard.

1.8.2   Memory requirements

Linux requires very little memory to run compared to other advanced operating systems. You should have at the very least 4 megabytes of RAM; however, it is strongly suggested that you have 8 megabytes. The more memory you have, the faster the system will run.

Linux can support the full 32-bit address range of the 386/486; in other words, it will utilize all of your RAM automatically.

Linux will run happily with only 8 megabytes of RAM, including all of the bells and whistles such as X Windows, Emacs, and so on. However, having more memory is almost as important as having a faster processor. 16 megabytes is more than enough for personal use; 32 megabytes or more may be needed if you are expecting a heavy user load on the system.

Most Linux users allocate a portion of their hard drive as swap space, which is used as virtual RAM. Even if you have a great deal of physical RAM in your machine, you may wish to use swap space. While swap space is no replacement for actual physical RAM, it can allow your system to run larger applications by swapping out inactive portions of code to disk. The amount of swap space that you should allocate depends on several factors; we'll come back to this question in Section **??**.

1.8.3   Hard drive and SCSI controller requirements

You do not need to have a hard drive to run Linux; you can run a minimal system completely from floppy. However, this is slow and very limited, and many users have access to hard drive storage anyway. You must have an AT-standard (16-bit) controller. There is support in the kernel for XT-standard (8 bit) controllers; however, most controllers used today are AT-standard. Linux should support all MFM, RLL, SCSI and IDE controllers. Most, but not all, ESDI controllers are supported—only those which do ST506 hardware emulation.

The general rule for non-SCSI hard drive and floppy controllers is that if you can access the drive from MS-DOS or another operating system, you should be able to access it from Linux.

Linux also supports a wide number of popular SCSI drive controllers. Supported SCSI controllers includes:

- Adaptec AHA-152x, AHA-1542, AHA-1740, AIC7xxx, AHA-274x, AHA-2842, AHA-2940, AHA-2940W, AHA-2940U, AHA-2940UW, AHA-2944D, AHA-2944WD, AHA-3940, AHA-3940W, AHA-3985, AHA-3985W

- Western Digital 7000FASST SCSI support.

- AdvanSys SCSI support.

- AMD AM53/79C974 SCSI support.

- Buslogic MultiMaster SCSI support.

- DTC (Data Technology Corp) 3180/3280 SCSI support.

- DPT EATA-DMA SCSI support. (Boards such as PM2011, PM2021, PM2041, PM3021, PM2012B, PM2022, PM2122, PM2322, PM2042, PM3122, PM3222, PM3332, PM2024, PM2124, PM2044, PM2144, PM3224, PM3334.)

- DPT EATA-ISA/EISA SCSI support. (Boards such as PM2011B/9X, PM2021A/9X, PM2012A, PM2012B, PM2022A/9X, PM2122A/9X, PM2322A/9X)

- DPT EATA-PIO SCSI support. (PM2001 and PM2012A)

- Future Domain TMC-16x0 SCSI support.

- Always IN2000 SCSI support.

- IOMEGA PPA3 parallel port SCSI support. (also supports the parallel port version of the ZIP drive)

- NCR 53c406a SCSI support.

- NCR 5380 and 53c400 SCSI support.

- NCR 53c7xx, 53c8xx SCSI support. (Most NCR PCI SCSI controllers use this driver)

- Pro Audio Spectrum/Studio 16 SCSI support.

- ISA/VLB/PCMCIA Qlogic FastSCSI! support. (also supports the Control

- Concepts SCSI cards based on the Qlogic FASXXX chip)

- Qlogic PCI SCSI controllers.

- Seagate ST01/ST02, Future Domain TMC-885/950 SCSI support.

- Trantor T128/T128F/T228 SCSI support.

- UltraStor 14F, 24F, and 34F SCSI support.

Clones which are based on these cards should work as well.

1.8.4   Hard drive space requirements

Of course, to install Linux, you'll need to have some amount of free space on your
hard drive. Linux will support multiple hard drives in the same machine; you can
allocate space for Linux across multiple drives if necessary.

The *amount* of hard drive space that you will require depends greatly on your
needs and the amount of software that you're installing. Linux is relatively small as
UNIX implementations go; you could run a complete system in 25 to 40 megabytes
of space on your drive. However, if you want to have room for expansion, and
for larger packages such as X Windows, you will need around 400 megabytes for a
complete system. If you plan to allow multiple users to use the machine, you will
need to allocate storage for their files.

Also, unless you have a large amount of physical RAM (32 megabytes or more),
you will more than likely want to allocate swap space, to be used as virtual RAM.

You can run a minimal system with less than 40 megabytes; a complete system
with all of the bells and whistles in 100 megabytes or less; and a very large system with room for many users and space for future expansion in the range of 500
megabytes. Again, these figures are meant only as a ballpark approximation; you
will have to look at your own needs and goals in order to determine your specific
storage requirements.

1.8.5   Monitor and video adaptor requirements

Linux supports all standard Hercules, CGA, EGA, VGA, IBM monochrome, and
Super VGA video cards and monitors for the default text-based interface. In general, if the video card and monitor coupling works under another operating system

such as MS-DOS, it should work fine with Linux. Original IBM CGA cards suffer from "snow" under Linux, which is not pleasant to use.

Graphical environments such as the X Window System have video hardware requirements of their own. Instead of listing these requirements here, we relegate the discussion to Section 5.1.1. In short, to run the X Window System on your Linux machine, you will need one of the video cards listed in that section.

1.8.6 Miscellaneous hardware

The above sections described the hardware which is required to run a Linux system. However, most users have a number of "optional" devices such as tape and CD-ROM storage, sound boards, and so on, and are interested in whether or not this hardware is supported by Linux. Read on.

1.8.6.1 Mice and other pointing devices

For the most part, you will only be using a mouse under a graphical environment such as the X Window System. However, several Linux applications not associated with a graphics environment do make use of the mouse.

Linux supports all standard serial mice, including Logitech, MM series, Mouseman, Microsoft (2-button) and Mouse Systems (3-button). Linux also supports Microsoft, Logitech, and ATIXL busmice. The PS/2 (and C&T 82C710) mouse interface is supported as well.

All other pointing devices, such as trackballs, which emulate the above mice, should work as well.

1.8.6.2 CD-ROM drives

All SCSI CDROM drives work if the controller is supported. As long as you have a SCSI adaptor supported by Linux, then your CD-ROM drive should work.

All ATAPI/IDE CDROM drives work with Linux.

The following proprietary-interface CDROM drives are also supported by Linux:

- Aztech CDA268-01A, Orchid CD-3110, Okano/Wearnes CDD110, Conrad TXC,

- CyCDROM CR520, CR540 CDROM drives.

- Sony CDU31/33a, CDU531/535, CDU-541.

- Philips/LMS cm206 CDROM with cm260 adapter card.

- Goldstar R420 CD-ROM (sometimes sold in a 'Reveal Multimedia Kit').

- Non-IDE Mitsumi CDROM drives.

- NEC CDR-74

- Texel DM-3024

- Optics Storage 8000 AT CDROM (the 'DOLPHIN' drive).

- Sanyo CDR-H94A CDROM drives.

- Matsushita, Kotobuki, Panasonic, CreativeLabs (Sound Blaster),

- Longshine and Teac NON-IDE CDROM drives.

Linux supports the standard ISO-9660 filesystem for CD-ROMs.

1.8.6.3   Tape drives

There are several types of tape drives available on the market. Most of them use the
SCSI interface, these should be supported by Slackware Linux without a problem.
Among the verified SCSI tape drives are:

- Sankyo CP150SE

- Tandberg 3600

- Wangtek 5525ES, 5150ES, and 5099EN with the PC36 adaptor.

- QIC-02 drives should be supported as well.

Floppy tape drives are also supported in Slackware Linux. Here's a list:

- Alloy Retriever 250

- Archive 5580i/XL9250i

- Colorado DJ-10/DJ-20 (aka: Jumbo 120/Jumbo 250)

- HP Colorado T1000

- Conner C250MQ(T)

- TSM420R, TSM850R, TST800R, TST3200R

- Escom/Archive (Hornet) 31250Q,

- Irwin 80SX/Insight 80Mb

- Iomega 250, Iomega Ditto Tape Insider 420,1700, 3200

- Mountain FS8000

- Reveal TB1400

- Summit SE 150/SE 250,

- Tallgrass FS300

- Memorex tape drive backup system

- Wangtek 3040F, 3080F

1.8.6.4 Printers

Linux supports the complete range of parallel printers. If you are able to access
your printer via the parallel port from MS-DOS or another operating system, you
should be able to access it from Linux as well. The Linux printing software consists
of the UNIX standard `lp` and `lpr` software. This software also allows you to print
remotely via the network, if you have one available.

Printers supported by Ghostscript: Apple Imagewriter, C. Itoh M8510, Canon
BubbleJet BJ10e, BJ200, Canon LBP-8II, LIPS III, DEC LA50/70/75/75plus, DEC
LN03, LJ250, Epson 9 pin, 24 pin, LQ series, Stylus, AP3250, HP 2563B, HP De-
signJet 650C, HP DeskJet/Plus/500, HP DeskJet 500C/520C/550C/1200C color,
HP LaserJet/Plus/II/III/4, HP PaintJet/XL/XL300 color, IBM Jetprinter color,
IBM Proprinter, Imagen ImPress, Mitsubishi CP50 color, NEC P6/P6+/P60, Oki-
data MicroLine 182, Ricoh 4081, SPARCprinter, StarJet 48 inkjet printer, Tektronix
4693d color 2/4/8 bit, Tektronix 4695/4696 inkjet plotter, Xerox XES printers
(2700, 3700, 4045, etc.)

1.8.6.5   Modems

As with printer support, Linux supports the full range of serial modems, both internal and external. There is a great deal of telecommunications software available for Linux, including Kermit, pcomm, minicom, and Seyon. If your modem is accessible from another operating system on the same machine, you should be able to access it from Linux with no difficulty.

1.8.7   Ethernet cards

Many popular Ethernet cards and LAN adaptors are supported by Linux. These include:

- 3com 3c503, 3c503/16

- Novell NE1000, NE2000

- Western Digital WD8003, WD8013

- Hewlett Packard HP27245, HP27247, HP27250

- D-Link DE-600

- LANNET LEC-45

- Alta Combo

- Artisoft LANtastic AE-2

- Asante Etherpak 2001/2003,

- D-Link Ethernet II

- LTC E-NET/16 P/N 8300-200-002

- Network Solutions HE-203,

- SVEC 4 Dimension Ethernet

- 4-Dimension FD0490 EtherBoard 16

- 3c501, 3c503, 3c505, 3c507, 3c509/3c579, 3c59x (592/595/597) "Vortex",

- AMD LANCE, PCnet AT1500, NE2100, Western Digital WD80*3,

- SMC Ultra, SMC 9194, AT1700, Cabletron E21xx, DEPCA, DE10x, DE200,

- DE201, DE202, DE422, EtherWORKS 3 (DE203, DE204, DE205),

- EtherExpress 16, EtherExpressPro, FMV-181/182/183/184,

- HP PCLAN+ 27247B, 27252A, HP PCLAN 27245, other 27xxx series,

- HP 10/100VG PCLAN (ISA, EISA, PCI), ICL EtherTeam 16i/32,

- NE2000, NE1000, NI5210, NI6510, SEEQ8005, SKG16,

- Ansel Communications EISA 3200, Apricot Xen-II on board ethernet,

- DE425, DE434, DE435, DE450, DE500, DECchip Tulip (dc21x4x) PCI,

- Digi Intl. RightSwitch SE-X, Zenith Z-Note, AT-LAN-TEC/RealTek pocket adaptor

- D-Link DE600 pocket adaptor, D-Link DE620 pocket adaptor, Token Ring, ARCnet.

Clones which are compatible with any of the above cards should work as well.

1.8.8 Sound cards

- Pro Audio Spectrum 16, Pro Audio Studio 16

- Logitech Sound Man 16

- Media Vision Jazz16 based cards: Pro Sonic 16, Logitech SoundMan Wave

- Sound Blasters: SB 1.0 to 2.0, SB Pro, SB 16, SB16 compatible cards by other manufacturers than Creative.

- Gravis Ultrasound: GUS, GUS + the 16 bit option, GUS MAX, GUS ACE (No MIDI port and audio recording), GUS PnP (Partially supported).

- MPU-401 and compatibles, Windows Sound System (MSS/WSS), 6850 UART MIDI,

- Yamaha FM synthesizers (OPL2, OPL3 and OPL4).

- PSS based cards (AD1848 + ADSP-2115 + Echo ESC614 ASIC).

- MediaTrix AudioTrix Pro

- Ensoniq SoundScape and compatibles (but not PnP).

- MAD16 and Mozart based cards

- Audio Excel DSP16

- Crystal CS4232 based cards such as AcerMagic S23

- TB Tropez Plus

- PC motherboards (Compaq, HP, Intel, ...)

- Turtle Beach Maui and Tropez.

1.8.9   ISDN support

- ICN 2B, 4B

- PCBIT-D

- Teles/NICCY1016PC/Creatix.

1.8.10   Non-intelligent multiport serial cards

- AST FourPort and clones (4 port)

- Accent Async-4 (4 port),

- Arnet Multiport-8 (8 port)

- Bell Technologies HUB6 (6 port)

- Boca BB-1004, 1008 (4, 8 port) - no DTR, DSR, and CD, Boca BB-2016 (16 port), Boca IO/AT66 (6 port), Boca IO 2by4 (4 serial / 2 parallel, uses 5 IRQ's),

- Computone ValuePort (4, 6, 8 port) (AST FourPort compatible),

- DigiBoard PC/X (4, 8, 16 port)

- Comtrol Hostess 550 (4, 8 port),

- PC-COMM 4-port (4 port)

- SIIG I/O Expander 4S (4 port, uses 4 IRQ's),

- STB 4-COM (4 port)

- Twincom ACI/550

- Usenet Serial Board II (4 port).

1.8.11   Intelligent multiport serial cards

- Digiboard PC/Xx

- Cyclades async mux

- Stallion

- SDL RISCom/8.

1.9   Sources of Linux Information

As you have probably guessed, there are many sources of information about Linux available apart from this book. In particular, there are a number of books, not specific to Linux but rather about UNIX in general, that will be of importance, especially to those readers without previous UNIX experience. If you are new to the UNIX world, we seriously suggest that you take the time to peruse one of these books before you attempt to brave the jungles of Linux. Specifically, the book *Learning the UNIX Operating System*, by Grace Todino and John Strang, is a good place to start.

Many of the following sources of information are available online in some electronic form. That is, you must have access to an online network, such as the Internet, USENET, or Fidonet, in order to access the information contained therein. If you do not have online access to any of this material, you might be able to find someone kind enough to give you hardcopies of the documents in question. Read on.

1.9.1   Online documents

If you have access to the Internet, there are many Linux documents available via anonymous FTP from archive sites all over the world. If you do not have direct Internet access, these documents may still be available to you: many Linux distributions on CD-ROM contain all of the documents mentioned here. Also, they are distributed on many other networks, such as Fidonet and CompuServe. If you are able to send mail to Internet sites, you may be able to retrieve these files using one of the `ftpmail` servers which will electronically mail you the documents or files from FTP archive sites. See Appendix B for more information on using `ftpmail`.

There is a great number of FTP archive sites which carry Linux software and related documents. A list of well-known Linux archive sites is given in Appendix B. In order to reduce network traffic, you should always use the FTP site which is geographically (network-wise) closest to you.

Appendix A contains a listing of some of the Linux documents which are available via anonymous FTP. The filenames will differ depending on the archive site in question; most sites keep Linux-related documents in the docs subdirectory of their Linux archive space. For example, on the FTP site sunsite.unc.edu, Linux files are stored in the directory /pub/Linux, with Linux-related documentation being found in /pub/Linux/docs.

Examples of available online documents are the *Linux FAQ*, a collection of frequently asked questions about Linux; the Linux *HOWTO* documents, each describing a specific aspect of the system—including the *Installation HOWTO*, the *Printing HOWTO*, and the *Ethernet HOWTO*; and, the Linux META-FAQ, a list of other sources of Linux information on the Internet.

Most of these documents are also regularly posted to one or more Linux-related USENET newsgroups; see Section 1.9.4 below.

1.9.2   Linux on the World Wide Web

The Linux Documentation Home Page is available for World Wide Web users at the URL

        http://sunsite.unc.edu/mdw/linux.html

This page contains many HOWTOs and other documents in HTML format, as well as pointers to other sites of interest to Linux users.

The Linux Organization Web Pages is available for World Wide Web users at the URL

        http://www.linux.org/

This page contains many HOWTOs and other documents in HTML format, as well as pointers to other sites of interest to Linux users.

1.9.3 Books and other published works

At this time, there are few published works specifically about Linux. Most note-worthy are the books from the Linux Documentation Project, a project carried out over the Internet to write and distribute a bona fide set of "manuals" for Linux. These manuals are analogues to the documentation sets available with commercial versions of UNIX: they cover everything from installing Linux, to using and running the system, programming, networking, kernel development, and more.

The Linux Documentation Project manuals are available via anonymous FTP from the Internet, as well as via mail order from several sources. Appendix A lists the manuals which are available and covers means of obtaining them in detail.

There are not many books specifically about Linux currently available. How-ever, there are a large number of books about UNIX in general which are certainly applicable to Linux—as far as using and programming the system is concerned, Linux does not differ greatly from other implementations of UNIX. In short, almost everything you want to know about using and programming Linux can be found in sources meant for a general UNIX audience. In fact, this book is meant to be complemented by the large library of UNIX books currently available; here, we present the most important Linux-specific details and hope that you will look to other sources for more in-depth information.

Armed with a number of good books about using UNIX, as well as the book you hold in your hands, you should be able to tackle just about anything. Appendix A includes a list of highly-recommended UNIX books, both for UNIX newcomers and UNIX wizards alike.

There is also a monthly magazine about Linux, called the *Linux Journal*. It is distributed worldwide, and is an excellent way to keep in touch with the many goings-on in the Linux community—especially if you do not have access to USENET news (see below). See Appendix A for information on subscribing to the *Linux Journal*.

1.9.4 USENET newsgroups

USENET is a worldwide electronic news and discussion forum with a heavy con-tingent of so-called "newsgroups"—discussion areas devoted to a particular topic. Much of the development of Linux has been done over the waves of the Internet and USENET, and not surprisingly there are a number of USENET newsgroups available for discussions about Linux.

The original Linux newsgroup was `alt.os.linux`, and was created to move some of the discussions about Linux out of `comp.os.minix` and the various mailing lists. Soon, the traffic on `alt.os.linux` grew to be large enough that a newsgroup in the `comp` hierarchy was warranted; a vote was taken in February of 1992, and `comp.os.linux` was created.

`comp.os.linux` quickly became one of the most popular (and loudest) USENET groups; more popular than any other `comp.os` group. In December of 1992, a vote was taken to split the newsgroup in order to reduce traffic; only `comp.os.linux.announce` passed this vote. In July of 1993, the group was finally split into the new hierarchy. Almost 2000 people voted in the `comp.os.linux` reorganization, making it one of the largest USENET Call For Votes ever.

If you do not have direct USENET access, but are able to send and receive electronic mail from the Internet, there are mail-to-news gateways available for each of the newsgroups below.

comp.os.linux.announce

`comp.os.linux.announce` is a moderated newsgroup for announcements and important postings about the Linux system (such as bug reports, important patches to software, and so on). If you read any Linux newsgroups at all, read this one. Often, the important postings in this group are not crossposted to other groups. This group also contains many periodic postings about Linux, including many of the online documents described in the last section and listed in Appendix A.

Postings to this newsgroup must be approved by the moderators, Matt Welsh and Lars Wirzenius. If you wish to submit and article to this group, in most cases you can simply post the article as you normally would (using `Pnews` or whatever posting software that you have available); the news software will automatically forward the article to the moderators for approval. However, if your news system is not set up correctly, you may need to mail the article directly; the submission address is `linux-announce@tc.cornell.edu`.

The rest of the Linux newsgroups listed below are unmoderated.

comp.os.linux.help

This is the most popular Linux newsgroup. It is for questions and answers about using, setting up, or otherwise running a Linux system. If you are having problems with Linux, you may post to this newsgroup, and hopefully receive a reply from someone who might be able to help. However, it is strongly suggested that you read all of the available Linux documentation before posting questions to this newsgroup.

`comp.os.linux.admin`

This newsgroup is for questions and discussion about running a Linux system, most commonly in an active, multi-user environment. Any discussion about administrative issues of Linux (such as packaging software, making backups, handling users, and so on) is welcome here.

`comp.os.linux.development`

This is a newsgroup for discussions about development of the Linux system. All issues related to kernel and system software development should be discussed here. For example, if you are writing a kernel driver and need help with certain aspects of the programming, this would be the place to ask. This newsgroup is also for discussions about the direction and goals behind the Linux development effort, as described (somewhat) in Section 1.6.

It should be noted that this newsgroup is not (technically) for discussions about development of software *for* Linux, but rather for discussions of development *of* Linux. That is, issues dealing with applications programming under Linux should be discussed in another Linux newsgroup; `comp.os.linux.development` is about developing the Linux system itself, including the kernel, system libraries, and so on.

`comp.os.linux.misc`

This newsgroup is for all discussion which doesn't quite fit into the other available Linux groups. In particular, advocacy wars (the incessant "Linux versus Windows NT" thread, for example), should be waged here, as opposed to in the technical Linux groups. Any nontechnical or metadiscourse about the Linux system should remain in `comp.os.linux.misc`.

It should be noted that the newsgroup `comp.os.linux`, which was originally the only Linux group, has been superseded by the new hierarchy of groups. If you have access to `comp.os.linux`, but not to the newer Linux groups listed above, encourage your news administrator to create the new groups on your system.

1.9.5   Internet mailing lists

If you have access to Internet electronic mail, you can participate in a number of
mailing lists even if you do not have USENET access. Note that if you are not
directly on the Internet, you can join one of these mailing lists as long as you are
able to exchange electronic mail with the Internet (for example, UUCP, FidoNET,
CompuServe, and other networks all have access to Internet mail).

The "Linux Activists" mailing list is primarily for Linux developers and people
interested in aiding the development process. This is a "multi-channel" mailing
list, in which you join one or more "channels" based on your particular interests.
Some of the available channels include: `NORMAL`, for general Linux-related issues;
`KERNEL`, for kernel development; `GCC`, for discussions relating to the `gcc` compiler
and library development; `NET`, for discussions about the TCP/IP networking code;
`DOC`, for issues relating to writing and distributing Linux documentation; and more.

For more information about the Linux Activists mailing list, send mail to

```
linux-activists@niksula.hut.fi
```

You will receive a list of currently available channels, including information on how
to subscribe and unsubscribe to particular channels on the list.

Quite a few special-purpose mailing lists about and for Linux exist as well.
The best way to find out about these is to watch the Linux USENET newsgroups
for announcements, as well as to read the list of publicly-available mailing lists,
periodically posted to the USENET group `news.answers`.

1.10   Getting Help

You will undoubtedly require some degree of assistance during your adventures in
the Linux world. Even the most wizardly of UNIX wizards occasionally is stumped
by some quirk or feature of Linux, and it's important to know how and where to
find help when you need it.

The primary means of getting help in the Linux world are via Internet mailing
lists and USENET newsgroups, as discussed in Section 1.9. If you don't have online
access to these sources, you might be able to find comparable Linux discussion
forums on other online services, such as on local BBS's, CompuServe, and so on.

A number of businesses are providing commercial support for Linux. This will
allow you to pay a "subscription fee" which will allow you to call the consultants for

help with your Linux problems. Appendix **??** contains a list of Linux vendors, some of which provide commercial support. However, if you have access to USENET and Internet mail, you may find the free support found there to be just as useful.

Keeping the following suggestions in mind will greatly improve your experiences with Linux and will guarantee you more success in finding help to your problems.

Consult all available documentation. . . first! The first thing you should do when encountering a problem is consult the various sources of information listed in Section 1.9 and Appendix A. These documents were laboriously written for people like you—people who need help with the Linux system. Even books written for UNIX in general are applicable to Linux, and you should take advantage of them. More than likely, you will find the answer to your problems somewhere in this documentation, as impossible as it may seem.

If you have access to USENET news or any of the Linux-related mailing lists, be sure to actually *read* the information there before posting for help with your problem. Many times, solutions to common problems are not easy to find in documentation, and instead are well-covered in the newsgroups and mailing lists devoted to Linux. If you only post to these groups, and don't actually read them, you are asking for trouble.

Learn to appreciate self-maintenance. In most cases, it is preferable to do as much independent research and investigation into the problem as possible before seeking outside help. After all, you asked for it, by running Linux in the first place! Remember that Linux is all about hacking and fixing problems yourself. It is not a commercial operating system, nor does it try to look like one. Hacking won't kill you. In fact, it will teach you a great deal about the system to investigate and solve problems yourself—maybe even enough to one day call yourself a Linux guru. Learn to appreciate the value of hacking the system, and how to fix problems yourself. You can't expect to run a complete, homebrew Linux system without some degree of handiwork.

Remain calm. It is vital to refrain from getting frustrated with the system, at all costs. Nothing is earned by taking an axe—or worse, a powerful electromagnet—to your Linux system in a fit of anger. The authors have found that a large punching bag or similar inanimate object is a wonderful way to relieve the occasional stress attack. As Linux matures and distributions become more reliable, we hope that this problem will go away. However, even commercial UNIX implementations can be tricky at times. When all else fails, sit back, take a few deep breaths, and go after the problem again when you feel relaxed. Your mind and conscience will be clearer.

Refrain from posting spuriously. Many people make the mistake of posting or mailing messages pleading for help prematurely. When encountering a problem, do not—we repeat, do *not*—rush immediately to your nearest terminal and post a message to one of the Linux USENET newsgroups. Often, you will catch your own mistake five minutes later and find yourself in the curious situation of defending your own sanity in a public forum. Before posting anything any of the Linux mailing lists or newsgroups, first attempt to resolve the problem yourself and be absolutely certain what the problem is. Does your system not respond when switched on? Perhaps the machine is unplugged.

If you do post for help, make it worthwhile. If all else fails, you may wish to post a message for help in any of the number of electronic forums dedicated to Linux, such as USENET newsgroups and mailing lists. When posting, remember that the people reading your post are not there to help you. The network is not your personal consulting service. Therefore, it is important to remain as polite, terse, and informative as possible.

How can one accomplish this? First, you should include as much (relevant) information about your system and your problem as possible. Posting the simple request, "I cannot seem to get e-mail to work" will probably get you nowhere unless you include information on your system, what software you are using, what you have attempted to do so far and what the results were. When including technical information, it is usually a good idea to include general information on the version(s) of your software (Linux kernel version, for example), as well as a brief summary of your hardware configuration. However, don't overdo it—including information on the brand and type of monitor that you have probably is irrelevant if you're trying to configure networking software.

Secondly, remember that you need to make some attempt—however feeble—at solving your problem before you go to the Net. If you have never attempted to set up electronic mail, for instance, and first decide to ask folks on the Net how to go about doing it, you are making a big mistake. There are a number of documents available (see the Section 1.9) on how to get started with many common tasks under Linux. The idea is to get as far along as possible on your own and *then* ask for help if and when you get stuck.

Also remember that the people reading your message, however helpful, may occasionally get frustrated by seeing the same problem over and over again. Be sure to actually read the Linux newsgroups and mailing lists before posting your problems. Many times, the solution to your problem has been discussed repeatedly, and all that's required to find it is to browse the current messages.

Lastly, when posting to electronic newsgroups and mailing lists, try to be as polite as possible. It is much more effective and worthwhile to be polite, direct, and informative—more people will be willing to help you if you master a humble tone. To be sure, the flame war is an art form across many forms of electronic communication, but don't allow that to preoccupy your and other people's time. Save the network undue wear and tear by keeping bandwidth as low as possible, and by paying as much attention to other sources of information which are available to you. The network is an excellent way to get help with your Linux problems—but it is important to know how to use the network *effectively*.

Chapter 2

Installing Slackware Linux

Linux is a multiuser, multitasking operating system that was developed by Linus Torvalds and hundreds of volunteers around the world working over the Internet.

The Linux operating system now runs on several machine architectures, including Intel 80x86, SPARC, m68k, PowerPC, and DEC Alpha. The Slackware distribution of Linux runs on Intel (and compatible) 386, 486, Pentium, and Pentium Pro based PCs. Linux is modeled after the UNIX operating system. The Slackware distribution contains a full program development system with support for C, C++, Fortran-77, LISP, and other languages, full TCP/IP networking with NFS, SLIP, PPP, a full implementation of the X Window System, and much more.

2.1 Sources of documentation

If you're new to Slackware, you'll be happy to know there is a **lot** of documentation and help available both on the Internet and on the CDROM itself.

One of the primary sources of Linux information is a collection of documents known as the "Linux HOWTOs." You can find these on the Internet at sunsite.unc.edu, in the `/pub/Linux/docs/HOWTO` directory.

Other useful documentation at that site includes:

`/pub/Linux/docs/FAQ` – answers to Frequently Asked Questions about Linux

`/pub/Linux/docs/LDP/` – Manuals written by the Linux Documentation Project.

Of course, these documents are also available on the Slackware CDROM in the /docs directory, or on `ftp.cdrom.com` in `/pub/linux/slackware/docs`.

2.2   Hardware requirements

Most PC hardware will work fine with Slackware, but there are a few exceptions. Slackware does not support the MCA (Microchannel Architecture) motherboards used in some IBM machines (most notably PS/2s).

Some Plug-and-Play devices also cause problems under Slackware. In some cases you can work around this by letting DOS initialize the card and then starting Slackware with the Loadlin utility.

Here's a basic list of what you'll need to install Slackware:

Four megabytes (4MB) or more or RAM. If you only have four megabytes, you'll want to make sure you disable shadow RAM in your system's CMOS settings, as the couple hundred kilobytes of memory freed can make the difference between a successful installation or a failed one. If you have eight or more megabytes of RAM, you'll be just fine.

You also will need some disk space to install Slackware. For a complete installation, you'll probably want to devote a 250 MB or larger partition completely to Slackware. You can make a smaller subset of Slackware fit into as little as 20 MB, although an average installation uses around 100 to 200 MB. The amount of disk space required varies dramatically depending on the amount of software you've chosen to install, the number of users on your machine, and the amount of swap space you've given Slackware. If you haven't installed Slackware before, you may have to experiment. If you've got the drive space, again, more is going to be better than not enough. Also, you can always install only the first software set (the A series containing only the basic system utilities) and then install more software later once your system is running.

If you use SCSI, Slackware supports most SCSI controllers. Check the list of bootdisks in the `bootdsks.144/README.TXT` file to see if there's a bootdisk for your controller. You also might consult the `SCSI-HOWTO` for specific information about your controller.

To install from the CDROM, you'll need a supported CDROM drive. Again, check the `bootdsks.144/README.TXT` file to see if your drive is listed. If it's not, you still have an excellent chance of finding a bootdisk through trial and error that works with it anyway, since many CDROM drives sold by brand-X companies contain electronics manufactured by one of the companies that make a supported drive. Also, more and more drives made today use the ATAPI/IDE standard – these drives will all work fine under Slackware.

2.3 Slackware space requirements

Slackware divides the installable software into categories. In the early days most people installed Slackware from floppy disk, so I often refer to the categories as "disk sets." Only the A series is mandatory, but you can't do very much on a system that only has the A series installed. Usually, you won't install the entire disk series, but will pick which packages you wish to install. Here's an overview of the software that's available for installation, along with the amount of drive space you'd need to install the entire set:

- **Disk Set A**
  The base Slackware system. Contains enough utilities to get Slackware running and have comm programs, editors, and installation utilities available. Installing the entire A series requires 20 MB.

- **Disk Set AP**
  Linux applications. These are some useful programs, including better editors, file quota utilities, a spell checker, man pages (and the groff package needed to process them), a Norton Commander clone called the Midnight Commander, extra shells, and other utilities. Installing the entire AP series uses 15 MB.

- **Disk Set D**
  Program development. This series contains compilers, interpreters, and translators for C, C++, Objective-C, Fortran-77, Common LISP, Pascal, Perl, and more, as well as utilities needed to use them. You need this series if you plan to recompile your kernel (or anything else). Installing the entire D series will require 48 MB. If you omit a.out support, you need 40 MB.

- **Disk Set E**
  GNU Emacs 19.31. This is a text editor with about a million extra features that allow you to read your mail, news, edit and compile programs, and just about anything else you might need to do. Installing the entire E series will require 28 MB.

- **Disk Set F**

  Answers to Frequently Asked Questions about Linux. This series will install useful Linux documentation, including the Linux HOWTOs, on your machine under /usr/doc/faq. Installing the F series requires about 2 MB.

- **Disk Set K**

  Linux kernel source. This package contains source code for the 2.0.0 Linux kernel. You'll need this (along with the C compiler and utilities from the D series) if you want to recompile your Linux kernel. Installing the K series will require 23 MB, and you'll need more to compile it.

- **Disk Set N**

  Networking. This package contains TCP/IP and UUCP support for Slackware, including packages to support SLIP/PPP, mail programs such as sendmail, pine, and elm, news readers like tin, trn, and nn, the Apache Web server, and Web browsers. Installing the entire N series will use 15 MB.

- **Disk Set T**

  The NTeX TeX distribution. TeX is a typesetting language that you can use to format and print high-quality output on many types of printers. Installing the entire T series requires 45 MB.

- **Disk Set TCL**

  Tcl/Tk/TclX scripting languages, and the TkDesk file manager. The TCL series needs about 6 MB.

- **Disk Set X**

  The X Window System, from XFree86 3.1.2. This series provides a system for supporting GUIs (Graphical User Interfaces) under Slackware. The entire X series requires 38 MB.

- **Disk Set XAP**

  Applications for the X Window System. Extra programs for X, such as a couple of file managers (xfm, xfilemanager), a window manager that makes X resemble Windows95 (fvwm95), the Arena web browser, image editing and processing apps, a fractal generator (xfractint), communications programs, and more. Installing the entire XAP series will require about 12 MB.

- **Disk Set XD**

  Extra development tools for X. This series contains libraries used to make static X applications, and a link kit used to compile X servers. (This series is not needed to compile X applications) Installing the XD series will use about 13 MB.

- **Disk Set XV**

  xview3.2p1-X11R6. The XView series adds support for the Open Look window manager (commonly used on Sun systems), and for compiling XView applications. The XV series uses 11 MB.

- **Disk Set Y**

  The Y series contains a collection of games for Slackware. Installing the entire Y series will use about 11 MB.

You must install the Disk Set A set. You probably also want to install the AP, D, and N series, as well as the X, XAP, and possibly the XV sets if you wish to run the X Window System. The Y series is fun if you have the space for it.

2.3.1   Creating the installation floppies

NOTE: The Walnut Creek official Slackware CDROM has a provision for installing **without** creating `boot` and `root` floppies. You'll still need one formatted high-density floppy disk to complete the installation. The 'setup' program will use it to create a bootdisk with which will start the installed system. See the "Floppyless Installation" section for more details.

If you still want to do a regular floppy install. You must install Slackware from a set of startup floppies. These are the **boot** and **root** disks. The bootdisk contains the Linux kernel, so you'll need to choose a bootdisk matched to your hardware. The rootdisk contains a small Linux filesystem and the installation software. Later, you'll also need a third formatted floppy disk when the system generates a custom bootdisk to start your Slackware system.

If you use a 3.5" floppy drive, you'll find the bootdisk images on the CDROM in the `bootdsks.144` (for 1.44 MB) directory. If you use a 5.25" floppy drive, you'll find the bootdisk images in the `bootdsks.12` directory.

USING THE VIEW PROGRAM: If you have MS-DOS on your machine, you can greatly simplify the process of selecting and creating your boot and root disks by running the **VIEW.EXE** program on the CDROM. This will let you look at the lists of boot and root disks (showing the hardware each supports) and will write out the disks automatically. To see a list of bootdisks for your machine, start **VIEW.EXE** under MS-DOS.

NOTE: Writing out the boot and root disks will not work correctly under Windows95. Start your machine in real MS-DOS mode before attempting to create the disks.

Use the view program to switch into a directory containing Slackware bootdisks. If you have a 1.44 MB floppy drive, bootdsks.144 is the directory to use. Move the selection bar with the arrow keys until bootdsks.144/ is highlighted, and then hit enter to move into the directory. If you have a 1.2 MB floppy drive, move into the bootdsks.12/ directory instead. Once you're in one of the bootdsks.*/ directories, move down another level into one of the ide-bat/ or scsi-bat/ directories. These contain MS-DOS batch files to write out the bootdisks. Use the scsi-bat/ directory if your machine has a SCSI controller card, or the ide-bat/ directory if it only has IDE. You'll see a list of the bootdisks you can use. Use the view program to select one that supports the hardware you've got. You'll be prompted to insert a formatted floppy disk, and then hit a key. If all goes well, your floppy drive should start chugging away, writing the bootdisk image onto the floppy disk.

There are two main categories of Slackware bootdisks, those that support SCSI (and IDE) controllers, and those that only support IDE. The disks that only contain IDE support have a .I extension to the filename, while those with IDE and SCSI support have a .S extension. Note that **all** of the Slackware bootdisks have full support for IDE (including IDE/ATAPI CDROM drives). A detailed list of bootdisks for Slackware follows:

2.3.2   Boot disc description

IDE Slackware bootdisks:

- **aztech.i**
  Aztech CDA268-01A, Orchid CD-3110, Okano/Wearnes CDD110, Conrad TXC, CyCDROM CR520, CR540

- **bare.i**
  (none, just IDE support)

- **cdu31a.i**
  Sony CDU31/33a CDROM

- **cdu535.i**
  Sony CDU531/535 CDROM

- **cm206.i**
  Philips/LMS cm206 CDROM with cm260 adapter card

- **goldstar.i**
  Goldstar R420 CDROM (sometimes sold in a 'Reveal Multimedia Kit')

- **mcd.i**
  NON-IDE Mitsumi CDROM support

- **mcdx.i**
  Improved NON-IDE Mitsumi CDROM support

- **net.i**
  Ethernet support

- **optics.i**
  Optics Storage 8000 AT CDROM (the 'DOLPHIN' drive)

- **sanyo.i**
  Sanyo CDR-H94A CDROM support

- **sbpcd.i**
  Matsushita, Kotobuki, Panasonic, CreativeLabs (Sound Blaster), Longshine and Teac NON-IDE CDROM support

- **xt.i** MFM hard drive support

SCSI/IDE Slackware bootdisks:

- **7000fast.s**
  Western Digital 7000 FAST SCSI support

- **advansys.s**
  AdvanSys SCSI support

- **aha152x.s**
  Adaptec 152x SCSI support

- **aha1542.s**
  Adaptec 1542 SCSI support

- **aha1740.s**
  Adaptec 1740 SCSI support

- **aha2x4x.s**
  Adaptec AIC7xxx SCSI support (For these cards: AHA-274x, AHA-2842, AHA-2940, AHA-2940W, AHA-2940U, AHA-2940UW, AHA-2944D, AHA-2944WD, AHA-3940, AHA-3940W, AHA-3985, AHA-3985W)

- **am53c974.s**
  AMD AM53/79C974 SCSI support

- **aztech.s**

  All supported SCSI controllers, plus CDROM support for Aztech CDA268-
  01A, Orchid CD-3110, Okano/Wearnes CDD110, Conrad TXC, CyCDROM
  CR520, CR540

- **buslogic.s**

  Buslogic MultiMaster SCSI support

- **cdu31a.s**

  All supported SCSI controllers, plus CDROM support for Sony CDU31/33a

- **cdu535.s**

  All supported SCSI controllers, plus CDROM support for Sony CDU531/535

- **cm206.s**

  All supported SCSI controllers, plus Philips/LMS cm206 CDROM with cm260
  adapter card

- **dtc3280.s**

  DTC (Data Technology Corp) 3180/3280 SCSI support

- **eata_dma.s**

  DPT EATA-DMA SCSI support (Boards such as PM2011, PM2021, PM2041,
  PM3021, PM2012B, PM2022, PM2122, PM2322, PM2042, PM3122, PM3222,
  PM3332, PM2024, PM2124, PM2044, PM2144, PM3224, PM3334.)

- **eata_isa.s**

  DPT   EATA-ISA/EISA   SCSI   support   (Boards
  such as PM2011B/9X, PM2021A/9X, PM2012A, PM2012B, PM2022A/9X,
  PM2122A/9X, PM2322A/9X)

- **eata_pio.s**

  DPT EATA-PIO SCSI support (PM2001 and PM2012A)

- **fdomain.s**

  Future Domain TMC-16x0 SCSI support

- **goldstar.s**

  All supported SCSI controllers, plus Goldstar R420 CDROM (sometimes sold
  in a 'Reveal Multimedia Kit')

- **in2000.s**

  Always IN2000 SCSI support

- **iomega.s**
  IOMEGA PPA3 parallel port SCSI support (also supports the parallel port version of the ZIP drive)

- **mcd.s**
  All supported SCSI controllers, plus standard non-IDE Mitsumi CDROM support

- **mcdx.s**
  All supported SCSI controllers, plus enhanced non-IDE Mitsumi CDROM support

- **n53c406a.s**
  NCR 53c406a SCSI support

- **n_5380.s**
  NCR 5380 and 53c400 SCSI support

- **n_53c7xx.s**
  NCR 53c7xx, 53c8xx SCSI support (Most NCR PCI SCSI controllers use this driver)

- **optics.s**
  All supported SCSI controllers, plus support for the Optics Storage 8000 AT CDROM (the 'DOLPHIN' drive)

- **pas16.s**
  Pro Audio Spectrum/Studio 16 SCSI support

- **qlog_fas.s**
  ISA/VLB/PCMCIA Qlogic FastSCSI! support (also supports the Control Concepts SCSI cards based on the Qlogic FASXXX chip)

- **qlog_isp.s**
  Supports all Qlogic PCI SCSI controllers, except the PCI-basic, which the AMD SCSI driver supports

- **sanyo.s**
  All supported SCSI controllers, plus Sanyo CDR-H94A CDROM support

- **sbpcd.s**
  All supported SCSI controllers, plus Matsushita, Kotobuki, Panasonic, CreativeLabs (Sound Blaster), Longshine and Teac NON-IDE CDROM support

- **scsinet.s**

  All supported SCSI controllers, plus full ethernet support

- **seagate.s**

  Seagate ST01/ST02, Future Domain TMC-885/950 SCSI support

- **trantor.s**

  Trantor T128/T128F/T228 SCSI support

- **ultrastr.s**

  UltraStor 14F, 24F, and 34F SCSI support

- **ustor14f.s**

  UltraStor 14F and 34F SCSI support

You'll want to choose a bootdisk from the list that supports your installation media (such as a CDROM drive) and the hard drive you'll be installing to. For example, to install from an IDE CDROM drive to an IDE hard drive, you'd use the `BARE.I` disk. Or, for a system with an NCR 53c810 SCSI controller, SCSI CDROM, and SCSI hard drive, you'd use the `n_53c7xx.s` bootdisk.

Disks with network support are usually used to install from NFS, so you don't need to be concerned with whether the installed system will require ethernet drivers at this point. When selecting the bootdisk, you only need to think about what you need to get the system installed. You can add additional drivers after installation by recompiling the Linux kernel, or by loading the support in the form of kernel modules.

Once you've selected your bootdisk, you'll need to write it out to a floppy disk. The easiest way to do this is to use the MS-DOS **VIEW.EXE** program on the CDROM.

Use the view program to navigate into either the `bootdsks.12` or `bootdsks.144` directory. From there, move into either the `SCSI-BAT` or `IDE-BAT` directory, depending on whether you've got a SCSI controller in your system. Here, you'll see a list of options. To create a bootdisk, select one of the choices with the view program. Then follow the on-screen prompts to put a formatted floppy in your drive and write out the disk image.

You also can create the disk manually under DOS using the **RAWRITE.EXE** program. This utility copies a file onto a floppy disk directly, track by track. To use RAWRITE, just put a formatted high density floppy disk into your boot drive, change to the `bootdsks.144` or `bootdsks.12` directory on the CDROM (depending on which size disk you use), and use the RAWRITE command to write out the disk:

```
C:\> E:    (or D:, or whatever drive letter your CDROM uses)

E:\> CD BOOTDSKS.144

E:\> DIR A:
```

(NOTE: On some machines RAWRITE.EXE will incorrectly try to use an incorrect sector size unless you make DOS look at the disk first with the DIR command.)

```
E:\BOOTDSKS.144> RAWRITE BARE.I A:
```

In the example above, you'll notice the image written out is **BARE.I**. You'll want to replace that with the name of the disk you've chosen to use.

Making the floppy disks from Linux or UNIX is also no problem. In most cases you can just stick a formatted floppy disk in the drive and then send the image to the drive with 'cat':

```
$ cat bare.i > /dev/fd0    (The exact name of the floppy device varies
                           depending on the system used)
```

You also can write out the disk under Linux or UNIX using the 'dd' command. This might work better in some cases than 'cat', since it ensures that the correct sector size is used:

```
$ dd if=bare.i of=/dev/(rdfd0, rdf0c, fd0, or whatever) obs=18k
```

Once you've created your bootdisk, you need to pick a rootdisk. You will find these on the CDROM in the rootdsks directory. If you plan to install Slackware on its own partition, you'll probably want to use the COLOR.GZ rootdisk.

If you want to install Slackware on an existing MS-DOS partition in a \LINUX directory, then you'll want to use the **UMSDOS.GZ** rootdisk. Usually you'll want to use one of those two rootdisks, although there are other disks that support more complex installation procedures, such as installing from tape or via NFS through a PCMCIA ethernet card. A list of Slackware rootdisks follows:

SCSI/IDE Slackware bootdisks:

- **COLOR.GZ**

  This is the default Slackware installation disk, used to install Slackware Linux to its own partition. The name COLOR.GZ comes from the color menus used to install Slackware.

- **UMSDOS.GZ**

  This is similar to the COLOR disk, but installs using UMSDOS – a filesystem
  that allows you to install Slackware into a directory on an existing MS-DOS
  partition. This isn't as fast as using a native Linux filesystem, and can use
  more drive space because of limitations in the way DOS stores small files.
  The big advantage of using UMSDOS is that you can try Slackware without
  repartitioning your hard drive. This is much easier for the beginner, and
  potentially a lot less dangerous to your system.

- **TEXT.GZ**

  This is a text-based version of the install program. Although many users
  prefer the COLOR.GZ disk, this version can be useful for troubleshooting
  because it displays error messages on the screen – COLOR.GZ often covers
  error messages with menus before you can read them. I derived the installation
  scripts used by this disk from older versions of Slackware.

- **TAPE.GZ**

  I designed this image to support installation from tape. Tape installation
  remains experimental, but if you'd like to try it, see the README file on
  tape installation found in the rootdsks directory. This requires access to a
  machine with GNU tar running Linux or UNIX to make the tape.

- **PCMCIA.GZ**

  This is a version of the TEXT.GZ rootdisk with added support for PCMCIA
  ethernet cards. You should use this disk to install to a laptop through the
  network using NFS.

Once you've selected the rootdisk you want to use, you write it out to a formatted
floppy – as you did with the bootdisk. Again, you can use the **VIEW.EXE** program
to create the rootdisk. From within the **VIEW.EXE** program, change into the
rootdsks directory on the CDROM. Then, select an appropriate rootdisk such as
`COLOR.GZ`, and use **VIEW.EXE** to select it. Place a formatted floppy disk in your
drive and press enter to write the rootdisk image to the disk.

NOTE: Looking at the rootdisk images, you'll notice they end in `.GZ`. This
stands for GNU zip, a utility used to compress the rootdisk images. Do not uncompress the rootdisk before writing it out. The uncompressed images won't fit on 1.2
MB floppy disks.

Now you should have two installation disks prepared, a bootdisk and a rootdisk.

If you haven't done so already, you also should format a high density diskette that you will use to make an emergency bootdisk for your system when you are finished with the installation.

2.4 Preparing a partition for Slackware

If you plan to install Slackware onto its own hard drive partition (this offers optimal performance), then you'll need to prepare one or more partitions for it. If you're planning to use the UMSDOS system, then you can skip to the next section.

A partition is a section of a hard drive that has been set aside for use by an operating system. You can have up to four primary partitions on a single hard drive. If you need more than that, you can make what is called an "extended partition." This is actually a way to make one of the primary partitions contain several sub-partitions.

Usually there won't be any free space on your hard drive. Instead, you will have already partitioned it for the use of other operating systems, such as MS-DOS or OS/2. Before you can make your Linux partitions, you'll need to remove one or more of your existing drive partitions to make room for it. Removing a partition destroys the data on it, so you'll want to back it up first.

If you've got a large DOS partition that you'd like to shrink to make space for Slackware, there's a program called `FIPS` in the `INSTALL` directory on the CDROM. This utility allows you to shrink the size of a DOS partition without destroying the data on it. The idea is to use a disk defragmenter utility to compress all of your data into the first part of the partition. MS-DOS versions 6.0 and above include DEFRAG (a reduced-feature version of Norton Speedisk) which works well for this purpose. Then you use `FIPS` to set a new end point for the partition, leaving free space that you can make into Linux partitions. Even though `FIPS` is usually safe to use, it's a good practice to back up all of the data on the drive. You can find a detailed guide to using `FIPS` on the CDROM in `\INSTALL\FIPS\FIPS.DOC` If you plan to use `FIPS` to resize your DOS partition, refer to the `FIPS` guide for further repartitioning instructions.

To read the `FIPS` documentation from the MS-DOS view program, move into the install directory, then into the `FIPS` directory, and then select `FIPS.DOC` to bring up the documentation on the screen.

Once you've finished repartitioning, you can go on to the section on Installing the Slackware distribution.

If you plan to repartition your system manually, you'll need to back up the data on any partitions you plan to change. The usual tool for deleting/creating partitions is the **FDISK** program. Most PC operating systems have a version of this tool, and if you're running DOS or OS/2 it's probably best to use the repartitioning tool from that OS. Usually DOS uses the entire drive. Use DOS fdisk to delete the partition. Then create a smaller primary DOS partition, leaving enough space to install Linux (hopefully 200 MB or so, and about another 16 MB for swap space). You'll then need to reinstall DOS on your new DOS partition, and then restore your backup.

2.5   Using Linux fdisk to create a Linux partition

(If you're using the floppyless installation, you won't need to use the boot and root disks as described below. Instead, skip to the "Floppyless Installation" in section 2.5.1.)

At this point, you should have a large chunk of unpartitioned space on your hard drive that you'll be making into partitions for Slackware. To do this, place the Slackware bootdisk in your machine and reboot your machine. The disk will display a screenful of information and give you the opportunity to enter extra kernel flags to help configure your hardware. Most users won't need to enter anything special here. However, if your hardware isn't detected properly (and you're sure the bootdisk you're using contains the correct support) then see the file **BOOTING.TXT** on the CDROM for instructions on using this feature. If you don't need to enter any kernel parameters (and you probably don't), then just hit enter to begin loading the kernel. You'll see a message like this displayed on the screen as the kernel loads:

```
LILO loading ramdisk........
```

The kernel will then boot. As the kernel probes your machine to determine its hardware configuration, you'll see plenty of diagnostic information printed to the screen. Eventually it will display this message:

```
VFS: Insert root floppy disk to be loaded into ramdisk and press
ENTER
```

Now take the bootdisk out of the drive, replace it with the rootdisk, and hit enter. Your computer will load the Slackware rootdisk into memory, and then you'll get a login prompt. Log into the system as "root."

2.5.1 Floppyless Installation

If you're using the floppyless installation from the Slackware Linux , use this procedure to get to the login prompt. From the MS-DOS prompt, change to the directory
/kernels on the CDROM. There should be subdirectories within the /kernels directory each containing a kernel image. Change to the directory containing the boot
kernel image you wish to use. Depending on the type of installation you wish to use,
run either the color.bat (for installing to a Linux partition) or the umsdos.bat
(for installing to a MS-DOS partition) batch file. Once you select one of these, your
system will attempt to load Linux. If successful, you'll get a login prompt. Log in as
root, and then continue with the installation process as described below. Once you
select one of these, your system will attempt to load Linux. If successful, you'll get
a login prompt. Log in as root, and then continue with the installation process as
described below. **NOTE**: Many DOS drivers (such as memory managers, etc) can
interfere with the process of booting Linux directly from the CDROM. If you run
into problems, you can try to disable as many DOS drivers as possible and then try
again. If you use Windows95, you can do this by hitting the F8 key as your machine
starts to boot. You'll be presented with a menu – choose option 5 for a command
line only interface. DOS will then ask if you wish to process your CONFIG.SYS.
Answer yes, and you'll be asked to confirm each DOS driver as it loads. If you have
emm386, QEMM, 386MAX, or other memory managers listed, hit ESC as DOS asks if
you'd like to load them. In general, you should avoid loading anything except the
drivers for your CDROM drive. Then, try to load a kernel and rootdisk again using
the procedure described above.

2.5.2 Creating Linux partitions

Now you're ready to create your root Linux partition. To do this, you'll use the
Linux version of fdisk. By default, Linux fdisk creates partitions on the first IDE
hard drive (/dev/hda1). If you need to partition a different hard drive, you need
to specify the name of the device when you start fdisk. For example:

```
fdisk /dev/hda        (Repartition the first IDE hard drive)
fdisk /dev/hdb        (Repartition the second IDE hard drive)
fdisk /dev/sda        (Repartition the first SCSI hard drive)
fdisk /dev/sdb        (Repartition the second SCSI hard drive)
```

Once you've started fdisk, it will display a command prompt. First look at your
existing partition table with the 'p' command:

```
Command (m for help): p


Disk /dev/sda: 255 heads, 63 sectors, 92 cylinders
Units = cylinders of 16065 * 512 bytes


    Device Boot   Begin   Start    End   Blocks   Id  System
/dev/sda1       1     1     32   257008+   6  DOS 16-bit >= 32M
```

If you used FIPS to split a DOS partition, you'll see two primary DOS partitions instead of one. The second DOS partition is empty, so you'll want to go ahead and delete it to make free space for your Linux root and swap partitions. To do this, use the 'd' command. You'll be asked which partition number you want to delete. This will probably be the second partition on the drive, but check the partition size to make sure its the right one.

```
Next, you'll want to use the 'n' command to create a primary
partition.  This will be your root Linux partition.


Command (m for help): n
Command action
   e   extended
   p   primary partition (1-4)


You'll want to enter 'p' to make a primary partition.


Partition number (1-4): 2
```

Here, you enter "2" since DOS is already using the first primary partition. Fdisk will first ask you which cylinder the partition should start on. Fdisk knows where your last partition left off and will suggest the first available cylinder on the drive as the starting point for the new partition. Go ahead and accept this value. Then, fdisk will want to know what size to make the partition. You can specify this in a couple of ways, either by entering the ending cylinder number directly, or by entering a size. In this case, we'll enter a size. To do this, you need to enter +sizeM – in this case, +450M. Here's what the screen looks like as these figures are entered:

```
First cylinder (33-92): 33
Last cylinder or +size or +sizeM or +sizeK (33-92): +450M
```

You have now created your primary Linux partition with a size of 450 MB. Next, you'll want to make a Linux swap partition. You do this the same way. First, enter another "n" to make a primary partition:

```
Command (m for help): n
Command action
e    extended
p    primary partition (1-4)
```

Enter "p" to select a primary partition. Partition 1 is in use by DOS, and you've already used partition 2 for Linux, so you'll want to enter "3" for the new partition number:

```
Partition number (1-4):  3
```

Since this is the last partition we plan to make on this hard drive, we'll specify the end cylinder manually this time. Here are the entries for this:

```
First cylinder (90-92):  90
Last cylinder or +size or +sizeM or +sizeK (33-92):  92
```

Now we need to set the type of partition to 82, used for Linux swap. The reason we didn't need to set a partition type the last time is that unless otherwise specified Linux fdisk automatically sets the type of all new partitions to 83 (Linux native). To set the partition type, use the "t" command:

```
Command (m for help):  t
Partition number (1-4):  3
Hex code (type L to list codes):  82
```

Now you're ready to save the updated partition table information onto your hard drive. Use the **p** command again to check the results and be sure you're satisfied with them:

```
Command (m for help):  p

Disk /dev/sda:  255 heads, 63 sectors, 92 cylinders
Units = cylinders of 16065 * 512 bytes

Device Boot Begin Start End Blocks Id System
/dev/sda1 1 1 32 257008+ 6 DOS 16-bit >= 32M
```

```
/dev/sda2 33 33 89 465885 83 Linux native
/dev/sda3 90 90 92 16065 82 Linux swap
```

This looks good, so we'll use the **w** command to write the data out to the drive's partition table. If you want to exit without updating the partition table (if you've made a mistake), then you can exit without changing anything by using the **q** command instead.

When you exit fdisk using the **w** command, fdisk recommends that you reboot the machine to be sure that the changes you've made take effect. Unless you've created extended partitions, you can go ahead and run setup without rebooting.

Note: Sometimes fdisk will give you a message like "This drive has more than 1024 cylinders" and warn about possible problems using partitions with DOS. This is because MS-DOS suffers from a limitation that only allows access to the first 1024 cylinders on a hard drive. Since LILO (the utility used to boot Linux from a hard drive) uses the BIOS routines for disk access, it's also affected by this limitation. This means that if your drive has more than 1024 cylinders, all DOS partitions need to reside between cylinder 1 and 1024. Linux has no problem with partitions that stretch beyond cylinder 1024, but LILO may have trouble booting kernels from them. If that happens, you can still set up Loadlin to boot from your DOS partition, or use a bootdisk to start Linux.

2.6   Installing the Slackware distribution

You are now ready to begin installing software onto your hard drive. To start this process, enter the command "setup" and hit enter:

```
# setup
```

This starts the installation program, and puts a full-color menu on your screen with the various options needed to install Slackware. In general, you'll want to start with the ADDSWAP option. Even if you've already created and activated a swap partition manually, you'll need to run this so Slackware adds the swap partition to your /etc/fstab file. If you don't add it, your system won't use the swap space when you reboot.

Installing a typical system involves running the following options from the setup menu in this order: ADDSWAP, TARGET, SOURCE, DISK SETS, INSTALL, and `CONFIGURE`. If you don't have a swap partition, you can just go ahead and start with the `TARGET` option.

For the rest of this section, we'll walk through a typical installation process.

The ADDSWAP option:

First, we select the `ADDSWAP` option. The system will scan for partitions marked as type "Linux swap" and will ask if you want to use them for swap space. Answer **YES**, and the system will ask if you wish to format the partition with mkswap. If you already did this manually then there will be no need to do it again. (Note: even if the partition is active, formatting doesn't hurt anything). Otherwise select **YES** to format the partition and then make it active. Once it's finished, setup will display a message showing the line it will add to `/etc/fstab` to configure the swap partition at boot time. Hit enter to continue, and setup will ask if you want to go on to the `TARGET` option. Answer **YES**.

NOTE: If you created a partition to use for swap space, but setup doesn't see it when it scans your drives, it's possible that the partition type hasn't been set in the partition table. Use the Linux "fdisk" program to list your partitions like this:

```
# fdisk -l

Disk /dev/sda: 255 heads, 63 sectors, 92 cylinders
Units = cylinders of 16065 * 512 bytes

    Device Boot   Begin    Start     End   Blocks   Id  System
    /dev/sda1      1        1        32    257008+   6  DOS 16-bit >= 32M
    /dev/sda2     33       33        89    465885   83  Linux native
    /dev/sda3     90       90        92     16065   83  Linux native
```

In this case, if /dev/sda3 is meant to be a Linux swap partition, you'll need to start fdisk on drive /dev/sda:

```
# fdisk /dev/sda

Command (m for help): t
Partition number (1-4): 3
Hex code (type L to list codes): 82

Command (m for help): w
```

This will change the third partition to type 82 (Linux swap) and write the partition table out to `/dev/sda`.

Now, if you run setup again, the ADDSWAP option should detect the Linux swap partition.

The TARGET option:

The next option on the setup menu is TARGET. This lets you select which partition(s) you'd like to install Slackware on, and will format them using the Linux Second Extended Filesystem. When you select the TARGET option, the system will scan for "Linux native" partitions on your hard drives using the fdisk program. If it doesn't find any, you'll need to make sure that you've created partitions using the fdisk program, and that the partitions are labeled as type 83 (Linux native). This is the same process shown above. If you've created one or more partitions for Slackware using Linux's fdisk program that you shouldn't have any problems, since Linux fdisk sets all new partitions to type 83 (Linux native) by default.

You will see a menu listing all the Linux native partitions. Use the arrow keys to select the partition you'd like to use for your root (or primary) Linux partition and hit enter. The setup program will then ask if you'd like to format the partition. If this is a new installation of Slackware, you'll need to do this. Otherwise, if you're installing software onto an existing Linux partition, you don't need to format the partition.

There are a few options you need to know about when you format Linux partitions. First, you'll need to decide whether or not you'd like to check the partition for bad blocks when you do the format. This is usually not necessary unless you know the drive in question has problems. Checking takes a long time compared to a normal format, so you'll probably want to just go ahead and use the "Format" menu option to format the drive normally. If you have drive problems later on, then you might want to try using the "Check" option to map the bad sectors on the drive.

Once you've picked your formatting mode, setup will prompt you to provide the inode density. On Linux filesystems, entries called "inodes" store the names of files and the locations of the blocks that make up the file. You need at least one inode for each file, so if you run out of inodes then you can't make any new files, even if there seems to be plenty of space on the drive. Inodes themselves take up space on your drive, so you need to consider how you will use the partition. Usually, the default value of one inode for every 4096 bytes on the drive is fine. But if you're planning to use the drive for a news feed or something that uses many small files, then you may wish to increase the inode density to one inode for every 2048 (or even 1024) bytes. Once you've selected the inode density, setup will go ahead and format your root Linux partition. You will then return to the menu showing the partitions available for Linux.

You'll notice that the partition you just formatted is now listed as "in use." If you made some other partitions for Slackware, you'll need to go through the same process of formatting them, selecting whether or not to check for bad blocks, and setting a reasonable inode density. With these partitions there will be an additional step – you'll need to select where you'd like to put the partition in your directory tree.

MS-DOS assigns a letter such as A:, B:, C:, etc, to each device. Unlike DOS, Linux makes your devices visible somewhere under the root directory (/). You might have /dev/hda1 for your root partition (/) and put /dev/hda2 somewhere underneath it, such as under your /home directory. When prompted for a mount location, just enter a directory such as /home, and hit enter. As you format each additional partition and place it in the filesystem tree, you'll be returned to the partition selection menu. When you've prepared all of your Linux partitions, select "Cancel" to go on to the SOURCE option.

The SOURCE option:

The next option is SOURCE, where you select the physical media from which you will install Slackware.

Source displays a menu offering the choice of installation from floppy disk, NFS, a hard drive partition, a directory, or from CDROM. Make sure your Slackware CDROM is in your drive, and select option 5: Installing from CDROM. Next, the system will ask you what type of CDROM drive you have. Select your drive from the menu provided. Setup will then try to access the Slackware CDROM. If this is successful, setup will ask you if you wish to go on to the next option, DISK SETS, elsewhere in this chapter. The Disk sets option lets you select the software you want to install.

2.6.1 Setup was not successful accessing your CDROM drive.

If setup is not successful in accessing the CDROM drive, you'll need to figure out why before you can go on. The most common reason for this is that you used a bootdisk that doesn't support the CDROM drive. In this case, you'll have to figure out the correct disk to use. Refer to the list of bootdisks elsewhere in this chapter and the drives they support.

Another common mistake is selecting the wrong option when asked which type of CDROM drive you have. Some manufacturers make different versions of their drives, and it can be difficult to know which version you've got without trying a few different options. For example, Mitsumi makes several models of CDROM drives; some of these come with their own interface card, and need the Linux Mitsumi driver (and are selected as a Mitsumi drive from the menu), while most of the recent Mitsumi drives plug directly onto the computer's IDE interface (and are selected as an `ATAPI/IDE` CDROM drive).

For `ATAPI/IDE` drives, you also need to know which device entry your computer uses to access the drive. Sometimes the system's hard drive will be the master device on the IDE interface, while the CDROM is connected as the slave device. In this example, the hard drive is `/dev/hda`, and the CDROM drive is `/dev/hdb`.

Scanning for IDE CDROM drive

If you have no idea which device an IDE CDROM drive is connected to, you can try to have the system scan for it. You also can look at the messages generated by the system as it boots – you should see a message that Slackware detected your CDROM drive along with information about what type of drive it is. You can look at these messages by using the right shift key together with the PageUp and PageDown keys to scroll the screen up and down. If you don't see a message about your drive, you're probably using the wrong bootdisk. If you're not sure which bootdisk you need to use, try these steps:

If your CDROM drive is connected to a SCSI controller, try using the `SCSI.S` disk. This contains most of the Linux SCSI drivers, and should identify which controller your system uses. Then make the bootdisk especially for your controller to use for the installation process.

If you have an IDE controller, keep trying the various IDE bootdisks. Watch the screen for a message saying that Slackware detected your CDROM drive.

If Slackware still won't detect your drive, look at the file `BOOTING.TXT` on the CDROM. This contains a list of extra parameters you can pass to the kernel when you boot a Slackware bootdisk. These parameters can be handy to force hardware detection when the autoprobing fails. For example, you can tell the kernel to look for a Sony CDU31a drive by entering the following command line on the bootdisk's first prompt:

```
ramdisk cdu31a=0x1f88,0,PAS
```

This tells the kernel that you've got a Sony CDU31a drive connected to an interface card at address 0x1f88, interrupts are disabled, and the interface card is a Pro Audio Spectrum.

The documentation that comes with the Linux kernel also lists examples for other types of hardware. You can find these on the Slackware CDROM in the `/docs/kernel-2.0` directory.

2.6.2 Installing Slackware from MS-DOS

If you can't get your CDROM detected by Linux, it's possible that the kernel doesn't support it. Linux supports most hardware, but some is not (most notably plug-and-play devices). If you've tried everything and still can't use the CDROM drive, you can still install Slackware. You do this by copying files from the CDROM onto a DOS partition, and then installing the software from there.

The Linux `Installation-HOWTO` (`INSTALL.TXT` on the CDROM) gives an in-depth discussion of this, but here's a brief description of the steps involved:

- (1) Under MS-DOS, create a directory to install from, such as `C:\SLACK`.

- (2) Copy the disk sets you wish to install from the CDROM into the `C:\SLACK` directory with `XCOPY`. For instance, you'd use this command to copy the A series from the CDROM to your DOS partition from a CDROM assigned a drive letter of E:

  `XCOPY E:\SLAKWARE\A* C:\SLACK /S`

  This will copy the software into subdirectories of `C:\SLACK` named A1, A2, A3, etc. Do the same for any other disk sets you wish to install.

- (3) Run setup. When you get to the SOURCE option, tell it you want to install from a hard drive partition. Enter the source device (such as `/dev/hda1`) and the directory to install from (in this case, `/slack`) and then proceed with the installation as normal.

The DISK SETS option:

The Disk sets option lets you select the software you want to install.

When you start the `DISK SETS` option, you'll see a menu where you can choose which categories of software you're interested in installing. The first series (called the A series) contains the base filesystem structure and binaries that are crucial for your system to boot and run properly. You must install the A series. Make sure that at least the selection for series A has an [X] next to it. Use the cursor keys and the space bar to select other disk sets to install.

Once you've selected the general categories of software you wish to install, hit enter and you'll go on to the INSTALL option.

The INSTALL option:

This option goes through the categories of software you've chosen and installs it.

The first question the INSTALL option will ask is what type of prompting you'd like to use during the installation process. A menu will show several options, including NORMAL, MENU, CUSTOM, PATH, EXPERT, and NONE.

Most people will want to use NORMAL, MENU, or EXPERT mode. The NORMAL mode installs all of the required packages in each series, and for each of the others puts a menu on the screen allowing the user to answer **YES** (install the package), **NO** (do not install the package), or **SKIP** (skip ahead to the next series). The menu will print a description of the package to help the user decide. Installing using the NORMAL mode is verbose, so it can be tedious.

For users that can decide which packages they want from less information, the MENU option is a good choice. The MENU option displays a menu before installing each series and lets the user toggle items on or off with the spacebar. When you install a series using the MENU option, you do not see the required packages on the screen at all, and packages that go together are combined into a single menu choice. Once you have selected the software, you hit enter and all the software is installed automatically.

The EXPERT option is similar to the MENU option, but assumes you want control over every package that could get installed. The EXPERT mode lets you toggle packages individually, allowing the user to make bad decisions like turning off crucial packages or installing a package that's part of a larger set of software without installing the other parts. If you know exactly what you need, the EXPERT mode offers the maximum amount of flexibility. If you don't know what you need, using the EXPERT mode will allow you to install a system that's missing crucial files.

The CUSTOM and PATH options are only used if you've created "tagfiles" for installation. In the first directory of each disk set is a file called "tagfile" containing a list of all the packages in that series, as well as a flag marking whether the package should be installed automatically, skipped, or the user should be prompted to decide. This is useful for situations where you need to install large numbers of machines (such as in a computer lab), but most users will not need to create tagfiles. If you are interested in using them, look at one of the tagfiles with an editor.

The last option to consider is NONE, or no prompting mode. If you select this mode, then setup assumes you want to install all the packages from the selected disk sets and just goes ahead with it. This is fast and easy. It also may result in filling up your hard drive with lots of software that you don't need.

If you're new to Slackware, you'll probably want to select the MENU option as the easiest way to install. If you think you need the extra information offered by the NORMAL mode, go ahead and use that.

Once you have selected a prompting mode, the system begins the installation process. If you've chosen MENU or EXPERT mode, you'll see a menu of software to choose from right away – use the arrow keys and spacebar to pick what you need, and then hit enter to install it. If you've chosen the NORMAL mode, the installation will begin immediately, continuing until it finds optional packages (install will ask you about each of these).

If you've selected too much software, it's possible that your hard drive may run out of space during installation. If this happens, you'll know it because you'll see error messages on the screen as setup tries to install the packages. In such as case, you'll have to reinstall selecting less software. You can avoid this problem by choosing a reasonable amount of software to begin with, and installing more software later once your system is running. Installing software on a running Slackware system is even easier than the initial installation – just type "setup" at a prompt, select CDROM as the source, and select and install some more software.

Once you have installed the software on your system, you'll need to go on to the CONFIGURE option.

The CONFIGURE option:

The CONFIGURE option of setup does the basic configuration your system needs, such as creating links for your mouse and modem, setting your timezone, etc.

The CONFIGURE option will first ensure that you've installed a usable Linux kernel on your hard drive. There are a couple of generic kernels that come with the A series called IDE and SCSI, but the best kernel to install is the one from your bootdisk. To do this, select the "bootdisk" option on the kernel installation menu. The menu will prompt you to reinsert your installation bootdisk and hit enter, and then setup will copy the kernel from the bootdisk to your hard drive.

If you don't want to use that kernel, you can pick a kernel from a menu of kernels available on the CDROM, but if you install the wrong kernel the machine likely won't boot. I recommend you install the bootdisk kernel. Since you used it successfully to install Slackware, you know it will work on the installed system as well.

NOTE: If you install a kernel on your system that doesn't boot correctly, you can still boot your system with the installation bootdisk. To do this, you need to enter some information on the bootdisk's boot prompt. For example, if your root partition is on `/dev/sda1`, you'd enter this to boot your system:

```
mount root=/dev/sda1 ro
```

The "ro" option makes the root partition initially load as read-only so Linux can safely check the filesystem. If you're using the UMSDOS filesystem, use "rw" (for read-write) instead.

Once you've installed a kernel, you'll be asked if you want to make a bootdisk for your new system. This is a very good idea for emergencies, so insert a formatted floppy disk and use the "lilo" option to create a bootdisk for your system.

Next, you'll be asked if you have a modem. If you do, pick the device from the list shown. This will make a link in `/dev` point to the correct device, such as `/dev/modem -> /dev/cua1`. Similarly, you'll be asked if you have a mouse. Pick the mouse type from the menu, and setup will create a /dev/mouse link.

After this, other installation scripts will run depending on which packages you've installed. For instance, if you installed sendmail you'll be asked if you're running TCP/IP or UUCP.

2.6.3   LILO - Linux loader

LILO is the Linux Loader, a program that allows you to boot Linux (and other operating systems) directly from your hard drive. If you installed the LILO package, you now have an opportunity to set it up.

Installing LILO can be dangerous. If you make a mistake it's possible to make your hard drive unbootable. If you're new to Linux, it might be a good idea to skip LILO installation and use the bootdisk to start your system at first. You can install LILO later after you've had a chance to read the information about it in `/usr/lib/lilo`. If you do decide to go ahead and install LILO, be sure you have a way to boot all the operating systems on your machine in case something goes wrong. If you can't boot DOS again, use the DOS command `FDISK /MBR` to remove LILO from your master boot record.

If you decide you want to install LILO from the Slackware LILO configuration menu, here's how you do it. LILO uses a configuration file called `/etc/lilo.conf` to hold the information about your bootable partitions. To create this file, first select `BEGIN` to enter the basic information about where to install LILO. The first menu will ask if you have extra parameters you'd like passed to the Linux kernel at boot time. If you need any extra parameters enter them here.

Next, decide where you want LILO installed. Usually you'll want to install LILO on the boot drive's MBR (master boot record). If you use a different boot manager (like the one that comes with OS/2) then you'll want to install LILO on your root Linux partition and then add that partition to the boot manager menu using its configuration tool. Under OS/2, this is the fdisk program.

NOTE: If you use the EZ-DRIVE utility (a disk manager program supplied with some large IDE drives to make them usable with DOS) then do not install LILO to the MBR. If you do, you may disable EZ-DRIVE and render your disk unusable with DOS. Instead, install LILO to the superblock of your root Linux partition, and use fdisk to make the partition bootable. (With MS-DOS fdisk, this is called setting the 'active' partition)

The next menu lets you set a delay before the system boots into the default operating system. If you're using LILO to boot more than one operating system (such as DOS and Linux) then you'll need to set a delay so you can pick which OS you'd like to boot. If you press the SHIFT key during the delay, LILO will display a prompt where you can type a label (typically DOS or Linux) to select which OS to boot. If you set the delay to 'Forever', the system will display a prompt at boot time and wait for you to enter a choice.

Next, you need to add entries for each operating system that LILO can boot. The first entry you make will be the machine's default operating system. You can add either a DOS, Linux or OS/2 partition first. For example, let's say you select "Linux." The system will display your Linux partitions and ask which one of them you'd like to boot. Enter the name of your root Linux partition. Then, you'll be prompted to enter a label. This is the name you will enter at the boot time LILO prompt to select which partition you want to boot. A good choice for this is "Linux".

Adding a DOS or OS/2 partition is similar. To add a DOS partition to the LILO configuration file, select the DOS option. The system will display your DOS partitions and ask which one of them you'd like to boot with LILO. Enter the name of your primary DOS partition. Then enter a label for the partition, like DOS. Once you've added all of your bootable partitions, install LILO by selecting the "Install" option.

2.6.4   Networking

Another configuration menu allows you to configure your machine's networking setup. First, enter a hostname for your machine. The default hostname after installation is "darkstar," but you can enter any name you like. Next, you'll be asked to provide a domain name. If you're running a stand-alone machine (possibly using a dialup link to an Internet Service Provider) then you can pick any name you like. The default domain name is "frop.org". If you are going to add the machine to a local network, you'll need to use the same domain name as the rest of the machines on your network. If you're not sure what this is, contact your network administrator for help. Once you've specified the hostname and domain name, you'll be asked if you want to set up the machine to only use loopback. If you don't have an ethernet card, just use loopback. Otherwise, say NO. Then the setup program will ask for your machine's IP address, gateway address, netmask, and nameserver. Again, if you don't know what numbers you should be using, ask the person in charge of the network to help provide the information.

Once you've completed all the configuration menus, you can exit setup and reboot your machine. Simply press ctrl-alt-delete and the kernel will kill any programs that are running, unmount your filesystems and restart the machine.

2.7   Booting the installed Slackware system

If you've installed LILO, make sure you don't have a disk in your floppy drive. When your machine reboots it should start LILO. Otherwise, insert the bootdisk made for your system during the configuration process and use it to boot.

The kernel will go through the startup process, detecting your hardware, checking your partitions and starting various processes. Eventually you'll be given a login prompt:

```
darkstar login:

Log into the new system as root.
Welcome to Linux 2.0.0
darkstar login:  root
last login:  Mon Jul 1 10:37:39 on ttgl
Linux 2.0.0.
You have mail.
```

```
darkstar:  ~#
```

2.8 Post-installation configuration

Once the system is running, most of the work is complete. However, there are still a few programs you'll need to configure. We'll cover the most important of these in this section.

/etc/rc.d/rc.modules

This file contains a list of Linux kernel modules. A kernel module is like a device driver under DOS. You can think of the `/etc/rc.d/rc.modules` file as similar to DOS's `CONFIG.SYS`. The file specifies which modules the system needs to load to support the machine's hardware. After booting your machine, you may find that some of your hardware isn't detected (usually an ethernet card) then you'll need to load the correct module to provide the support.

To do this, edit the `/etc/rc.d/rc.modules` file with a text editor such as 'vi' or 'emacs'. You'll see a list of modules, one per line. Most of these lines will have a # at the beginning of them – this causes the line to be ignored. As an example, let's say your machine has a 3com 3c509 ethernet card. To activate support for this card, find the line with '3c509' in it, and remove the # from the beginning of the line. Then save the changed file. When you reboot the system, the module will load and the kernel will recognize the card.

There's a lot more information out there about kernal modules, including lists of module names and the cards they support. You will also find extra options you can add to the module lines to configure the hardware om different ways. This documentation is on the Slackware CDROM in the /docs directory. Useful files include `/docs/mini/Kerneld`, `/cdrom/docs/kernel-2.0/modules.txt`, and `/cdrom/docs/kernel-2.0/networking/net-modules.txt`.

2.8.1 User accounts

You should make a user account for yourself. Use this account unless you have system administration tasks to do that require the special powers of the root account. Using the root account for everyday tasks is dangerous, since you could damage or erase important files with a simple typing error. When you use a normal user account, you can't cause any major damage to the system since it won't let you erase or change important system files. To make a user account, use the **adduser** program. Just type `adduser` at a prompt, and follow the instructions. Going with the default selections for user ID, group ID, and shell should be just fine for most users.

2.8.2   Securing your machine

When you first boot a newly installed Slackware system, there is no password for the root account. You should change this immediately. To do this, use the `passwd` command:

```
darkstar:~ # passwd
```

The system will prompt you to enter a password for the root account.

When choosing passwords for a Linux system that is connected to a network you should pick a **strong** password. However, passwords only help protect a system from remote tresspassing. It's easy to gain access to a system if someone has physical access to the console.

If you forget the root password, take the original `boot` and `root` disks you used to install and start up the system as if you were going to reinstall linux. At the prompt, you can manually mount the root Linux partition from your hard drive and remove the root password. For example, I might do the following (assuming my root partition is (`/dev/hda2`):

```
# mount /dev/hda2 /mnt
# cp /mnt/etc/passwd /mnt/etc/passwd.bk
# cp /mnt/etc/passwd.OLD /mnt/etc/passwd
```

This will make a backup of your password file and copy a default password file (without a root password) over the current one. Now you should be able to reboot and login as root.

Here are some pointers on selecting **strong** passwords.

1. Never use your name, birthdate, license plate, your dog or child's name or anything relating to yourself as a password. These are the first things a cracker will try.

2. Don't use a password that is any variation of your login name.

3. Do not use words from the dictionary, syllables of two different words concatenated together or "password" as your password.

4. Do not write your password down and stick it to your terminal.

5. Do not use a number as your password like 123456 or a password shorter than six characters.

Here are some examples of strong passwords:

```
*^fg!:1?        ()lsp%@9       i6v917&#        ++c$!jke       *!zd/mn1
```

Here are some weak passwords:

```
irule god root sex power password unix
```

2.9 Installing Slackware Linux with other operating systems.

2.9.1 Installing Linux with OS/2 and DOS on the same disk.

This section is based on the Linux + OS/2 (+ DOS) mini-HOWTO, version 0.2. May 20, 1996. by Hamish Moffatt (moffatt@yallara.cs.rmit.edu.au)

Warning

The instructions in this document will change the boot loader on your computer. During the course of these instructions some mistakes may make your system unable to boot either Linux or OS/2 or DOS, or perhaps none of the above. Make sure you have your Linux boot and root disks, your OS/2 Installation and Disk 1 diskettes, and your DOS Setup disks if relevant handy before you begin. The writer takes no responsibility for any damage incurred during the process of these instructions; there is no warranty, guarantee etc whatsoever.

- (1) Introduction

  When I first got interested in Linux, in about August 95, I was told that while it should be possible to have OS/2 Boot Manager and Linux coexist, it "just didn't work." When I actually got around to installing OS/2 and Linux together on a new PC, it turned out that it works perfectly and isn't actually too hard. This mini-HOWTO should help you get these two working together.

Note: in this document, I will describe how to have OS/2 Boot Manager boot Linux (via LILO). There is a short section later on on having LILO (Linux's loader and boot manager) boot OS/2.

- (2) Before you read this document

In this document I assume you have already installed OS/2 (and also DOS if you wish) on your system. If you've already installed Linux but not OS/2, or both OS/2 and Linux, see section 4 or 5 respectively.

Note that you need to have OS/2 Boot Manager installed. If you have OS/2 and DOS on the same partition (and you switch between them with BOOT /DOS and BOOT /OS2), then you're using Dual Boot, not Boot Manager. You need to read the LILO documentation or mini-HOWTO on booting another (non-Linux) operating system. This document is for Boot Manager only.

- (3) The actual installation

- (3.1) Some background

So, you have OS/2 and maybe DOS already installed. (In this document my examples will have DOS also installed). Your partition table might look something like this:

```
Device Boot Begin Start End Blocks Id System /dev/hda1 1 1
254 512032+ 6 DOS 16-bit >=32M /dev/hda2 256 256 786 1070496
5 Extended /dev/hda3 * 255 255 255 2016 a OS/2 Boot Manager
/dev/hda5 * 256 256 509 512032+ 7 OS/2 HPFS /dev/hda6 * 510
510 763 512032+ 83 Linux native /dev/hda7 * 764 764 786
46336+ 82 Linux swap
```

Here hda1 contains DOS, hda3 is Boot Manager, hda5 is the OS/2 (boot) partition, and hda6 is the Linux (boot) partition. If your OS/2 partition is FAT rather than HPFS, that's fine – these instructions apply just the same. Also, while OS/2 Boot Manager must be on **/dev/hda** somewhere, OS/2 and Linux could be on **/dev/hdb, hdc,** or **hdd,** etc. (OS/2 BootMan has no problems booting OS/2 from a second disk, so it should have no problems booting Linux from a second disk. I haven't been able to get DOS to boot from a second disk, though.)

- (3.2) Install Linux

At this point, you should install Linux. You are best to create your DOS and OS/2 (and extended, if necessary) partitions using OS/2's FDISK, then creating your Linux partitions with Linux's fdisk. Some people have reported that sometimes OS/2 thinks the partition table is corrupt and won't let you add Linux to the Boot Manager menu later, so you might have to try creating ALL your partitions with OS/2's FDISK, and using Linux's fdisk later to change the partitions to the right types. See the fdisk documentation for further information on changing partition types. (Thanks to bubeck@informatik.uni-tuebingen.de (Till Bubeck).)

Your distribution's installation program should ask you about installing LILO; Slackware's does. You do want LILO installed (OS/2 Boot Manager cannot boot Linux directly, since it's doesn't understand Linux's file system format. Also, adding LILO gives you a chance to choose between different versions of Linux, add boot parameters so Linux can find all your hardware, etc.)

- (3.3) Install LILO

Slackware will ask you **where** you want to install LILO; the SuperBlock (partition table, master boot record etc), the Linux partition's boot sector, etc. The boot manager that lives in the SuperBlock is your master boot manager - you want this to be OS/2's Boot Manager, so you need to install LILO (Linux's boot manager) in the boot sector of your Linux partition. In the partition table example above, this would be on /dev/hda6. (**Not** /dev/hda, which would be the master boot record, where OS/2 BootMan lives.)

Finish your Linux installation. If the installation hasn't run it for you, run /sbin/lilo. You **may** need to create your own /etc/lilo.conf, which is the LILO configuration file; it tells LILO where it can find the Linux kernel (the operating system itself) on your hard drive, etc. A very simple one might be

```
boot = /dev/hda6
delay = 50
vga = normal
ramdisk = 0

image = /vmlinuz
root = /dev/hda6
label = linux
read-only
```

boot specifies the partition where LILO will install itself; this should be `/dev/hdax`, not `/dev/hda` (or `hdb`, as appropriate).

- (3.4) Add Linux to OS/2's Boot Manager menu

Now you have Linux installed and ready to go, but after you reboot, you won't be able to boot it. All that's left now is to tell OS/2 Boot Manager about it. Reboot, and select OS/2 from the Boot Manager menu. (If you get a "LILO" prompt instead of Boot Manager, read section 3.5 below).

Boot up OS/2, and run `FDISK`. Move to your Linux partition (listed as **Type 83** – OS/2 doesn't seem to know Linux's partition types). Press Enter, and from the menu select **Add to Boot Manager menu**. Enter an appropriate name (eg Linux), then press F3, save and exit.

When you reboot, your OS/2 Boot Manager menu should include Linux. When you select it, you should see **LILO** for about five seconds, then Linux should boot. If it does, you're all finished. Enjoy!

- (3.5) If you get LILO rather than OS/2 Boot Manager when you reboot

If when you reboot, you get **LILO**, rather than OS/2 Boot Manager, then you've installed LILO in the superblock (`/dev/hda`), rather than on a partition (`/dev/hda6` or whatever). To fix this isn't too hard, luckily. Boot up your OS/2 Installation floppy, and exit to the command prompt. Run `FDISK`, then save and exit. Boot Manager should be back when you reboot. However, now you can't boot Linux again. Get out your Linux boot and root disks, and mount your Linux partition. You can either boot completely from diskettes, then type

```
mount /dev/hda6 /mnt
```

once you can log in, or (depending on your distribution), you can mount your hard drive instead of the root floppy. On Slackware, you can do this by typing

```
mount root=/dev/hda6
```

at the LILO prompt you get as soon as you've booted the boot disk.

Now, edit your LILO config (either `/mnt/etc/lilo.conf` or `/etc/lilo.conf`, depending on which of the above methods you used), and change the **boot =** line to say `/dev/hda6` (or whatever) instead of `/dev/hda`. Then run

```
/mnt/sbin/lilo -C /mnt/etc/lilo.conf
```

or

```
/sbin/lilo
```

depending on which method you used before. Reboot again, and OS/2 Boot Manager should be back. See section 3.4 on adding Linux to the OS/2 Boot Manager menu.

- (3.6) Advanced options

  If you want to save a few seconds during booting, you can get **delay = 0** instead of 50 in your `/etc/lilo.conf`. Using the delay gives you a chance to boot another operating system, but you're using OS/2 Boot Manager for that, so you may not need it. (However, LILO also gives you the chance to boot different Linux kernel versions, and you may want that).

  Actually, if you press shift immediately after you select Linux from the Boot Manager menu, you get the **LILO:** prompt anyway. LILO loads very quickly though, so this can be harder than it sounds.

- (4) If you've already installed Linux, but not OS/2 ...

- (4.1) Installing OS/2

  You have Linux installed, and when you boot your PC you get the LILO prompt. You want to install OS/2. This might actually be easier than installing OS/2 before Linux, actually.

  Boot Linux, and edit your `/etc/lilo.conf` file. Change the **boot =** line to the name of your linux partition, eg `/dev/hda6`, instead of the name of your boot drive, eg `/dev/hda`. Then run `/sbin/lilo` to install LILO again. This will install LILO in the boot sector of your Linux partition, so that OS/2 can boot it later.

  Now, install OS/2. When you create your OS/2 partitions in OS/2's `FDISK`, **do** install Boot Manager, and make sure you add your OS/2 (and DOS) partition to it. Also, add your Linux (`Type 83` in OS/2 `FDISK`) partition to the menu too. (Press Enter on the Linux partition, and select **Add to Boot Manager menu**, and enter a suitable description). You should now be all set to boot Linux and OS/2 from the Boot Manager menu.

- (4.2) Troubleshooting

  If, when you select Linux from the Boot Manager menu, you get Missing Operating System, Non-system disk or disk error, etc, then you didn't get LILO installed properly in your Linux partition's boot sector. Use your Linux boot (and maybe also root) disk to edit your `lilo.conf` file again as in section 4.1, and make sure you run `/sbin/lilo`. (Section 3.5 gives some information on how you can boot Linux from floppies and get access to your Linux partition on hard drive).

If you get LILO when you reboot, instead of OS/2 Boot Manager, then Boot-Man wasn't installed properly. Boot the OS/2 Installation disks again, quit to the command prompt F3, and run FDISK. Make sure Boot Manager is installed, and that the BootMan partition is marked Bootable.

- (5) You've already installed both OS/2 and Linux ...

Both LILO (Linux's boot manager and loader) and OS/2 BootMan like to be the master boot manager on your system. If you've already installed both of these using default options, then you probably can't boot one of these two at the moment (the one you installed first won't be bootable).

OS/2 BootMan **has** to be the master boot manager, but LILO can be moved so it only boots Linux.

- (5.1) If you can boot OS/2 but not Linux

You need to boot Linux (using your boot and root floppies if need be; see section 3.5 on how to get to your Linux hard disk partition from the boot/root disks).

Edit your /etc/lilo.conf and change **boot** = to the name of your Linux partition (eg /dev/hda6) rather than your boot drive (eg /dev/hda). Run /sbin/lilo. (Section 3.5 gives more details about getting to these files).

Now, boot OS/2 and run FDISK. Select your Linux partition (Type 83), and select **Add to Boot Manager menu** from the pop-up menu. You should now be all set.

If you reboot and Linux still isn't listed, check that you added it properly in the last step. If Linux is listed but you get missing system or non-system disk errors when you select it, you might not have got LILO installed correctly in the first part of 5.1.

- (5.2) If you can boot Linux but not OS/2

See the instructions in 5.1. To boot Linux, just boot from your hard drive as normal; to boot OS/2, use the Installation diskette, and exit to the command prompt F3 to run FDISK.

- (6) Getting LILO to boot OS/2 ...

Theoretically, LILO could boot OS/2; that is, at the LILO prompt you could hit Shift and enter OS2 or whatever. I have tried this, and it didn't work. However, my OS/2 is on /dev/hdb6, which may complicate things.

In `/etc/lilo.conf`, you need to add

`other = /dev/hda5 label = os2`

(if your OS/2 partition is `/dev/hda5`). You should also add

`table = /dev/hda`

(or `hdb`) so that Linux can check for the partition, but I got missing partition errors when running `/sbin/lilo`.

If your OS/2 is on your second hard drive, you also need to add

`loader = /boot/os2_d.b`

else `/sbin/lilo` won't run successfully (it requires a special loader to boot OS/2 from a second hard drive, and `os2_d.b` is it).

If you've been able to get this working, please let me know.

- (7) The end.

  The latest version of this mini-HOWTO should be at

  http://yallara.cs.rmit.edu.au/ moffatt/linux-os2/

2.9.2   Installing Linux with Windows 95 and Windows 3.1 on the same disk.

This section is based on the Windows 95 + Windows 3.x + Linux HOWTO, August, 1996. by Robert Goodwin (Robert.Goodwin@mcc.ac.uk)

- (0) Introduction

  This document was originally written in January 1996. I have incorporated various comments, information, and questions received since then. This document is also available in Japanese; see the collection of Japanese linux docs at `http://epsenewsc.gee.kyoto-u.ac.jp/JF/JF.html`

- (1) Booting Multiple Operating Systems

  If you want to boot multiple operating systems (and you don't want to have to boot them from floppy disk!), you need to use some sort of **boot manager**.

  Windows 95 doesn't really **have** a boot manager - it has boot options, but in my book a **boot manager** can be configured to boot anything.

  Lilo can be configured to boot almost anything, as can the OS/2 boot manager and the Windows NT boot manager. Which of these you use is really up to you; it depends what you want on your system. If you use the OS/2 manager, for example, it hides the other DOS partitions from you.

- (2) Why this HOWTO?

This document addresses the following issues:

How to get Windows 3.x to live on the same machine as Windows 95 without problems (and what those problems might otherwise be)

How to avoid problems on a machine with Windows 95 which can also remote boot DOS

How to install Windows 95 with Linux without having to reinstall lilo (with the tedious booting of Linux from floppy)

Although the Windows 95 filesystem lives on top of the standard DOS FAT, it does some pretty unpleasant things to it. Boot your Windows 95 machine from a bootable DOS floppy and get Norton to check the disk (but **don't** let it attempt any repairs or you'll mess up some **long** filenames)

I am currently required to support applications in the Windows 95 environment as well as under Windows 3.x (both run locally and network booted). I developed the setup described in this document to allow me to do all this with just one PC.

Don't ask how a Unix person ended up in this position...

- (3) Requirements

If you are prepared to tinker with the source to lilo (lilo 1.7 or later), it is possible to do all this with **one** hard disk. This works by changing the contents of the partition table as the system boots; if you don't feel confident about trying this, then don't!

Otherwise, you will need **two** hard disks. This is due to some DOS/Windows limitations with respect to booting and allocation of drive letters. Believe me, I tried to get it working with one. (but I didn't want to mess with the lilo source)

- (4) What you will end up with

A word on device names. I have seen systems which use /dev/hdc for the 3rd IDE disk (first IDE disk on secondary controller) and /dev/hdd for the fourth. I've also seen systems which use /dev/hd1a and /dev/hd1b (giving such partitions as /dev/hd1a3 etc). My system uses this second naming style, but I have changed to names to /dev/hdc and /dev/hdd to minimize confusion.

Here is a brief description of what I now have - watch those drive letters because they change...

If you use a secondary IDE controller, you may need to create the `/dev` entries yourself (`/dev/hdcd*` and `/dev/hdd*`) This might be the case if you add a second hard drive to a machine with one IDE disk and an IDE CDROM already installed; your second hard disk would be `/dev/hdc`. I have tried this arrangement with no problems.

I have:

`/dev/hda` - first hard disk
`/dev/hdb` - cd-rom drive
`/dev/hdc` - second hard disk

Option 1:
On powering up the machine, I can allow the boot ROM on the ethernet card to remote boot DOS. The **C** drive is the first DOS partition on the FIRST IDE disk (in my case `/dev/hda1`). The **D** drive is the first DOS partition on the SECOND IDE disk (in my case `/dev/hdc1`), and the **E** drive is the second DOS partition on the SECOND IDE disk (`/dev/hdc2`). The CD-ROM becomes **F**:

Option 2:
Allow lilo to boot the default system (Linux, naturally)

Option 3:
Interrupt lilo and ask for an option I call DOS. This boots DOS from `/dev/hda1`, and, as with option 1, the **C** drive is `/dev/hda1` the **D** drive is `/dev/hdc1` and the **E** drive is `/dev/hdc2`. The CD-ROM becomes **F**:

Option 4:
Interrupt lilo and ask for an option I call Windows 95. This boots Windows 95 from the first DOS partition on the SECOND IDE drive (in my case `/dev/hdc1`). Follow this carefully: the **C** drive is now the first DOS partition on the SECOND IDE disk (`/dev/hdc1`), the **D** drive is now the first DOS partition on the FIRST IDE disk (`/dev/hda1`), and the **E** drive remains the second DOS partition on the SECOND IDE disk (`/dev/hdc2`). The CD-ROM becomes **F**:

Notice that the **C** drive changes depending how you boot. This means that when you install Windows NT, you install it to `C:\WINDOWS`, and when you install Windows 3.x, you install it to `C:\WINDOWS` but this isn't the same place.

Also notice that the third DOS partition (which I use as a general data drive) is **E**: whichever way you boot, and that the CD-ROM stays constant too.

- (5) How to do it

  First of all, install Linux; it does not matter which drive you install it on; but since you are using two drives it makes sense to create a swap partition on each.

  Create a primary DOS partition on the second disk. Unfortunately, the DOS FDISK won't let you do this, so you must use the Linux `fdisk` to create the partition, set the type (6 for DOS 16 BIT FAT greater then 32Mb), set the partition as bootable, and **carefully** follow the advice on the man page for `fdisk`. This describes how to persuade DOS to recognise a partition created in this manner using the dd command to zero the first 512 bytes of the partition. (Basically, you use `dd if=/dev/zero of=/dev/XXXX, bs=512 count=1` where XXXX is the device but be **very** careful since this is a good way to trash a disk for example by putting `/dev/hda` instead of `/dev/hda1`!)

  Creating the primary DOS partition on the first hard disk can be done with the DOS FDISK. Any other required DOS partitions can similarly be created.

  Both of these primary partitions must be formatted as bootable DOS partitions; use `FORMAT C: /S` and `FORMAT D: /S` after having booted from a floppy. In order to avoid confusion, give the partitions meaningful volume labels!

  Edit `/etc/lilo.conf` to give you the option of booting from either of the two primary DOS partitions. I have appended an example to the end of this document. Note the use of the **loader** line in this example file. Which you choose to install as Windows 95 and which as DOS/Windows 3.x is up to you; I used the second hard disk for Windows 95 since network booting of the machine then gives the normal DOS drive as **C**. Also (and usefully), installing Windows 95 on the second hard disk avoids having to boot linux from a recovery disk and re-install lilo (why this should be is explained below). Remember to run lilo to install the options.

  If you are (sensibly) planning to install Windows 95 from CDROM, you will need to include the relevant drivers on the Windows 95 partition such that when you boot from it, the CDROM drive will be accessible.

  Now boot, using lilo, from the drive you wish to use for DOS/Windows 3.x and install the rest of DOS and Windows 3.x - the Windows installation should go to the `C:\WINDOWS` directory as per default.

  Once this is done, reboot the machine and, using lilo, boot from the Windows 95 partition. Perform your Windows 95 installation. The installation procedure may suggest `D:\WINDOWS` for installing Windows 95 because it searches the machine for existing WINDOWS versions - **don't** accept this, install Windows 95 to `C:\WINDOWS`.

Now for the neat part! Windows 95 is a rather arrogant system - when you install it, it assumes that it is the only operating system on the machine and proceeds to write its own MBR (Master Boot Record) to the hard disk. This is why you generally need to re-install lilo. If you have installed Windows 95 to the second hard disk, you have done something which the Microsoft programmers didn't consider.

On one machine where I performed this operation, Windows 95 wrote its replacement MBR to the MBR of the SECOND hard disk. On another, I never found any evidence of it at all. The practical upshot of this is that the MBR which matters, that of the first hard disk, is not disturbed. Thus when you reboot the machine, you will be greeted by the friendly and familiar LILO prompt.

Example Partition List:

```
/dev/hda1 * DOS partition (C: or D: depending upon boot)
/dev/hda2 Extended partition /dev/hda5 / /dev/hda6 swap
/dev/hda7 /home

/dev/hdc1 * Windows 95 partition (C: or D: depending upon
boot) /dev/hdc2 DOS partition (E: always) /dev/hdc3 swap
```

(Partitions with a * are set as bootable (or "active") by fdisk)

Example lilo.conf:

```
# /etc/lilo.conf
install = /boot/boot.b
compact
delay = 20    # optional, for systems that boot very quickly
#prompt             # use instead of delay to force response
# to boot prompt
#vga = normal # force sane state
#ramdisk = 0  # paranoia setting
#root = current     # use "current" root
boot = /dev/hda
image = /boot/vmlinuz
read-only
label = linux
other = /dev/hdc1
```

```
label = win95
loader= /boot/any_d.b
other = /dev/hda1
table = /dev/hda
label = dos
image = /boot/vmlinuz.old
label = linux.old
optional
read-only
```

- (6) Some Questions and Answers

Q: Does this scheme work for SCSI disks?
A: I have been told that this works, but have not been able to try it for myself.

Q: Does this scheme work if Linux is wholly on one disk, and DOS and Windows 95 are partitions of the other?
A: No - the DOS and Windows 95 bits both have to be the primary "DOS" partition of a disk. It is possible to get round this by recompiling LILO.

Q: I have downloaded a Windows 95 FAQ which speaks of the ability to boot between DOS and Windows 95. If I install Windows 3.x in a different directory from Windows it says I can run Windows 95 and Windows 3.x. in harmony. This is one partition.
A: Yes, this can be done. It may cause problems however. Windows 95 does some nasty things to the FAT drive and some operations you perform under your old DOS and old windows (3.x) can easily destroy the long-filename information. For example, defragmenting the drive using a DOS/Windows 3.x utility will do this. You are also introducing difficulties for yourself when things don't work; you have to worry about the INI files under each system **and** the Windows 95 registry.

Q: Does LBA matter?
A:Yes. Ugh! BIOS's after approx 1994 support LBA to get around a limit somewhere inside DOS which prevents DOS from being able to cope with cylinder numbers greater then1024. (This is covered in much greater detail in PC hardware FAQs). LBA fiddles the disk geometry, multiplying the number of heads by 2 or 4 (etc) in order to divide the apparent number of cylinders by 2 or 4 (etc) to a number less then1024. This works around this limit.

Linux can handle cylinders greater then1024 (provided that the partition from which you boot is below 1024 cylinders), so can handle large (great then 504Mb) disks even on old machines (pre-1994 BIOS). It can also handle large disks on BIOS's which do support LBA, whether or not LBA is enabled.

It is vital that ALL the OS's view each disk as having the same geometry - this is because the numbers in the partition table are **perceived** cylinder numbers, not the actual ones. Therefore, changing the BIOS setting to activate LBA will invalidate the existing contents of a disk.

If your linux system does not **see** the **correct** geometry (that is, the same that DOS **sees**), you will need to add a line to `lilo.conf append= "hd=x,y,z"` where x,y,z represent the disk geometry (see the relevant man pages).

Q: My BIOS only holds information on two HDDs, not four. Does this matter?
A: Maybe! Having 4 HDDs with old BIOS's under DOS required the use of driver software. Newer BIOS's hold information on 4 HDDs.

Linux can happily use 4 HDDs even with most of these older BIOS's, but if you put a DOS partition on disk 3 you will only be able to access it via linux.

This is relevant since many machines have an IDE drive, an IDE CD-ROM and, if you want to implement this document, another IDE drive too.

If you have found this document useful, please let me know.

Chapter 3

Slackware Linux Tutorial

3.1 Introduction

New users of UNIX and Linux may be a bit intimidated by the size and apparent complexity of the system before them. There are many good books on using UNIX out there, for all levels of expertise from novice to expert. However, none of these books covers, specifically, an introduction to using Linux. While 95% of using Linux is exactly like using other UNIX systems, the most straightforward way to get going on your new system is with a tutorial tailored for Linux. Herein is such a tutorial.

This chapter does not go into a large amount of detail or cover many advanced topics. Instead, it is intended to get the new Linux user running, on both feet, so that he or she may then read a more general book about UNIX and understand the basic differences between other UNIX systems and Linux.

Very little is assumed here, except perhaps some familiarity with personal computer systems, and MS-DOS. However, even if you're not an MS-DOS user, you should be able to understand everything here. At first glance, UNIX looks a lot like MS-DOS (after all, parts of MS-DOS were modeled on the CP/M operating system, which in turn was modeled on UNIX). However, only the very superficial features of UNIX resemble MS-DOS in any way. Even if you're completely new to the PC world, this tutorial should be of help.

And, before we begin: *Don't be afraid to experiment.* The system won't bite you. You can't destroy anything by working on the system. UNIX has some amount of security built in, to prevent "normal" users (the role which you will now assume) from damaging files which are essential to the system. Even so, the absolute worst thing that can happen is that you'll delete all of your files—and you'll have to go back and re-install the system. So, at this point, you have nothing to lose.

3.2   Basic UNIX Concepts

UNIX is a multitasking, multiuser operating system. This means that there can be many people using one computer at the same time, running many different applications. (This differs from MS-DOS, where only one person can use the system at any one time.) Under UNIX, for users to identify themselves to the system, they must **log in**, which entails two steps: Entering your **login name** (the name which the system identifies you as), and entering your **password**, which is your personal secret key to logging into your account. Because only you know your password, no one else can login to the system under your username.

On traditional UNIX systems, the system administrator will assign you a username and an initial password when you are given an account on the system. However, because you are the system administrator, you must set up your own account before you can login—see Section 3.2.1, below. For the following discussions, we'll use the imaginary username "`larry`".

In addition, each UNIX system has a **hostname** assigned to it. It is this hostname that gives your machine a name, gives it character and charm. The hostname is used to identify individual machines on a network, but even if your machine isn't networked, it should have a hostname. In Section 4.10.2 we'll cover setting your system's hostname. For our examples, below, the system's hostname is "`mousehouse`".

3.2.1   Creating an account

Before you can use the system, you must set up a user account for yourself. This is because it's usually not a good idea to use the `root` account for normal use. The `root` account should be reserved for running privileged commands and for maintaining the system, as discussed in Section 4.1.

In order to create an account for yourself, you need to login as `root` and use the `adduser` command. See Section 4.4 for information on this procedure.

3.2.2 Logging in

At login time, you'll see a prompt resembling the following on your screen:

```
mousehouse login:
```

Here, enter your username, and press the $\boxed{\texttt{Return}}$ key. Our hero, `larry`, would type the following:

```
mousehouse login:  larry
Password:
```

Now, enter your password. It won't be echoed to the screen when you login, so type carefully. If you mistype your password, you'll see the message

```
Login incorrect
```

and you'll have to try again.

Once you have correctly entered the username and password, you are officially logged into the system, and are free to roam.

3.2.3 Virtual consoles

The system's **console** is the monitor and keyboard connected directly to the system. (Because UNIX is a multiuser operating system, you may have other terminals connected to serial ports on your system, but these would not be the console.) Linux, like some other versions of UNIX, provides access to **virtual consoles** (or VC's), which allow you to have more than one login session from your console at a time.

To demonstrate this, login to your system (as demonstrated above). Now, press $\boxed{\texttt{alt-F2}}$. You should see the `login:` prompt again. You're looking at the second virtual console—you logged into the first. To switch back to the first VC, press $\boxed{\texttt{alt-F1}}$. *Voila!* You're back to your first login session.

A newly-installed Slackware Linux system probably allows you to access the first six VC's, using $\boxed{\texttt{alt-F1}}$ through $\boxed{\texttt{alt-F6}}$. However, it is possible to enable up to 12 VC's—one for each function key on your keyboard. As you can see, use of VC's can be very powerful—you can be working on several different VC's at once.

While the use of VC's is somewhat limiting (after all, you can only be looking at one VC at a time), it should give you a feel for UNIX's multiuser capabilities. While you're working on VC #1, you can switch over to VC #2 and start working on something else.

3.2.4   Shells and commands

For most of your explorations in the world of UNIX, you'll be talking to the system through the use of a **shell**. A shell is just a program which takes user input (e.g., commands which you type) and translates them into instructions. This can be compared to the `COMMAND.COM` program under MS-DOS, which does essentially the same thing. The shell is just one interface to UNIX. There are many possible interfaces—such as the X Window System, which lets you run commands by using the mouse and keyboard in conjunction.

As soon as you login, the system starts the shell, and you can type commands to it. Here's a quick example. Here, Larry logs in, and is left sitting at the shell **prompt**.

```
mousehouse login:  larry
Password:  larry's password
Welcome to Mousehouse!

/home/larry#
```

"`/home/larry#`" is the shell's prompt, indicating that it's ready to take commands. (More on what the prompt itself means later.) Let's try telling the system to do something interesting:

```
/home/larry# make love
make:  *** No way to make target 'love'.  Stop.
/home/larry#
```

Well, as it turns out `make` was the name of an actual program on the system, and the shell executed this program when given the command. (Unfortunately, the system was being unfriendly.)

This brings us to one burning question: What are commands? What happens when you type "`make love`"? The first word on the command line, "`make`", is the name of the command to be executed. Everything else on the command line is taken as arguments to this command. Examples:

/home/larry# *cp foo bar*

Here, the name of the command is "cp", and the arguments are "foo" and "bar".

When you type a command, the shell does several things. First of all, it looks at the command name, and checks to see if it is a command which is internal to the shell. (That is, a command which the shell knows how to execute itself. There are a number of these commands, and we'll go into them later.) The shell also checks to see if the command is an alias, or substitute name, for another command. If neither of these conditions apply, the shell looks for a program, on the disk, with the command's name. If it finds such a program, the shell runs it, giving the program the arguments specified on the command line.

In our example, the shell looks for the program called make, and runs it with the argument love. Make is a program often used to compile large programs, and it takes as arguments the name of a "target" to compile. In the case of "make love", we instructed make to compile the target love. Because make can't find a target by this name, it fails with a humorous error message, and we are returned to the shell prompt.

What happens if we type a command to a shell, and the shell can't find a program with the command name to run? Well, we can try it:

/home/larry# *eat dirt*
eat: command not found
/home/larry#

Quite simply, if the shell can't find a program with the name given on the command line (here, "eat"), it prints an error message which should be self-explanatory. You'll often see this error message if you mistype a command (for example, if you had typed "mkae love" instead of "make love").

3.2.5 Logging out

Before we delve much further, we should tell you how to log out of the system. At the shell prompt, use the command

/home/larry# *exit*

to logout. There are other ways of logging out as well, but this is the most foolproof one.

3.2.6   Changing your password

You should also be aware of how to change your password. The command `passwd` will prompt you for your old password, and your new password. It will ask you to reenter the new password for validation. Be careful not to forget your password—if you do, you will have to ask the system administrator to reset it for you. (If you're the system administrator, see Section 4.4.)

3.2.7   Files and directories

Under most operating systems (UNIX included), there is the concept of a **file**, which is just a bundle of information which is given a name (called a **filename**). Examples of files would be your history term paper, an e-mail message, or an actual program which can be executed. Essentially, anything which is saved on disk is saved in an individual file.

Files are identified by their filenames. For example, the file containing your history paper might be saved with the filename `history-paper`. These names usually identify the file and its contents in some form which is meaningful to you. There is no standard format for filenames as there is under MS-DOS and other operating systems; in general, filenames may contain any character (except /—see the discussion of pathnames, below), and are limited to 256 characters in length.

With the concept of files comes the concept of directories. A **directory** is just a collection of files. It can be thought of as a "folder" which contains many different files. Directories themselves are given names, with which you can identify them. Furthermore, directories are maintained in a tree-like structure; that is, directories may contain other directories.

A file may be referred to by its **pathname**, which is made up of the filename, preceded by the name of the directory which contains the file. For example, let's say that Larry has a directory called `papers`, which contains three files: `history-final`, `english-lit`, and `masters-thesis`. (Each of these three files contains information for three of Larry's ongoing projects.) To refer to the file `english-lit`, Larry can specify the file's pathname:

```
papers/english-lit
```

As you can see, the directory and file names are separated by a single slash (/). For this reason, filenames themselves cannot contain the / character. MS-DOS users

will find this convention familiar, although in the MS-DOS world, the backslash (\)
is used instead.

As mentioned, directories can be nested within each other as well. For example,
let's say that Larry has another directory, within `papers`, called `notes`. This directory contains the files `math-notes` and `cheat-sheet`. The pathname of the file
`cheat-sheet` would be

    papers/notes/cheat-sheet

Therefore, the pathname really is a "path" which you take to locate a certain
file. The directory above a given subdirectory is known as the **parent directory**.
Here, the directory `papers` is the parent of the `notes` directory.

3.2.8   The directory tree

Most UNIX systems have a standard layout for files, so that system resources and
programs can be easily located. This layout forms a directory tree, which starts at
the "/" directory, also known as "the root directory". Directly underneath / are
some important subdirectories: `/bin`, `/etc`, `/dev`, and `/usr`, among others. These
directories in turn contain other directories which contain system configuration files,
programs, and so on.

In particular, each user has a **home directory**, which is the directory set aside
for that user to store his or her files. In the examples above, all of Larry's files (such
as `cheat-sheet` and `history-final`) were contained in Larry's home directory.
Usually, user home directories are contained under `/home`, and are named for the
user who owns that directory. Therefore, Larry's home directory is `/home/larry`.

In Figure 3.2.8 a sample directory tree is represented. It should give you some
idea of how the directory tree on your system is organized.

3.2.9   The current working directory

At any given time, commands that you type to the shell are given in terms of your
current working directory. You can think of your working directory as the
directory in which you are currently "located". When you first login, your working
directory is set to your home directory—`/home/larry` in our case. Whenever you
reference a file, you may refer to it in relationship to your current working directory,
instead of specifying the full pathname of the file.

Here's an example. Larry has the directory `papers`, and `papers` contains the file `history-final`. If Larry wants to look at this file, he can use the command

  `/home/larry#` *more /home/larry/papers/history-final*

The `more` command simply displays a file, one screen at a time. However, because Larry's current working directory is `/home/larry`, he can instead refer to the file *relative* to his current location. The command would be

  `/home/larry#` *more papers/history-final*

Therefore, if you begin a filename (such as `papers/final`) with a character other than "/", the system assumes that you're referring to the file in terms relative to your current working directory. This is known as a **relative pathname**.

On the other hand, if you begin a filename with a "/", the system interprets this as a full pathname—that is, a pathname including the entire path to the file, starting from the root directory, `/`. This is known as an **absolute pathname**.

3.2.10   Referring to home directories

Under both `tcsh` and `bash`,[1] your home directory can be referred to using the tilde character ("~"). For example, the command

  `/home/larry#` *more ~/papers/history-final*

is equivalent to

  `/home/larry#` *more /home/larry/papers/history-final*

The "~" character is simply replaced with the name of your home directory by the shell.

In addition, you can specify other user's home directories with the tilde as well. The pathname "~karl/letters" translates to "/home/karl/letters" by the shell (if `/home/karl` is karl's home directory). The use of the tilde is simply a shortcut; there is no directory named "~"—it's just syntactic sugar provided by the shell.

---

[1]`tcsh` and `bash` are two *shells* running under Slackware Linux. The shell is the program which reads user commands and executes them; most Linux systems enable `bash` for new user accounts.

3.3 First Steps into UNIX

Before we begin, it is important to note that all file and command names on a UNIX system are case-sensitive (unlike operating systems such as MS-DOS). For example, the command make is very different than Make or MAKE. The same hold for file and directory names.

3.3.1 Moving around

Now that we can login, and know how to refer to files using pathnames, how can we change our current working directory, to make life easier?

The command for moving around in the directory structure is cd, short for "change directory". You'll notice that many often-used Unix commands are two or three letters. The usage of the cd command is:

cd ⟨directory⟩

where ⟨directory⟩ is the name of the directory which you wish to change to.

As we said, when you login, you begin in your home directory. If Larry wanted to move down into the **papers** subdirectory, he'd use the command

/home/larry# *cd papers*
/home/larry/papers#

As you can see, Larry's prompt changes to reflect his current working directory (so he knows where he is). Now that he's in the **papers** directory, he can look at his history final with the command

/home/larry/papers# *more history-final*

Now, Larry is stuck in the **papers** subdirectory. To move back up to the parent directory, use the command

/home/larry/papers# *cd ..*
/home/larry#

(Note the space between the "cd" and the "..".) Every directory has an entry named ".." which refers to the parent directory. Similarly, every directory has an entry named "." which refers to itself. Therefore, the command

```
/home/larry/papers# cd .
```

gets us nowhere.

You can also use absolute pathnames in the cd command. To cd into Karl's home directory, we can use the command

```
/home/larry/papers# cd /home/karl
/home/karl#
```

Also, using cd with no argument will return you to your own home directory.

```
/home/karl# cd
/home/larry#
```

3.3.2   Looking at the contents of directories

Now that you know how to move around directories you probably think, "So what?" The basic skill of moving around directories is fairly useless, so let's introduce a new command, ls. ls prints a listing of files and directories, by default from your current directory. For example:

```
/home/larry# ls
Mail
letters
papers
/home/larry#
```

Here we can see that Larry has three entries in his current directory: Mail, letters, and papers. This doesn't tell us much—are these directories or files? We can use the -F option on the ls command to tell us more.

```
/home/larry# ls -F
Mail/
letters/
papers/
/home/larry#
```

From the / appended to each filename, we know that these three entries are in fact subdirectories.

Using `ls -F` may also append "*" to the end of a filename. This indicates that the file is an **executable**, or a program which can be run. If nothing is appended to the filename using `ls -F`, the file is a "plain old file", that is, it's neither a directory, or an executable.

In general, each UNIX command may take a number of options in addition to other arguments. These options usually begin with a "-", as demonstrated above with `ls -F`. The -F option tells `ls` to give more information about the type of the files involved—in this case, printing a / after each directory name.

If you give `ls` a directory name, it will print the contents of that directory.

```
/home/larry# ls -F papers
english-lit
history-final
masters-thesis
notes/
/home/larry#
```

Or, for a more interesting listing, let's see what's in the system's /etc directory.

```
/home/larry# ls /etc
```

DIR_COLOR	ftpusers	mailcap	rpc
HOSTNAME	gateways	makedev.cfg	securetty
NETWORKING	gettydefs	motd	sendmail.cf
NNTP_INEWS_DOMAIN	group	msgs/	sendmail.st
X11@	host.conf	mtab	services
XF86Config	hosts	mtools.conf	shells
aliases	hosts.allow	named.boot	skel/
aliases.db	hosts.deny	networks	slip.hosts
at.deny	hosts.equiv	nntpserver	slip.login
bootptab	hosts.lpd	organization	snooptab
csh.cshrc	inet@	passwd	sudoers
csh.login	inetd.conf	passwd.OLD	syslog.conf
default/	inittab	passwd.old	termcap
devinfo	inittab.gettyps.sample pcmcia/		ttys
diphosts	issue	ppp/	utmp@
exports	issue.net	printcap	vga/

```
fastboot            ld.so.cache       profile         wtmp@
fdprm               ld.so.conf        protocols       yp.conf.example
fstab               lilo.conf         psdevtab        zprofile@
ftpaccess           localtime         rc.d/
ftpconversions      magic             resolv.conf
ftpgroups           mail.rc           rmt@
/home/larry#
```

(For those MS-DOS users out there, notice how the filenames can be longer than 8 characters, and can contain periods in any position. It is even possible to have more than one period in a filename.)

Let's `cd` up to the top of the directory tree, using "`cd ..`", and then down to another directory: `/usr/bin`.

```
/home/larry# cd ..
/home# cd ..
/# cd usr
/usr# cd bin
/usr/bin#
```

You can also move into directories in multiple steps, as in `cd /usr/bin`.

Try moving around various directories, using `ls` and `cd`. In some cases, you may run into a foreboding "`Permission denied`" error message. This is simply the concept of UNIX security kicking in: in order to `ls` or to `cd` into a directory, you must have permission to do so. We'll talk more about this in   Section 3.9.

3.3.3   Creating new directories

It's time to learn how to create directories. This involves the use of the `mkdir` command. Try the following:

```
/home/larry# mkdir foo
/home/larry# ls -F
Mail/
foo/
letters/
papers/
/home/larry# cd foo
```

```
/home/larry/foo# ls
/home/larry/foo#
```

Congrats! You've just made a new directory and moved into it. Since there aren't any files in this new directory, let's learn how to copy files from one place to another.

3.3.4 Copying files

Copying files is done with the command cp:

```
/home/larry/foo# cp /etc/termcap  .
/home/larry/foo# cp /etc/shells  .
/home/larry/foo# ls −F
shells     termcap
/home/larry/foo# cp shells bells
/home/larry/foo# ls −F
bells     shells     termcap
/home/larry/foo#
```

The cp command copies the files listed on the command line to the file or directory given as the last argument. Notice how we use the directory "." to refer to the current directory.

3.3.5 Moving files

A new command named mv moves files, instead of copying them. The syntax is very straightforward.

```
/home/larry/foo# mv termcap sells
/home/larry/foo# ls -F
bells     sells     shells
/home/larry/foo#
```

Notice how termcap no longer exists, but in its place is the file sells. This can be used to rename files, as we have just done, but also to move a file to a completely new directory.

◇   **Note:** mv and cp will overwrite the destination file (if it already exists) without asking you. Be careful when you move a file into another directory: there may already be a file with the same name in that directory, which you'll overwrite!

3.3.6   Deleting files and directories

You now have an ugly rhyme developing with the use of the ls command. To delete a file, use the rm command. ("rm" stands for "remove").

```
/home/larry/foo# rm bells sells
/home/larry/foo# ls -F
shells
/home/larry/foo#
```

We're left with nothing but shells, but we won't complain. Note that rm by default won't prompt you before deleting a file—so be careful.

A related command to rm is rmdir. This command deletes a directory, but only if the directory is empty. If the directory contains any files or subdirectories, rmdir will complain.

3.3.7   Looking at files

The commands more and cat are used for viewing the contents of files. more displays a file, one screenful at a time, while cat displays the whole file at once.

To look at the file shells, we can use the command

```
/home/larry/foo# more shells
```

In case you're interested what shells contains, it's a list of valid shell programs on your system. In Slackware Linux, this includes /bin/sh, /bin/bash, /bin/csh, /bin/zsh, /bin/ash, and /bin/tcsh. We'll talk about these different types of shells later.

While using more, press ⎡Space⎤ to display the next page of text, and ⎡b⎤ to display the previous page. There are other commands available in more as well, these are just the basics. Pressing ⎡q⎤ will quit more.

Quit more and try cat /etc/termcap. The text will probably fly by much too quickly for you to read it. The name "cat" actually stands for "concatenate", which is the real use of the program. The `cat` command can be used to concatenate the contents of several files and save the result to another file. This will be discussed later.

3.3.8   Getting online help

Almost every UNIX system, Slackware Linux included, provides a facility known as "manual pages", or "man pages" for short. These man pages contain online documentation for all of the various system commands, resources, configuration files, and so on.

The command used to access man pages is `man`. For example, if you're interested in finding out about the other options of the `ls` command, you can type

```
/home/larry#  man ls
```

and the man page for `ls` will be displayed.

Unfortunately, most of the man pages out there are written for those who already have some idea of what the command or resource does. For this reason, man pages usually only contain the hardcore technical details of the command, without a lot of tutorial. However, man pages can be an invaluable resource for jogging your memory if you forget the syntax of a command. Man pages will also tell you a lot about the commands which we won't tell you in this book.

I suggest that you try `man` for the commands we've already gone over, and whenever I introduce a new command. You'll notice some of these commands won't have man pages. This could be for several reasons. For one, the man pages haven't been written yet (the Linux Documentation Project is responsible for man pages under Linux as well. We are gradually accumulating most of the man pages available for the system). Secondly, the command might be an internal shell command, or an alias (as discussed in Section 3.2.4), in which case it would not have a man page of its own. One example is `cd`, which is a shell internal command. The shell actually processes the `cd`—there is no separate program which contains this command.

3.4   Summary of Basic Commands

This section introduces some of the most useful basic commands on a UNIX system, including those covered in the last section.

Note that options usually begin with a "-", and in most cases multiple one-letter options may be combined using a single "-". For example, instead of using the command `ls -l -F`, it is adequate to use `ls -lF`.

Instead of listing all of the options available for each of these commands, we'll only talk about those which are useful or important at this time. In fact, most of these commands have a large number of options (most of which you'll never use). You can use **man** to see the manual pages for each command, which list all of the available options.

Also note that many of these commands take a list of files or directories as arguments, denoted by "⟨*file1*⟩ ... ⟨*fileN*⟩". For example, the `cp` command takes as arguments a list of files to copy, followed by the destination file or directory. When copying more than one file, the destination must be a directory.

cd   Change the current working directory.
              Syntax: `cd` ⟨*directory*⟩
              ⟨*directory*⟩ is the directory to change to. ("." refers to the current directory, ".." the parent directory.)
              Example: `cd ../foo` sets the current directory to `../foo`.

ls   Displays information about the named files and directories.
              Syntax: `ls` ⟨*file1*⟩ ⟨*file2*⟩ ... ⟨*fileN*⟩
              Where ⟨*file1*⟩ through ⟨*fileN*⟩ are the filenames or directories to list.
              Options: There are more options than you want to think about. The most commonly used are `-F` (used to display some information about the type of the file), and `-l` (gives a "long" listing including file size, owner, permissions, and so on. This will be covered in detail later.)
              Example: `ls -lF /home/larry` will display the contents of the directory `/home/larry`.

cp   Copies file(s) to another file or directory.
              Syntax: `cp` ⟨*file1*⟩ ⟨*file2*⟩ ... ⟨*fileN*⟩ ⟨*destination*⟩
              Where ⟨*file1*⟩ through ⟨*fileN*⟩ are the files to copy, and ⟨*destination*⟩ is the destination file or directory.
              Example: `cp ../frog joe` copies the file `../frog` to the file or directory `joe`.

mv   Moves file(s) to another file or directory. This command does the equivalent of a copy followed by the deletion of the original. This can be used to rename files, as in the MS-DOS command `RENAME`.

Syntax: `mv` ⟨*file1*⟩ ⟨*file2*⟩ ... ⟨*fileN*⟩ ⟨*destination*⟩

Where ⟨*file1*⟩ through ⟨*fileN*⟩ are the files to move, and ⟨*destination*⟩ is the destination file or directory.

Example: `mv ../frog joe` moves the file `../frog` to the file or directory `joe`.

`rm` Deletes files. Note that when files are deleted under UNIX, they are unrecoverable (unlike MS-DOS, where you can usually "undelete" the file).

Syntax: `rm` ⟨*file1*⟩ ⟨*file2*⟩ ... ⟨*fileN*⟩

Where ⟨*file1*⟩ through ⟨*fileN*⟩ are the filenames to delete.

Options: `-i` will prompt for confirmation before deleting the file.

Example: `rm -i /home/larry/joe /home/larry/frog` deletes the files `joe` and `frog` in `/home/larry`.

`mkdir` Creates new directories.

Syntax: `mkdir` ⟨*dir1*⟩ ⟨*dir2*⟩ ... ⟨*dirN*⟩

Where ⟨*dir1*⟩ through ⟨*dirN*⟩ are the directories to create.

Example: `mkdir /home/larry/test` creates the directory `test` under `/home/larry`.

`rmdir` This command deletes empty directories. When using `rmdir`, your current working directory must not be within the directory to be deleted.

Syntax: `rmdir` ⟨*dir1*⟩ ⟨*dir2*⟩ ... ⟨*dirN*⟩

Where ⟨*dir1*⟩ through ⟨*dirN*⟩ are the directories to delete.

Example: `rmdir /home/larry/papers` deletes the directory `/home/larry/papers`, if it is empty.

`man` Displays the manual page for the given command or resource (that is, any system utility which isn't a command, such as a library function.) Syntax: `man` ⟨*command*⟩

Where ⟨*command*⟩ is the name of the command or resource to get help on.

Example: `man ls` gives help on the `ls` command.

`more` Displays the contents of the named files, one screenful at a time.

Syntax: `more` ⟨*file1*⟩ ⟨*file2*⟩ ... ⟨*fileN*⟩

Where ⟨*file1*⟩ through ⟨*fileN*⟩ are the files to display.

Example: `more papers/history-final` displays the file

papers/history-final.

less   Displays the contents of the named files, one screenful at a time.
                Syntax: less ⟨file1⟩ ⟨file2⟩ ...⟨fileN⟩
                Where ⟨file1⟩ through ⟨fileN⟩ are the files to display. Use arrow
                keys to scroll through the file.
                Example: less papers/history-final   displays   the   file
                papers/history-final.

cat   Officially used to concatenate files, cat is also used to display the
                entire contents of a file at once.
                Syntax: cat ⟨file1⟩ ⟨file2⟩ ...⟨fileN⟩
                Where ⟨file1⟩ through ⟨fileN⟩ are the files to display.
                Example: cat letters/from-mdw   displays   the   file
                letters/from-mdw.

echo   Simply echoes the given arguments.
                Syntax: echo ⟨arg1⟩ ⟨arg2⟩ ...⟨argN⟩
                Where ⟨arg1⟩ through ⟨argN⟩ are the arguments to echo.
                Example: echo "Hello world" displays the string "Hello
                world".

grep   Display all of the lines in the named file(s) matching the given
                pattern.
                Syntax: grep ⟨pattern⟩ ⟨file1⟩ ⟨file2⟩ ...⟨fileN⟩
                Where ⟨pattern⟩ is a regular expression pattern, and ⟨file1⟩ through
                ⟨fileN⟩ are the files to search.
                Example: grep loomer /etc/hosts will display all lines in the
                file /etc/hosts which contain the pattern "loomer".

3.5 Exploring the File System

The **file system** is the collection of files and the hierarchy of directories on your
system. I promised before to escort you around the filesystem and the time has
come.

You have the skills and the knowledge to make sense out of what I'm saying,
and you have a roadmap. (Refer to Figure 3.2.8 on page 154).

First, change to the root directory (cd /), and do an ls -F. You'll probably see these directories[2]: `bin`, `boot`, `cdrom`, `dev`, `etc`, `home`, `lib`, `lost+found`, `mnt`, `proc`, `root`, `sbin`, `shlib`, `tmp`, `usr`, and `var`.

Let's take a look at each of these directories.

`/bin`

`/bin` is short for "binaries", or executables. This is where many essential system programs reside. Use the command "`ls /bin`" to list the files here. If you look down the list you may see a few commands that you recognize, such as `cp`, `ls`, and `mv`. These are the actual programs for these commands. When you use the `cp` command, you're running the program `/bin/cp`.

Using `ls`, you'll see that most (if not all) of the files in `/bin` have an asterisk ("∗") appended to their filenames. This indicates that the files are executables, as described in Section 3.3.2.

`/dev`

Next on our stop is `/dev`. Take a look, again with `ls`.

The "files" in `/dev` are known as **device drivers**—they are used to access system devices and resources, such as disk drives, modems, memory, and so on. For example, just as you can read data from a file, you can read input from the mouse by accessing `/dev/mouse`.

The filenames beginning with `fd` are floppy disk devices. `fd0` is the first floppy disk drive, `fd1` the second. Now, the astute among you will notice that there are more floppy disk devices then just the two I've listed above: they represent specific types of floppy disks. For example, `fd1h1440` will access high-density, 3.5" diskettes in drive 1.

Here is a list of some of the most commonly used device files. Note that even though you may not have some of the devices listed below, the chances are that you'll have entries in `/dev` for them anyway.

- `/dev/console` refers to the system's console—that is, the monitor connected directly to your system.

- The various `/dev/ttyS` and `/dev/cua` devices are used for accessing serial ports. For example, `/dev/ttyS0` refers to "COM1" under MS-DOS. The `/dev/cua` devices are "callout" devices, which are used in conjunction with a modem.

---

[2]You may see others, and you might not see all of them. Don't worry. Every release of Linux differs in some respects.

- The device names beginning with `hd` access hard drives. `/dev/hda` refers to the *whole* first hard disk, while `hda1` refers to the first *partition* on `/dev/hda`.

- The device names beginning with `sd` are SCSI drives. If you have a SCSI hard drive, instead of accessing it through `/dev/hda`, you would access `/dev/sda`. SCSI tapes are accessed via `st` devices, and SCSI CD-ROM via `sr` devices.

- The device names beginning with `lp` access parallel ports. `/dev/lp0` refers to "LPT1" in the MS-DOS world.

- `/dev/null` is used as a "black hole"—any data sent to this device is gone forever. Why is this useful? Well, if you wanted to suppress the output of a command appearing on your screen, you could send that output to `/dev/null`. We'll talk more about this later.

- The device names beginning with `/dev/tty` refer to the "virtual consoles" on your system (accessed via by pressing `alt-F1`, `alt-F2`, and so on). `/dev/tty1` refers to the first VC, `/dev/tty2` refers to the second, and so on.

- The device names beginning with `/dev/pty` are "pseudo-terminals". They are used to provide a "terminal" to remote login sessions. For example, if your machine is on a network, incoming `telnet` logins would use one of the `/dev/pty` devices.

`/etc`   `/etc` contains a number of miscellaneous system configuration files. These include `/etc/passwd` (the user database), `/etc/group` (the groups database), `/etc/aliases` (the system email aliases) and so on.

`/sbin`   `sbin` is used for storing essential system binaries, to be used by the system administrator.

`/home`   `/home` contains user's home directories. For example, `/home/larry` is the home directory for the user "`larry`". On a newly-installed system, there may not be any users in this directory.

`/lib`   `/lib` contains **shared library images**. These files contain code which many programs share in common. Instead of each program containing its own copy of these shared routines, they are all stored in one common place, in /lib. This makes executable files smaller, and saves space on your system.

/proc   /proc is a "virtual filesystem", the files in which are stored in memory, not on the drive. They refer to the various **processes** running on the system, and allow you to get information about what programs and processes are running at any given time. We'll go into more detail in Section 3.11.1.

/tmp   Many programs have a need to generate some information and store it in a temporary file. The canonical location for these files is in /tmp.

/usr   /usr is a very important directory. It contains a number of sub-directories which in turn contain some of the most important and useful programs and configuration files used on the system.

The various directories described above are essential for the system to operate, but most of the things found in /usr are optional for the system. However, it is those optional things which make the system useful and interesting. Without /usr, you'd more or less have a boring system, only with programs like cp and ls. /usr contains most of the larger software packages and the configuration files which accompany them.

/usr/X386   /usr/X386 contains The X Window System, if you installed it. The X Window System is a large, powerful graphical environment which provides a large number of graphical utilities and programs, displayed in "windows" on your screen. If you're at all familiar with the Microsoft Windows or Macintosh environments, X Windows will look very familiar. The /usr/X386 directory contains all of the X Windows executables, configuration files, and support files. This will be covered in more detail in Section 5.1.

/usr/bin   /usr/bin is the real warehouse for software on any UNIX system. It contains most of the executables for programs not found in other places, such as /bin.

/usr/include   /usr/include contains **include files** for the C compiler. These files (most of which end in .h, for "header") declare data structure names, subroutines, and constants used when writing programs in C. Those files found in /usr/include/sys are generally used when

programming on the UNIX system level. If you are familiar with
the C programming language, here you'll find header files such as
`stdio.h`, which declares functions such as `printf()`.

/usr/include/g++

/usr/include/g++ contains include files for the C++ compiler
(much like `/usr/include`).

/usr/lib

`/usr/lib` contains the "stub" and "static" library equivalents to
the files found in `/lib`. When compiling a program, the program is
"linked" with the libraries found in `/usr/lib`, which then directs
the program to look in `/lib` when it needs the actual code in the
library. In addition, various other programs store configuration
files in `/usr/lib`.

/usr/local

`/usr/local` is a lot like `/usr`—it contains various programs and
files not essential to the system, but which make the system fun
and exciting. In general, those programs found in `/usr/local` are
specialized for your system specifically—that is, `/usr/local` differs
greatly between UNIX systems.

/usr/man

This directory contains the actual man pages. There are two subdirectories for every man page "section" (use the command `man`
`man` for details). For example, `/usr/man/man1` contains the source
(that is, the unformatted original) for man pages in section 1, and
`/usr/man/cat1` contains the formatted man pages for section 1.

/usr/src

`/usr/src` contains the source code (the uncompiled program) for
various programs on your system. The most important thing here
is `/usr/src/linux`, which contains the source code for the Linux
kernel.

/var

`/var` holds directories that often change in size or tend to grow.
Many of those directories used to reside in `/usr`, but since we
are trying to keep it relatively unchangeable, the directories that
change often have been moved to `/var`. Some of those directories
are:

/var/adm

`/var/adm` contains various files of interest to the system administrator, specifically system logs, which record any errors or problems
with the system. Other files record logins to the system, as well as

failed login attempts. This will be covered in Chapter 4.

`/var/spool`   `/var/spool` contains files which are to be "spooled" to another program. For example, if your machine is connected to a network, incoming mail will be stored in `/var/spool/mail`, until you read it or delete it. Outgoing or incoming news articles may be found in `/var/spool/news`, and so on.

3.6 Types of shells

As I have mentioned too many times before, UNIX is a multitasking, multiuser operating system. Multitasking is *very* useful, and once you get used to it, you'll use it all of the time. Before long, you'll be able to run programs in the "background", switch between multiple tasks, and "pipeline" programs together to achieve complicated results with a single command.

Many of the features we'll be covering in this section are features provided by the shell itself. Be careful not to confuse UNIX (the actual operating system) with the shell—the shell is just an interface to the underlying system. The shell provides a great deal of functionality on top of UNIX itself.

The shell is not only an interpreter for your interactive commands, which you type at the prompt. It is also a powerful programming language, which allows you to write **shell scripts**, to "batch" several shell commands together in a file. MS-DOS users will recognize the similarity to "batch files". Use of shell scripts is a very powerful tool, which will allow you to automate and expand your usage of UNIX. See Section 3.13.1 for more information.

There are several types of shells in the UNIX world. The two major types are the "Bourne shell" and the "C shell". The Bourne shell uses a command syntax like the original shell on early UNIX systems, such as System III. The name of the Bourne shell on most UNIX systems is `/bin/sh` (where `sh` stands for "shell"). The C shell (not to be confused with a sea shell) uses a different syntax, somewhat like the programming language C, and on most UNIX systems is named `/bin/csh`.

Under Linux, there are several variations of these shells available. The two most commonly used are the Bourne Again Shell, or "Bash" (`/bin/bash`), and Tcsh (`/bin/tcsh`). Bash is a form of the Bourne shell with many of the advanced features found in the C shell. Because Bash supports a superset of the Bourne shell syntax, any shell scripts written in the standard Bourne shell should work with

Bash. For those who prefer to use the C shell syntax, Slackware Linux supports
Tcsh, which is an expanded version of the original C shell.

The type of shell that you decide to use is mostly a religious issue. Some folks
prefer the Bourne shell syntax with the advanced features of Bash, and some prefer
the more structured C shell syntax. As far as normal commands, such as `cp` and `ls`,
are concerned, the type of shell you're using doesn't matter—the syntax is the same.
Only when you start to write shell scripts or use some of the advanced features of
the shell do the differences between shell types begin to matter.

As we're discussing some of the features of the shell, below, we'll note those
differences between Bourne and C shells. However, for the purposes of this manual,
most of those differences are minimal. (If you're really curious at this point, read
the man pages for `bash` and `tcsh`).

3.7   Wildcards

A key feature of most Unix shells is the ability to reference more than one filename
using special characters. These so-called **wildcards** allow you to refer to, say, all
filenames which contain the character "n".

The wildcard "∗" refers to any character or string of characters in a filename.
For example, when you use the character "∗" in a filename, the shell replaces it with
all possible substitutions from filenames in the directory which you're referencing.

Here's a quick example. Let's suppose that Larry has the files `frog`, `joe`, and
`stuff` in his current directory.

```
/home/larry# ls
frog      joe       stuff
/home/larry#
```

To access all files with the letter "o" in the filename, we can use the command

```
/home/larry# ls *o*
frog      joe
/home/larry#
```

As you can see, the use of the "∗" wildcard was replaced with all substitutions
which matched the wildcard from filenames in the current directory.

The use of "*" by itself simply matches all filenames, because all characters match the wildcard.

```
/home/larry# ls *
frog      joe      stuff
/home/larry#
```

Here are a few more examples.

```
/home/larry# ls f*
frog
/home/larry# ls *ff
stuff
/home/larry# ls *f*
frog      stuff
/home/larry# ls s*f
stuff
/home/larry#
```

The process of changing a "*" into filenames is called **wildcard expansion** and is done by the shell. This is important: the individual commands, such as `ls`, *never* see the "*" in their list of parameters. The shell expands the wildcard to include all of the filenames which match. So, the command

```
/home/larry# ls *o*
```

is expanded by the shell to actually be

```
/home/larry# ls frog joe
```

One important note about the "*" wildcard. Using this wildcard will *not* match filenames which begin with a single period ("."). These files are treated as "hidden" files—while they are not really hidden, they don't show up on normal `ls` listings, and aren't touched by the use of the "*" wildcard.

Here's an example. We already mentioned that each directory has two special entries in it: "." refers to the current directory, and ".." refers to the parent directory. However, when you use `ls`, these two entries don't show up.

```
/home/larry# ls
frog      joe      stuff
/home/larry#
```

If you use the -a switch with ls, however, you can display filenames which begin
with ".". Observe:

```
/home/larry# ls -a
.          ..        .bash_profile    .bashrc    frog    joe    stuff
/home/larry#
```

Now we can see the two special entries, "." and "..", as well as two other "hidden"
files—.bash_profile and .bashrc. These two files are startup files used by bash
when larry logs in. More on them in Section 3.13.3.

Note that when we use the "*" wildcard, none of the filenames beginning with
"." are displayed.

```
/home/larry# ls *
frog      joe      stuff
/home/larry#
```

This is a safety feature: if the "*" wildcard matched filenames beginning with ".",
it would also match the directory names "." and "..". This can be dangerous
when using certain commands.

Another wildcard is "?". The "?" wildcard will only expand a single character.
Thus, "ls ?" will display all one character filenames, and "ls termca?" would
display "termcap" but *not* "termcap.backup". Here's another example:

```
/home/larry# ls j?e
joe
/home/larry# ls f??g
frog
/home/larry# ls ????f
stuff
/home/larry#
```

As you can see, wildcards allow you to specify many files at one time. In the
simple command summary, in Section 3.4, we said that the cp and mv commands
actually can copy or move multiple files at one time. For example,

```
/home/larry# cp /etc/s* /home/larry
```

will copy all filenames in /etc beginning with "s" to the directory /home/larry.
Therefore, the format of the cp command is really

> cp ⟨file1⟩ ⟨file2⟩ ⟨file3⟩ ... ⟨fileN⟩ ⟨destination⟩

where ⟨file1⟩ through ⟨fileN⟩ is a list of filenames to copy, and ⟨destination⟩ is the destination file or directory to copy them to. `mv` has an identical syntax.

Note that if you are copying or moving more than one file, the ⟨destination⟩ must be a directory. You can only copy or move a *single* file to another file.

3.8 UNIX Plumbing

3.8.1 Standard input and output

Many UNIX commands get input from what is known as **standard input** and send their output to **standard output** (often abbreviated as "stdin" and "stdout"). Your shell sets things up so that standard input is your keyboard, and standard output is the screen.

Here's an example using the command `cat`. Normally, `cat` reads data from all of the filenames given on the command line and sends this data directly to stdout. Therefore, using the command

> /home/larry/papers# *cat history-final masters-thesis*

will display the contents of the file `history-final` followed by `masters-thesis`.

However, if no filenames are given to `cat` as parameters, it instead reads data from stdin, and sends it back to stdout. Here's an example.

> /home/larry/papers# *cat*
> *Hello there.*
> Hello there.
> *Bye.*
> Bye.
> `ctrl-D`
> /home/larry/papers#

As you can see, each line that the user types (displayed in italics) is immediately echoed back by the `cat` command. When reading from standard input, commands know that the input is "finished" when they receive an EOT (end-of-text) signal. In general, this is generated by pressing `ctrl-D`.

Here's another example. The command `sort` reads in lines of text (again, from
stdin, unless files are given on the command line), and sends the sorted output to
stdout. Try the following.

```
/home/larry/papers# sort
bananas
carrots
apples
ctrl-D
apples
bananas
carrots
/home/larry/papers#
```

Now we can alphabetize our shopping list... isn't UNIX useful?

3.8.2   Redirecting input and output

Now, let's say that we wanted to send the output of `sort` to a file, to save our
shopping list elsewhere. The shell allows us to **redirect** standard output to a
filename, using the ">" symbol. Here's how it works.

```
/home/larry/papers# sort > shopping-list
bananas
carrots
apples
ctrl-D
/home/larry/papers#
```

As you can see, the result of the `sort` command isn't displayed, instead it's saved
to the file `shopping-list`. Let's look at this file.

```
/home/larry/papers# cat shopping-list
apples
bananas
carrots
/home/larry/papers#
```

Now we can sort our shopping list, and save it, too! But let's suppose that we were
storing our unsorted, original shopping list in the file **items**. One way of sorting

the information and saving it to a file would be to give **sort** the name of the file to read, in lieu of standard input, and redirect standard output as we did above. As so:

```
/home/larry/papers# sort items > shopping-list
/home/larry/papers# cat shopping-list
apples
bananas
carrots
/home/larry/papers#
```

However, there's another way of doing this. Not only can we redirect standard output, but we can redirect standard *input* as well, using the "**<**" symbol.

```
/home/larry/papers# sort < items
apples
bananas
carrots
/home/larry/papers#
```

Technically, **sort < items** is equivalent to **sort items**, but the former allows us to demonstrate the point: **sort < items** behaves as if the data in the file **items** was typed to standard input. The shell handles the redirection. **sort** wasn't given the name of the file (**items**) to read; as far as **sort** is concerned, it was still reading from standard input as if you had typed the data from your keyboard.

This introduces the concept of a **filter**. A filter is a program which reads data from standard input, processes it in some way, and sends the processed data to standard output. Using redirection, standard input and/or standard output can be referenced from files. **sort** is a simple filter: it sorts the incoming data and sends the result to standard output. **cat** is even simpler: it doesn't do anything with the incoming data, it simply outputs whatever was given to it.

3.8.3 Using pipes

We've already demonstrated how to use **sort** as a filter. However, these examples assumed that you had data in a file somewhere, or were willing to type the data to standard input yourself. What if the data you wanted to sort came from the output of another command, such as **ls**? For example, using the **-r** option with **sort** sorts

the data in reverse-alphabetical order. If you wanted to list the files in your current
directory in reverse order, one way to do it would be:

```
/home/larry/papers# ls
english-list
history-final
masters-thesis
notes
/home/larry/papers# ls > file-list
/home/larry/papers# sort -r file-list
notes
masters-thesis
history-final
english-list
/home/larry/papers#
```

Here, we saved the output of ls in a file, and then ran sort -r on that file. But
this is unwieldy and causes us to use a temporary file to save the data from ls.

The solution is to use **pipelining**. Pipelining is another feature of the shell
which allows you to connect a string of commands in a "pipe", where the stdout
of the first command is sent directly to the stdin of the second command, and so
on. Here, we wish to send the stdout of ls to the stdin of sort. The "|" symbol is
used to create a pipe:

```
/home/larry/papers# ls | sort -r
notes
masters-thesis
history-final
english-list
/home/larry/papers#
```

This command is much shorter, and obviously easier to type.

Another useful example—using the command

```
/home/larry/papers# ls /usr/bin
```

is going to display a long list a files, most of which will fly past the screen too
quickly for you to read them. Instead, let's use more to display the list of files in
/usr/bin.

/home/larry/papers# *ls /usr/bin | more*

Now you can page down the list of files at your own leisure.

But the fun doesn't stop here! We can pipe more than two commands together. The command **head** is a filter which displays the first lines from an input stream (here, input from a pipe). If we wanted to display the last filename in alphabetical order in the current directory, we can use:

/home/larry/papers# *ls | sort -r | head -1*
notes
/home/larry/papers#

where **head -1** simply displays the first line of input that it receives (in this case, the stream of reverse-sorted data from **ls**).

3.8.4 Non-destructive redirection

Using ">" to redirect output to a file is destructive: in other words, the command

/home/larry/papers# *ls > file-list*

overwrites the contents of the file **file-list**. If, instead, you redirect with the symbol ">>", the output will be appended to the named file, instead of overwriting it.

/home/larry/papers# *ls >> file-list*

will append the output of the **ls** command to **file-list**.

Just keep in mind that redirection and using pipes are features provided by the shell—the shell provides this handy syntax using ">" and ">>" and "|". It has nothing to do with the commands themselves, but the shell.

3.9 File Permissions

3.9.1 Concepts of file permissions

Because there are multiple users on a UNIX system, in order to protect individual user's files from tampering by other users, UNIX provides a mechanism known as **file permissions**. This mechanism allows files and directories to be "owned" by a particular user. As an example, because Larry created the files in his home directory, Larry owns those files, and has access to them.

UNIX also allows files to be shared between users and groups of users. If Larry so desired, he could cut off access to his files, such that no other user could access them. However, on most systems the default is to allow other users to read your files, but not modify or delete them in any way.

As explained above, every file is owned by a particular user. However, files are also owned by a particular **group**, which is a system-defined group of users. Every user is placed into at least one group when that user is created. However, the system administrator may also grant the user access to more than one group.

Groups are usually defined by the type of users which access the machine. For example, on a university UNIX system, users may be placed into the groups student, staff, faculty or guest. There are also a few system-defined groups (such as bin and admin) which are used by the system itself to control access to resources—very rarely do actual users belong to these system groups.

Permissions fall into three main divisions: read, write, and execute. These permissions may be granted to three classes of users: the owner of the file, the group to which the file belongs, and to all users, regardless of group.

Read permission allows a user to read the contents of the file, or in the case of directories, to list the contents of the directory (using ls). Write permission allows the user to write to and modify the file. For directories, write permission allows the user to create new files or delete files within that directory. Finally, execute permission allows the user to run the file as a program or shell script (if the file happens to be a program or shell script, that is). For directories, having execute permission allows the user to cd into the directory in question.

3.9.2   Interpreting file permissions

Let's look at an example to demonstrate file permissions. Using the ls command with the -l option will display a "long" listing of the file, including file permissions.

```
/home/larry/foo# ls -l stuff

-rw-r--r--    1 larry     users          505 Mar 13 19:05 stuff

/home/larry/foo#
```

The first field printed in the listing represents the file permissions. The third field is the owner of the file (`larry`), and the fourth field is the group to which the file belongs (`users`). Obviously, the last field is the name of the file (`stuff`), and we'll cover the other fields later.

This file is owned by `larry`, and belongs to the group `users`. Let's look at the file permissions. The string `-rw-r--r--` lists, in order, the permissions granted to the file's owner, the file's group, and everybody else.

The first character of the permissions string ("`-`") represents the type of file. A "`-`" just means that this is a regular file (as opposed to a directory or device driver). The next three letters ("`rw-`") represent the permissions granted to the file's owner, `larry`. The "`r`" stands for "read" and the "`w`" stands for "write". Thus, `larry` has read and write permission to the file `stuff`.

As we mentioned, besides read and write permission, there is also "execute" permission—represented by an "`x`". However, there is a "`-`" here in place of the "`x`", so Larry doesn't have execute permission on this file. This is fine, the file `stuff` isn't a program of any kind. Of course, because Larry owns the file, he may grant himself execute permission for the file if he so desires. This will be covered shortly.

The next three characters, `r--`, represent the group's permissions on the file. The group which owns this file is `users`. Because only an "`r`" appears here, any user which belongs to the group `users` may read this file.

The last three characters, also `r--`, represent the permissions granted to every other user on the system (other than the owner of the file and those in the group `users`). Again, because only an "`r`" is present, other users may read the file, but not write to it or execute it.

Here are some other examples of group permissions.

`-rwxr-xr-x`   The owner of the file may read, write, and execute the file. Users in the file's group, and all other users, may read and execute the file.

`-rw-------`   The owner of the file may read and write the file. No other user can access the file.

`-rwxrwxrwx`   All users may read, write, and execute the file.

3.9.3   Dependencies

It is important to note that the permissions granted to a file also depend on the permissions of the directory in which the file is located. For example, even if a file is set to `-rwxrwxrwx`, other users cannot access the file unless they have read and execute access to the directory in which the file is located. For example, if Larry wanted to restrict access to all of his files, he could simply set the permissions on his home directory `/home/larry` to `-rwx------`. In this way, no other user has access to his directory, and all files and directories within it. Larry doesn't need to worry about the individual permissions on each of his files.

In other words, to access a file at all, you must have execute access to all directories along the file's pathname, and read (or execute) access to the file itself.

Usually, users on a UNIX system are very open with their files. The usual set of permissions given to files is `-rw-r--r--`, which will allow other users to read the file, but not change it in any way. The usual set of permissions given to directories is `-rwxr-xr-x`, which will allow other users to look through your directories, but not create or delete files within them.

However, many users wish to keep other users out of their files. Setting the permissions of a file to `-rw-------` will not allow any other user to access the file. Likewise, setting the permissions of a directory to `-rwx------` will keep other users out of the directory in question.

3.9.4   Changing permissions

The command `chmod` is used to set the permissions on a file. Only the owner of a file may change the permissions on that file. The syntax of `chmod` is:

> chmod {a,u,g,o}{+,-}{r,w,x} ⟨filenames⟩

Briefly, you supply one or more of **a**ll, **u**ser, **g**roup, or **o**ther. Then you specify whether you are adding rights (+) or taking them away (-). Finally, you specify one or more of **r**ead, **w**rite, and **e**xecute. Some examples of legal commands are:

`chmod a+r stuff`
> Gives all users read access to the file.

`chmod +r stuff`
> Same as above—if none of a, u, g, or o is specified, a is assumed.

```
chmod og-x stuff
```
> Remove execute permission from users other than the owner.

```
chmod u+rwx stuff
```
> Allow the owner of the file to read, write, and execute the file.

```
chmod o-rwx stuff
```
> Remove read, write, and execute permission from users other than the owner and users in the file's group.

3.10 Managing file links

Links allow you to give a single file multiple names. Files are actually identified to the system by their **inode number**, which is just the unique filesystem identifier for the file[3]. A directory is actually a listing of inode numbers with their corresponding filenames. Each filename in a directory is a **link** to a particular inode.

3.10.1 Hard links

The `ln` command is used to create multiple links for one file. For example, let's say that you have the file `foo` in a directory. Using `ls -i`, we can look at the inode number for this file.

```
# ls -i foo
22192 foo
#
```

Here, the file `foo` has an inode number of 22192 in the filesystem. We can create another link to `foo`, named `bar`:

```
# ln foo bar
```

With `ls -i`, we see that the two files have the same inode.

```
# ls -i foo bar
22192 bar    22192 foo
#
```

---

[3]The command `ls -i` will display file inode numbers.

Now, accessing either `foo` or `bar` will access the same file. If you make changes to `foo`, those changes will be made to `bar` as well. For all purposes, `foo` and `bar` are the same file.

These links are known as *hard links* because they directly create a link to an inode. Note that you can only hard-link files on the same filesystem; symbolic links (see below) don't have this restriction.

When you delete a file with `rm`, you are actually only deleting one link to a file. If you use the command

    # *rm foo*

then only the link named `foo` is deleted; `bar` will still exist. A file is only actually deleted on the system when it has no links to it. Usually, files have only one link, so using the `rm` command deletes the file. However, if a file has multiple links to it, using `rm` will only delete a single link; in order to delete the file, you must delete all links to the file.

The command `ls -l` will display the number of links to a file (among other information).

```
# ls -l foo bar
-rw-r--r--   2 root     root         12 Aug  5 16:51 bar
-rw-r--r--   2 root     root         12 Aug  5 16:50 foo
#
```

The second column in the listing, "2", specifies the number of links to the file.

As it turns out, a directory is actually just a file containing information about link-to-inode translations. Also, every directory has at least two hard links in it: "." (a link pointing to itself), and ".." (a link pointing to the parent directory). The root directory (/) ".." link just points back to /.

3.10.2   Symbolic links

Symbolic links are another type of link, which are somewhat different than hard links. A symbolic link allows you to give a file another name, but it doesn't link the file by inode.

The command `ln -s` will create a symbolic link to a file. For example, if we use the command

> # *ln -s foo bar*

we will create the symbolic link `bar` pointing to the file `foo`. If we use `ls -i`, we will see that the two files have different inodes, indeed.

> # *ls -i foo bar*
> 22195 bar   22192 foo
> #

However, using `ls -l`, we see that the file `bar` is a symlink pointing to `foo`.

> # *ls -l foo bar*
> lrwxrwxrwx   1 root   root   3 Aug 5 16:51 bar -> foo
> -rw-r--r--   1 root   root   12 Aug 5 16:50 foo
> #

The permission bits on a symbolic link are not used (they always appear as `rwxrwxrwx`). Instead, the permissions on the symbolic link are determined by the permissions on the target of the symbolic link (in our example, the file `foo`).

Functionally, hard links and symbolic links are similar, but there are some differences. For one thing, you can create a symbolic link to a file which doesn't exist; the same is not true for hard links. Symbolic links are processed by the kernel differently than hard links are, which is just a technical difference but sometimes an important one. Symbolic links are helpful because they identify what file they point to; with hard links, there is no easy way to determine which files are linked to the same inode.

Links are used in many places on the Linux system. Symbolic links are especially important to the shared library images in `/lib`. See Section 4.7.2 for more information.

3.11 Job Control

3.11.1 Jobs and processes

Job control is a feature provided by many shells (Bash and Tcsh included) which allows you to control multiple running commands, or **jobs**, at once. Before we can delve much further, we need to talk about **processes**.

Every time you run a program, you start what is known as a *process*—which is just a fancy name for a running program. The command `ps` displays a list of currently running processes. Here's an example:

```
/home/larry# ps

  PID TT STAT  TIME COMMAND
   24 3 S     0:03 (bash)
  161 3 R     0:00 ps

/home/larry#
```

The `PID` listed in the first column is the **process ID**, a unique number given to every running process. The last column, `COMMAND`, is the name of the running command. Here, we're only looking at the processes which Larry is currently running[4]. These are `bash` (Larry's shell), and the `ps` command itself. As you can see, `bash` is running concurrently with the `ps` command. `bash` executed `ps` when Larry typed the command. After `ps` is finished running (after the table of processes is displayed), control is returned to the `bash` process, which displays the prompt, ready for another command.

A running process is known as a *job* to the shell. The terms *process* and *job* are interchangeable. However, a process is usually referred to as a "job" when used in conjunction with **job control**—a feature of the shell which allows you to switch between several independent jobs.

In most cases users are only running a single job at a time—that being whatever command they last typed to the shell. However, using job control, you can run several jobs at once, switching between them as needed. How might this be useful? Let's say that you're editing a text file and need to suddenly interrupt your editing and do something else. With job control, you can temporarily suspend the editor, and back at the shell prompt start to work on something else. When you're done, you can start the editor back up, and be back where you started, as if you never left the editor. This is just one example. There are many practical uses for job control.

3.11.2   Foreground and background

Jobs can either be in the **foreground** or in the **background**. There can only be one job in the foreground at any one time. The foreground job is the job which

---

[4]There are many other processes running on the system as well—"`ps -aux`" lists them all.

you interact with—it receives input from the keyboard and sends output to your screen. (Unless, of course, you have redirected input or output, as described in Section 3.8). On the other hand, jobs in the background do not receive input from the terminal—in general, they run along quietly without need for interaction.

Some jobs take a long time to finish, and don't do anything interesting while they are running. Compiling programs is one such job, as is compressing a large file. There's no reason why you should sit around being bored while these jobs complete their tasks; you can just run them in the background. While the jobs are running in the background, you are free to run other programs.

Jobs may also be **suspended**. A suspended job is a job that is not currently running, but is temporarily stopped. After you suspend a job, you can tell the job to continue, in the foreground or the background as needed. Resuming a suspended job will not change the state of the job in any way—the job will continue to run where it left off.

Note that suspending a job is not equal to *interrupting* a job. When you interrupt a running process (by hitting your interrupt key, which is `ctrl-C`)[5], it kills the process, for good. Once the job is killed, there's no hope of resuming it; you'll have to re-run the command. Also note that some programs trap the interrupt, so that hitting `ctrl-C` won't immediately kill the job. This is to allow the program to perform any necessary cleanup operations before exiting. In fact, some programs simply don't allow you to kill them with an interrupt at all.

3.11.3 Backgrounding and killing jobs

Let's begin with a simple example. The command `yes` is a seemingly useless command which sends an endless stream of y's to standard output. (This is actually useful. If you piped the output of `yes` to another command which asked a series of yes and no questions, the stream of y's would confirm all of the questions.)

Try it out.

```
/home/larry# yes
y
y
y
```

---

[5]The interrupt key can be set using the `stty` command. The default on Slackware Linux is `ctrl-C`.

```
y
y
```

The y's will continue *ad infinitum*. You can kill the process by hitting your interrupt
key, which is usually ctrl-C . So that we don't have to put up with the annoying
stream of y's, let's redirect the standard output of yes to /dev/null. As you
may remember, /dev/null acts as a "black hole" for data. Any data sent to it
will disappear. This is a very effective method of quieting an otherwise verbose
program.

```
/home/larry# yes > /dev/null
```

Ah, much better. Nothing is printed, but the shell prompt doesn't come back. This
is because yes is still running, and is sending those inane y's to /dev/null. Again,
to kill the job, hit the interrupt key.

Let's suppose that we wanted the yes command to continue to run, but wanted
to get our shell prompt back to work on other things. We can put yes into the
background, which will allow it to run, but without need for interaction.

One way to put a process in the background is to append an "&" character to
the end of the command.

```
/home/larry# yes > /dev/null &
[1] 164
/home/larry#
```

As you can see, we have our shell prompt back. But what is this "[1] 164"? And
is the yes command really running?

The "[1]" represents the **job number** for the yes process. The shell assigns a
job number to every running job. Because yes is the one and only job that we're
currently running, it is assigned job number 1. The "164" is the process ID, or
PID, number given by the system to the job. Either number may be used to refer
to the job, as we'll see later.

You now have the yes process running in the background, continuously sending
a stream of y's to /dev/null. To check on the status of this process, use the shell
internal command jobs.

```
/home/larry# jobs
[1]+  Running                 yes >/dev/null  &
/home/larry#
```

Sure enough, there it is. You could also use the `ps` command as demonstrated above to check on the status of the job.

To terminate the job, use the command `kill`. This command takes either a job number or a process ID number as an argument. This was job number 1, so using the command

        /home/larry# *kill %1*

will kill the job. When identifying the job with the job number, you must prefix the number with a percent ("%") character.

Now that we've killed the job, we can use `jobs` again to check on it:

        /home/larry# *jobs*

        [1]+ Terminated   yes >/dev/null

        /home/larry#

The job is in fact dead, and if we use the `jobs` command again nothing should be printed.

You can also kill the job using the process ID (PID) number, which is printed along with the job ID when you start the job. In our example, the process ID is 164, so the command

        /home/larry# *kill 164*

is equivalent to

        /home/larry# *kill %1*

You don't need to use the "%" when referring to a job by its process ID.

3.11.4 Stopping and restarting jobs

There is another way to put a job into the background. You can start the job normally (in the foreground), **stop** the job, and then restart it in the background.

First, start the **yes** process in the foreground, as you normally would:

        /home/larry# *yes > /dev/null*

Again, because **yes** is running in the foreground, you shouldn't get your shell prompt
back.

Now, instead of interrupting the job with ⎡ctrl-C⎤, we'll *suspend* the job. Suspending a job doesn't kill it: it only temporarily stops the job until you restart it.
To do this, you hit the suspend key, which is usually ⎡ctrl-Z⎤.

```
/home/larry# yes > /dev/null
ctrl-Z
[1]+  Stopped                      yes >/dev/null
/home/larry#
```

While the job is suspended, it's simply not running. No CPU time is used for the
job. However, you can restart the job, which will cause the job to run again as if
nothing ever happened. It will continue to run where it left off.

To restart the job in the foreground, use the command **fg** (for "foreground").

```
/home/larry# fg
yes >/dev/null
```

The shell prints the name of the command again so you're aware of which job you
just put into the foreground. Stop the job again, with ⎡ctrl-Z⎤. This time, use the
command **bg** to put the job into the background. This will cause the command to
run just as if you started the command with "&" as in the last section.

```
/home/larry# bg
[1]+ yes >/dev/null &
/home/larry#
```

And we have our prompt back. **jobs** should report that **yes** is indeed running, and
we can kill the job with **kill** as we did before.

How can we stop the job again? Using ⎡ctrl-Z⎤ won't work, because the job is
in the background. The answer is to put the job in the foreground, with **fg**, and
then stop it. As it turns out you can use **fg** on either stopped jobs or jobs in the
background.

There is a big difference between a job in the background and a job which is
stopped. A stopped job is not running—it's not using any CPU time, and it's not
doing any work (the job still occupies system memory, although it may be swapped
out to disk). A job in the background is running, and using memory, as well as

completing some task while you do other work. However, a job in the background may try to display text on to your terminal, which can be annoying if you're trying to work on something else. For example, if you used the command

/home/larry# *yes &*

without redirecting stdout to **/dev/null**, a stream of y's would be printed to your screen, without any way of interrupting it (you can't use $\boxed{\texttt{ctrl-C}}$ to interrupt jobs in the background). In order to stop the endless y's, you'd have to use the **fg** command, to bring the job to the foreground, and then use $\boxed{\texttt{ctrl-C}}$ to kill it.

Another note. The **fg** and **bg** commands normally foreground or background the job which was last stopped (indicated by a "+" next to the job number when you use the command **jobs**). If you are running multiple jobs at once, you can foreground or background a specific job by giving the job ID as an argument to **fg** or **bg**, as in

/home/larry# *fg %2*

(to foreground job number 2), or

/home/larry# *bg %3*

(to background job number 3). You can't use process ID numbers with **fg** or **bg**.

Furthermore, using the job number alone, as in

/home/larry# *%2*

is equivalent to

/home/larry# *fg %2*

Just remember that using job control is a feature of the shell. The commands **fg**, **bg** and **jobs** are internal to the shell. If for some reason you use a shell which does not support job control, don't expect to find these commands available.

In addition, there are some aspects of job control which differ between Bash and Tcsh. In fact, some shells don't provide job control at all—however, most shells available for Linux support job control.

3.12   Using the vi Editor

A **text editor** is simply a program used to edit files which contain text, such as a letter, C program, or a system configuration file. While there are many such editors available for Linux, the only editor which you are guaranteed to find on any UNIX system is vi— the "visual editor". vi is not the easiest editor to use, nor is it very self-explanatory. However, because it is so common in the UNIX world, and at times you may be required to use it, it deserves some documentation here.

Your choice of an editor is mostly a question of personal taste and style. Many users prefer the baroque, self-explanatory and powerful **Emacs**—an editor with more features than any other single program in the UNIX world. For example, Emacs has its own built-in dialect of the LISP programming language, and has many extensions (one of which is an "Eliza"-like AI program). However, because Emacs and all of its support files are relatively large, you may not have access to it on many systems. vi, on the other hand, is small and powerful, but more difficult to use. However, once you know your way around vi, it's actually very easy. It's just the learning curve which is sometimes difficult to cross.

This section is a coherent introduction to vi—we won't discuss all of its features, just the ones you need to know to get you started. You can refer to the man page for vi if you're interested in learning about more of this editor's features. Or, you can read the book *Learning the* vi *Editor* from O'Reilly and Associates. See Appendix A for information.

3.12.1   Concepts

While using vi, at any one time you are in one of three modes of operation. These modes are known as *command mode*, *insert mode*, and *last line mode*.

When you start up vi, you are in *command mode*. This mode allows you to use certain commands to edit files or to change to other modes. For example, typing "x" while in command mode deletes the character underneath the cursor. The arrow keys move the cursor around the file which you're editing. Generally, the commands used in command mode are one or two characters long.

You actually insert or edit text within *insert mode*. When using vi, you'll probably spend most of your time within this mode. You start insert mode by using a command such as "i" (for "insert") from command mode. While in insert mode, you are inserting text into the document from your current cursor location. To end insert mode and return to command mode, press `esc`.

Last line mode is a special mode used to give certain extended commands to vi. While typing these commands, they appear on the last line of the screen (hence the name). For example, when you type ":" from command mode, you jump into last line mode, and can use commands such as "wq" (to write the file and quit vi), or "q!" (to quit vi without saving changes). Last line mode is generally used for vi commands which are longer than one character. In last line mode, you enter a single-line command and press ⎡enter⎤ to execute it.

3.12.2   Starting vi

The best way to understand these concepts is to actually fire up vi and edit a file. In the example "screens" below, we're only going to show a few lines of text, as if the screen was only six lines high (instead of twenty-four).

The syntax for vi is

> vi ⟨filename⟩

where ⟨filename⟩ is the name of the file that you wish to edit.

Start up vi by typing

> /home/larry# *vi test*

which will edit the file **test**. You should see something like

```
~
_
~

~

~

~

~
"test" [New file]
```

The column of "~" characters indicates that you are the end of the file.

3.12.3   Inserting text

You are now in command mode; in order to insert text into the file, press ⎡i⎤ (which will place you into insert mode), and begin typing.

```
Now is the time for all good men to come to the aid of the
party.
~
~
~
~
~
```

While inserting text, you may type as many lines as you wish
(pressing `return` after each, of course), and you may correct mistakes using the
backspace key.

To end insert mode, and return to command mode, press `esc`.

While in command mode, you can use the arrow keys to move around the file.
Here, because we only have one line of text, trying to use the up- or down-arrow
keys will probably cause `vi` to beep at you.

There are several ways to insert text, other than using the i command. For
example, the a command inserts text beginning *after* the current cursor position,
instead of on the current cursor position. For example, use the left arrow key to
move the cursor between the words "good" and "men".

```
Now is the time for all good men to come to the aid of the
party.
~
~
~
~
~
```

Press `a`, to start insert mode, type "wo", and then hit `esc` to return to command
mode.

```
Now is the time for all good women to come to the aid of the
party.
~
~
~
~
~
```

To begin inserting text at the line below the current one, use the o command.
For example, press `o` and type another line or two:

```
Now is the time for all good women to come to the aid of the
party.
Afterwards, we'll go out for pizza and beer.
~
~
~
~
```

Just remember that at any time you're either in command mode (where commands such as i, a, or o are valid), or in insert mode (where you're inserting text, followed by [esc] to return to command mode), or last line mode (where you're entering extended commands, as discussed below).

3.12.4   Deleting text

From command mode, the x command deletes the character under the cursor. If you press [x] five times, you'll end up with:

```
Now is the time for all good women to come to the aid of the
party.
Afterwards, we'll go out for pizza and_
~
~
~
~
```

Now press [a], insert some text, followed by [esc]:

```
Now is the time for all good women to come to the aid of the
party.
Afterwards, we'll go out for pizza and Diet Coke.
~
~
~
~
```

You can delete entire lines using the command dd (that is, press [d] twice in a row). If your cursor is on the second line, and you type dd,

```
Now is the time for all good women to come to the aid of the
party.
~
~
~
~
~
```

To delete the word which the cursor is on, use the `dw` command. Place the cursor on the word "good", and type `dw`.

```
Now is the time for all women to come to the aid of the
party.
~
~
~
~
~
```

3.12.5   Changing text

You can replace sections of text using the `R` command. Place the cursor on the first letter in "party", press [R], and type the word "hungry".

```
Now is the time for all women to come to the aid of the
hungry.
~
~
~
~
~
```

Using `R` to edit text is much like the `i` and `a` commands, but `R` overwrites text, instead of inserting it.

The `r` command replaces the single character under the cursor. For example, move the cursor to the beginning of the word "Now", and type `r` followed by `C`, you'll have:

```
Cow is the time for all women to come to the aid of the
hungry.
~
~
~
~
~
```

The "~" command changes the case of the letter under the cursor from upper-to lower-case, and vise versa, For example, if you place the cursor on the "o" in "Cow", above, and repeatedly press ⌷~⌷, you'll end up with:

```
COW IS THE TIME FOR ALL WOMEN TO COME TO THE AID OF THE
HUNGRY.
~
~
~
~
~
```

3.12.6 Moving commands

You already know how to use the arrow keys to move around the document. In addition, you can use the h, j, k, and l commands to move the cursor left, down, up, and right, respectively. This comes in handy when (for some reason) your arrow keys aren't working correctly.

The w command moves the cursor to the beginning of the next word; the b moves it to the beginning of the previous word.

The 0 (that's a zero) command moves the cursor to the beginning of the current line, and the $ command moves it to the end of the line.

When editing large files, you'll want to move forwards or backwards through the file a screenful at a time. Pressing ⌷ctrl-F⌷ moves the cursor one screenful forward, and ⌷ctrl-B⌷ moves it a screenful back.

In order to move the cursor to the end of the file, type G. You can also move to an arbitrary line; for example, typing the command 10G would move the cursor to line 10 in the file. To move to the beginning of the file, use 1G.

You can couple moving commands with other commands, such as deletion. For example, the command d$ will delete everything from the cursor to the end of the line; dG will delete everything from the cursor to the end of the file, and so on.

3.12.7   Saving files and quitting vi

To quit vi without making changes to the file, use the command :q!. When you
type the ":", the cursor will move to the last line on the screen; you'll be in last
line mode.

```
COW IS THE TIME FOR ALL WOMEN TO COME TO THE AID OF THE
HUNGRY.
~

~

~

~

~

:_
```

In last line mode, certain extended commands are available. One of them is q!,
which quits vi without saving. The command :wq saves the file and then exits vi.
The command ZZ (from command mode, without the ":") is equivalent to :wq.
Remember that you must press ⌷enter⌷ after a command entered in last line mode.

To save the file without quitting vi, just use :w.

3.12.8   Editing another file

To edit another file, use the :e command. For example, to stop editing test, and
edit the file foo instead, use the command

```
COW IS THE TIME FOR ALL WOMEN TO COME TO THE AID OF THE
HUNGRY.
~

~

~

~

~

:e foo_
```

If you use :e without saving the file first, you'll get the error message

```
No write since last change (":edit!" overrides)
```

which simply means that vi doesn't want to edit another file until you save the first one. At this point, you can use :w to save the original file, and then use :e, or you can use the command

```
COW IS THE TIME FOR ALL WOMEN TO COME TO THE AID OF THE
HUNGRY.
~
~
~
~
~
:e!  foo_
```

The "!" tells vi that you really mean it—edit the new file without saving changes to the first.

3.12.9 Including other files

If you use the :r command, you can include the contents of another file in the current file. For example, the command

```
:r foo.txt
```

would insert the contents of the file foo.txt in the text at the current cursor location.

3.12.10 Running shell commands

You can also run shell commands from within vi. The :r! command works like :r, but instead of reading a file, it inserts the output of the given command into the buffer at the current cursor location. For example, if you use the command

```
:r!  ls -F
```

you'll end up with

```
COW IS THE TIME FOR ALL WOMEN TO COME TO THE AID OF THE
HUNGRY.
letters/
misc/
papers/
~
~
```

You can also "shell out" of vi, in other words, run a command from within vi, and return to the editor when you're done. For example, if you use the command

    :! ls -F

the ls -F command will be executed, and the results displayed on the screen, but not inserted into the file which you're editing. If you use the command

    :shell

vi will start an instance of the shell, allowing you to temporarily put vi "on hold" while you execute other commands. Just logout of the shell (using the exit command) to return to vi.

3.12.11   Getting help

vi doesn't provide much in the way of interactive help (most UNIX programs don't), but you can always read the man page for vi. vi is a visual front-end to the ex editor; it is ex which handles many of the last-line mode commands in vi. So, in addition to reading the man page for vi, see ex as well.

3.13   Customizing your Environment

The shell provides many mechanisms to customize your work environment. As we've mentioned before, the shell is more than a command interpreter—it is also a powerful programming language. While writing shell scripts is an extensive subject, we'd like to introduce you to some of the ways that you can simplify your work on a UNIX system by using these advanced features of the shell.

As we have mentioned before, different shells use different syntaxes when executing shell scripts. For example, Tcsh uses a C-like syntax, while Bourne shells use another type of syntax. In this section, we won't be running into many of the differences between the two, but we will assume that shell scripts are executed using the Bourne shell syntax.

3.13.1 Shell scripts

Let's say that you use a series of commands often, and would like to shorten the amount of required typing by grouping all of them together into a single "command". For example, the commands

```
/home/larry#  cat chapter1 chapter2 chapter3 > book
/home/larry#  wc -l book
/home/larry#  lp book
```

would concatenate the files **chapter1**, **chapter2**, and **chapter3** and place the result in the file **book**. Then, a count of the number of lines in **book** would be displayed, and finally **book** would be printed with the **lp** command.

Instead of typing all of these commands, you could group them into a **shell script**. We described shell scripts briefly in Section 3.13.1. The shell script used to run all of these commands would look like

```
#!/bin/sh
# A shell script to create and print the book

cat chapter1 chapter2 chapter3 > book
wc -l book
lp book
```

If this script was saved in the file **makebook**, you could simply use the command

```
/home/larry#  makebook
```

to run all of the commands in the script. Shell scripts are just plain text files; you can create them with an editor such as **emacs** or **vi** [6].

Let's look at this shell script. The first line, "**#!/bin/sh**", identifies the file as a shell script, and tells the shell how to execute the script. It instructs the shell to pass the script to **/bin/sh** for execution, where **/bin/sh** is the shell program itself.

---

[6]**vi** is covered in Section 3.12.

Why is this important? On most UNIX systems, `/bin/sh` is a Bourne-type shell, such as Bash. By forcing the shell script to run using `/bin/sh`, we are ensuring that the script will run under a Bourne-syntax shell (instead of, say, a C shell). This will cause your script to run using the Bourne syntax even if you use Tcsh (or another C shell) as your login shell.

The second line is a *comment*. Comments begin with the character "#" and continue to the end of the line. Comments are ignored by the shell—they are commonly used to identify the shell script to the programmer.

The rest of the lines in the script are just commands, as you would type them to the shell directly. In effect, the shell reads each line of the script and runs that line as if you had typed it at the shell prompt.

Permissions are important for shell scripts. If you create a shell script, you must make sure that you have execute permission on the script in order to run it[7]. The command

> `/home/larry#` *chmod u+x makebook*

can be used to give yourself execute permission on the shell script `makebook`.

3.13.2   Shell variables and the environment

The shell allows you to define **variables**, as most programming languages do. A variable is just a piece of data which is given the name.

◇ Note that Tcsh, as well as other C-type shells, use a different mechanism for setting variables than is described here. This discussion assumes the use of a Bourne shell, such as Bash (which you're probably using). See the Tcsh man page for details.

When you assign a value to a variable (using the "=" operator), you can access the variable by prepending a "$" to the variable name, as demonstrated below.

> `/home/larry#` *foo="hello there"*

The variable `foo` is given the value "`hello there`". You can now refer to this value by the variable name, prefixed with a "$" character. The command

> `/home/larry#` *echo $foo*
> `hello there`
> `/home/larry#`

---

[7]When you create text files, the default permissions usually don't include execute permission.

produces the same results as

> /home/larry# *echo "hello there"*
> hello there
> /home/larry#

These variables are internal to the shell. This means that only the shell can access these variables. This can be useful in shell scripts; if you need to keep track of a filename, for example, you can store it in a variable, as above. Using the command **set** will display a list of all defined shell variables.

However, the shell allows you to **export** variables to the **environment**. The environment is the set of variables which all commands that you execute have access to. Once you define a variable inside the shell, exporting it makes that variable part of the environment as well. The **export** command is used to export a variable to the environment.

◇   Again, here we differ between Bash and Tcsh. If you're using Tcsh, another syntax is used for setting environment variables (the **setenv** command is used). See the Tcsh man page for more information.

The environment is very important to the UNIX system. It allows you to configure certain commands just by setting variables which the commands know about.

Here's a quick example. The environment variable **PAGER** is used by the **man** command. It specifies the command to use to display man pages one screenful at a time. If you set **PAGER** to be the name of a command, it will use that command to display the man pages, instead of **more** (which is the default).

Set **PAGER** to "cat". This will cause output from **man** to be displayed to the screen all at once, without breaking it up into pages.

> /home/larry# *PAGER="cat"*

Now, export **PAGER** to the environment.

> /home/larry# *export PAGER*

Try the command **man ls**. The man page should fly past your screen without pausing for you.

Now, if we set **PAGER** to "more", the **more** command will be used to display the man page.

/home/larry# *PAGER="more"*

Note that we don't have to use the `export` command after we change the value of
`PAGER`. We only need to export a variable once; any changes made to it thereafter
will automatically be propagated to the environment.

The man pages for a particular command will tell you if the command uses
any environment variables; for example, the `man` man page explains that `PAGER` is
used to specify the pager command. Some commands share environment variables;
for example, many commands use the `EDITOR` environment variable to specify the
default editor to use when one is needed.

The environment is also used to keep track of important information about your
login session. An example is the `HOME` environment variable, which contains the
name of your home directory.

/home/larry/papers# *echo $HOME*
/home/larry

Another interesting environment variable is `PS1`, which defines the main shell
prompt. For example,

$ *PS1="\t \h:\w > "*

might give a prompt like:

15:53:15 paranoid:˜>

`PS1` is the variable that needs to be set in order to customize you prompt. In the
above example the parameters between the double quotes express what `PS1` should
be set to. The '`\t`' parameter stands for the current time, the '`\h`' parameter
represents the hostname and the '`\w`' parameter will return the current working
directory. In this case the current working directory was displayed as a tilde (˜),
which is an abbreviation for the current users home directory. You can put just
about any other characters you want in the prompt, in the example above I use a
greater than symbol (>) Below is a list of the other variables that may be useful:

```
\t   the current time in HH:MM:SS format
\d   the date in "Weekday Month Date" format (e.g., "Tue May 26")
\n   newline
\s   the name of the shell, the basename of $0 (the portion
```

```
following the final slash)
\w   the current working directory
\W   the basename of the current working directory
\u   the username of the current user
\h   the hostname
\#   the command number of this command
\!   the history number of this command
\$   if the effective UID is 0, a #, otherwise a $
\nnn  the character corresponding to the octal number nnn
\\   a backslash
\[   begin a sequence of non-printing characters, which could be
used to embed a terminal control sequence into the prompt
\]   end a sequence of non-printing characters
```

The **bash** man page describes the syntax used for setting the prompt.

3.13.2.1 The PATH environment variable

When you use the `ls` command, how does the shell find the `ls` executable itself? In fact, `ls` is found in `/bin/ls` on most systems. The shell uses the environment variable PATH to locate executable files for commands which you type.

For example, your PATH variable may be set to:

```
/bin:/usr/bin:/usr/local/bin:.
```

This is a list of directories for the shell to search, each directory separated by a ":". When you use the command `ls`, the shell first looks for `/bin/ls`, then `/usr/bin/ls`, and so on.

Note that the PATH has nothing to do with finding regular files. For example, if you use the command

```
/home/larry# cp foo bar
```

The shell does not use PATH to locate the files `foo` and `bar`—those filenames are assumed to be complete. The shell only uses PATH to locate the `cp` executable.

This saves you a lot of time; it means that you don't have to remember where all of the command executables are stored. On many systems, executables are scattered about in many places, such as **/usr/bin**, **/bin**, or **/usr/local/bin**. Instead of

giving the command's full pathname (such as `/usr/bin/cp`), you can simply set
`PATH` to the list of directories that you want the shell to automatically search.

Notice that `PATH` contains ".", which is the current working directory. This
allows you to create a shell script or program and run it as a command from your
current directory, without having to specify it directly (as in `./makebook`). If a
directory isn't on your `PATH`, then the shell will not search it for commands to
run—this includes the current directory.

3.13.3   Shell initialization scripts

In addition to shell scripts that you create, there are a number of scripts that
the shell itself uses for certain purposes. The most important of these are your
initialization scripts, scripts automatically executed by the shell when you login.

The initialization scripts themselves are simply shell scripts, as described above.
However, they are very useful in setting up your environment by executing commands automatically when you login. For example, if you always use the `mail`
command to check your mail when you login, you place the command in your initialization script so it will be executed automatically.

Both Bash and Tcsh distinguish between a **login shell** and other invocations
of the shell. A login shell is a shell invoked at login time; usually, it's the only
shell which you'll use. However, if you "shell out" of another program, such as `vi`,
you start another instance of the shell, which isn't your login shell. In addition,
whenever you run a shell script, you automatically start another instance of the
shell to execute the script.

The initialization files used by Bash are: `/etc/profile` (set up by the system
administrator, executed by all Bash users at login time), `$HOME/.bash_profile`
(executed by a login Bash session), and `$HOME/.bashrc` (executed by all non-login
instances of Bash). If `.bash_profile` is not present, `.profile` is used instead.

Tcsh uses the following initialization scripts: `/etc/csh.login` (executed by all
Tcsh users at login time), `$HOME/.tcshrc` (executed a login time and by all new
instances of Tcsh), and `$HOME/.login` (executed at login time, following `.tcshrc`).
If `.tcshrc` is not present, `.cshrc` is used instead.

To fully understand the function of these files, you'll need to learn more about
the shell itself. Shell programming is a complicated subject, far beyond the scope of
this book. See the man pages for `bash` and/or `tcsh` to learn more about customizing
your shell environment.

3.14 So You Want to Strike Out on Your Own?

Hopefully we have provided enough information to give you a basic idea of how to use Slackware Linux. Keep in mind that most of the interesting and important aspects of Linux aren't covered here—these are the very basics. With this foundation, before long you'll be up and running complicated applications and fulfilling the potential of your system. If things don't seem exciting at first, don't despair—there is much to be learned.

One indispensable tool for learning about the system is to read the man pages. While many of the man pages may appear confusing at first, if you dig beneath the surface there is a wealth of information contained therein.

We also suggest reading a complete book on using a UNIX system. There is much more to UNIX than meets the eye—unfortunately, most of it is beyond the scope of this book. Some good UNIX books to look at are listed in Appendix A.

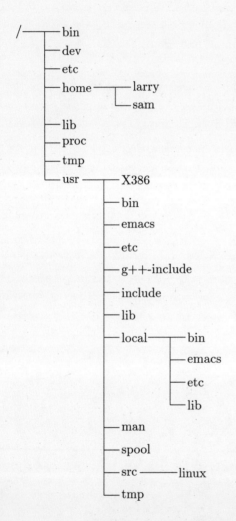

Figure 3.1: A typical (abridged) Unix directory tree.

Chapter 4

System Administration

This chapter is an overview to Linux system administration, including a number of advanced features which aren't necessarily for system administrators only. Just as every dog has its day, every system has its administrator, and running the system is a very important and sometimes time-consuming job, even if you're the only user on your system.

We have tried to cover here the most important things about system administration you need to know when you use Linux, in sufficient detail to get you comfortably started. In order to keep it short and sweet, we have only covered the very basics, and have skipped many important details. You should read the *Linux System Administrator's Guide* if you are serious about running Linux. It will help you understand better how things work, and how they hang together. At least skim through it so that you know what it contains and know what kind of help you can expect from it.

4.1 About Root, Hats, and the Feeling of Power

As you know, UNIX differentiates between different users, so that what they do to each other and to the system can be regulated (one wouldn't want anybody to be able to read one's love letters, for instance). Each user is given an **account**, which includes a username, home directory, and so on. In addition to accounts given to real people, there are special system-defined accounts which have special privileges. The most important of these is the **root account**, for the username root.

4.1.1   The root account

Ordinary users are generally restricted so that they can't do harm to anybody else on the system, just to themselves. File permissions on the system are arranged such that normal users aren't allowed to delete or modify files in directories shared by all users (such as /bin and /usr/bin. Most users also protect their own files with the appropriate file permissions so that other users can't access or modify those files.

There are no such restrictions on root. The user root can read, modify, or delete any file on the system, change permissions and ownerships on any file, and run special programs, such as those which partition the drive or create filesystems. The basic idea is that the person or people who run and take care of the system logs in as root whenever it is necessary to perform tasks that cannot be executed as a normal user. Because root can do anything, it is easy to make mistakes that have catastrophic consequences when logged in using this account.

For example, as a normal user, if you inadvertently attempt to delete all of the files in /etc, the system will not permit you to do so. However, when logged in as root, the system won't complain at all. It is very easy to trash your system when using root. The best way to prevent accidents is to:

- Sit on your hands before you press `return` on a command which may cause damage. For example, if you're about to clean out a directory, before hitting `return`, re-read the entire command and make sure that it is correct.

- Don't get accustomed to using root. The more comfortable you are in the role of the root user, the more likely you are to confuse your privileges with those of a normal user. For example, you might *think* that you're logged in as larry, when you're really logged in as root.

- Use a different prompt for the root account. You should change root's .bashrc or .login file to set the shell prompt to something other than your regular user prompt. For example, many people use the character "$" in prompts for regular users, and reserve the character "#" for the root user prompt.

- Only login as root when absolutely necessary. And, as soon as you're finished with your work as root, log out. The less you use the root account, the less likely you'll be to do damage on your system.

Of course, there is a breed of UNIX hackers out there who use root for virtually everything. But every one of them has, at some point, made a silly mistake as root and trashed the system. The general rule is, until you're familiar with the lack of restrictions on root, and are comfortable using the system without such restrictions, login as root sparingly.

Of course, everyone makes mistakes. Linus Torvalds himself once accidentally deleted the entire kernel directory tree on his system. Hours of work were lost forever. Fortunately, however, because of his knowledge of the filesystem code, he was able to reboot the system and reconstruct the directory tree by hand on disk.

Put another way, if you picture using the root account as wearing a special magic hat that gives you lots of power, so that you can, by waving your hand, destroy entire cities, it is a good idea to be a bit careful about what you do with your hands. Since it is easy to move your hand in a destructive way by accident, it is not a good idea to wear the magic hat when it is not needed, despite the wonderful feeling.

4.1.2   Abusing the system

Along with the feeling of power comes the tendency to do harm. This is one of the grey areas of UNIX system administration, but everyone goes through it at some point in time. Most users of UNIX systems never have the ability to wield this power—on university and business UNIX systems, only the highly-paid and highly-qualified system administrators ever login as root. In fact, at many such institutions, the root password is a highly guarded secret: it is treated as the Holy Grail of the institution. A large amount of hubbub is made about logging in as root; it is portrayed as a wise and fearsome power, given only to an exclusive cabal.

This kind of attitude towards the root account is, quite simply, the kind of thing which breeds malice and contempt. Because root is so fluffed-up, when some users have their first opportunity to login as root (either on a Linux system or elsewhere), the tendency is to use root's privileges in a harmful manner. I have known so-called "system administrators" who read other user's mail, delete user's files without warning, and generally behave like children when given such a powerful "toy".

Because root has such privilege on the system, it takes a certain amount of maturity and self-control to use the account as it was intended—to run the system. There is an unspoken code of honor which exists between the system administrator and the users on the system. How would you feel if your system administrator was reading your e-mail or looking over your files? There is still no strong legal precedent for electronic privacy on time-sharing computer systems. On UNIX systems, the `root` user has the ability to forego all security and privacy mechanisms on the system. It is important that the system administrator develop a trusting relationship with the users on the system. I can't stress that enough.

4.1.3   Dealing with users

UNIX security is rather lax by design. Security on the system was an afterthought— the system was originally developed in an environment where users intruding upon other users was simply unheard of. Because of this, even with security measures, there is still the ability for normal users to do harm.

System administrators can take two stances when dealing with abusive users: they can be either paranoid or trusting. The paranoid system administrator usually causes more harm than he or she prevents. One of my favorite sayings is, "Never attribute to malice anything which can be attributed to stupidity." Put another way, most users don't have the ability or knowledge to do real harm on the system. 90% of the time, when a user is causing trouble on the system (by, for instance, filling up the user partition with large files, or running multiple instances of a large program), the user is simply unaware that what he or she is doing is a problem. I have come down on users who were causing a great deal of trouble, but they were simply acting out of ignorance—not malice.

When you deal with users who are causing potential trouble, don't be accusative. The old rule of "innocent until proven guilty" still holds. It is best to simply talk to the user, and question about the trouble, instead of causing a confrontation. The last thing you want to do is be on the user's bad side. This will raise a lot of suspicion about you—the system administrator—running the system correctly. If a user believes that you distrust or dislike them, they might accuse you of deleting files or breaching privacy on the system. This is certainly not the kind of position that you want to be in.

If you do find that a user has been attempting to "crack" the system, or was intentionally doing harm to the system, don't return the malicious behavior with malice of your own. Instead, simply provide a warning—but be flexible. In many cases, you may catch a user "in the act" of doing harm to the system—give them a warning. Tell them not to let it happen again. However, if you *do* catch them causing harm again, be absolutely sure that it is intentional. I can't even begin to describe the number of cases where it appeared as though a user was causing trouble, when in fact it was either an accident or a fault of my own.

4.1.4 Setting the rules

The best way to run a system is not with an iron fist. That may be how you run the military, but UNIX was not designed for such discipline. It makes sense to lay down a simple and flexible set of guidelines for users—but remember, the fewer rules you have, the less chance there is of breaking them. Even if your rules for using the system are perfectly reasonable and clear, users will always at times break these rules without intending to. This is especially true in the case of new UNIX users, who are just learning the ropes of the system. It's not patently obvious, for example, that you shouldn't download a gigabyte of files and mail them to everyone on the system. Users need help understanding the rules, and why they are there.

If you do specify usage guidelines for your system, make sure that the reason behind a particular guideline is made clear. If you don't, then users will find all sorts of creative ways to get around the rule, and not know that they are in fact breaking it.

4.1.5 What it all means

We can't tell you how to run your system to the last detail. Most of the philosophy depends on how you're using the system. If you have many users, things are much different than if you only have a few users, or if you're the only user on the system. However, it's always a good idea—in any situation—to understand what being the system administrator really means.

Being the system administrator doesn't make you a UNIX wizard. There are many system admins out there who know very little about UNIX. Likewise, there are many "normal" users out there who know more about UNIX than any system administrator could. Also, being the system administrator does not allow you to use malice against your users. Just because the system gives you the privilege to mess with user files does not mean that you have any right to do so.

Lastly, being the system administrator is really not a big deal. It doesn't matter if your system is a little 386 or a Cray supercomputer. Running the system is the same, regardless. Knowing the `root` password isn't going to earn you money or fame. It will allow you to maintain the system, and keep it running. That's it.

4.2   Booting the System

There are several ways to boot the system, either from floppy or from the hard drive.

4.2.1   Using a boot floppy

Many people boot Linux using a "boot floppy" which contains a copy of the Linux kernel. This kernel has the Linux root partition coded into it, so it will know where to look on the hard drive for the root filesystem. (The rdev command can be used to set the root partition in the kernel image; see below.)

To create your own boot floppy, first locate the kernel image on your hard disk. It should be in the file /vmlinux.

Once you know where the kernel is, set the root device in the kernel image to the name of your Linux root partition with the rdev command. The format of the command is

    rdev ⟨kernel-name⟩ ⟨root-device⟩

where ⟨kernel-name⟩ is the name of the kernel image, and ⟨root-device⟩ is the name of the Linux root partition. For example, to set the root device in the kernel /etc/Image to /dev/hda2, use the command

    # rdev /vmlinux /dev/hda2

rdev can set other options in the kernel as well, such as the default SVGA mode to use at boot time. Just use "rdev -h" to get a help message.

After setting the root device, you can simply copy the kernel image to the floppy. Whenever copying data to a floppy, it's a good idea to MS-DOS format the floppy first. This lays down the sector and track information on the floppy, so it can be detected as either high or low density.

For example, to copy the kernel in the file /etc/Image to the floppy in /etc/fd0, use the command

    # cp /vmlinux /dev/fd0

This floppy should now boot Linux.

4.2.2 Using LILO

Another method of booting is to use LILO, a program which resides in the boot sector of your hard disk. This program is executed when the system is booted from the hard disk, and can automatically boot up Linux from a kernel image stored on the hard drive itself.

LILO can also be used as a first-stage boot loader for several operating systems, allowing you to select at boot time which operating system (such as Linux or MS-DOS) to boot. When you boot using LILO, the default operating system is booted unless you press ctrl , alt , or shift during the bootup sequence. If you press any of these keys, you will be provided with a boot prompt, at which you type the name of the operating system to boot (such as "linux" or "msdos"). If you press tab at the boot prompt, a listing of available operating systems will be provided.

The easy way to install LILO is to edit the configuration file, /etc/lilo.conf, and then run the command

> # */sbin/lilo*

The LILO configuration file contains a "stanza" for each operating system that you want to boot. The best way to demonstrate this is with an example LILO config file. The below setup is for a system which has a Linux root partition on /dev/hda1, and an MS-DOS partition on /dev/hda2.

```
# Tell LILO to modify the boot record on /dev/hda (the first
# non-SCSI hard drive). If you boot from a drive other than /dev/hda,
# change the following line.
boot = /dev/hda

# Name of the boot loader. No reason to modify this unless you're doing
# some serious hacking on LILO.
install = /boot/boot.b

# Have LILO perform some optimization.
compact

# Stanza for Linux root partition on /dev/hda1.
image = /etc/Image    # Location of kernel
   label = linux      # Name of OS (for the LILO boot menu)
   root = /dev/hda1   # Location of root partition
   vga = ask          # Tell kernel to ask for SVGA modes at boot time
```

```
# Stanza for MSDOS partition on /dev/hda2.
other = /dev/hda2     # Location of partition
   table = /dev/hda   # Location of partition table for /dev/hda2
   label = msdos      # Name of OS (for boot menu)
```

The first operating system stanza in the config file will be the default OS for
LILO to boot. You can select another OS to boot at the LILO boot prompt, as
discussed above.

Remember that every time you update the kernel image on disk, you should
rerun /sbin/lilo in order for the changes to be reflected on the boot sector of
your drive.

Also note that if you use the "root =" line, above, there's no reason to use rdev
to set the root partition in the kernel image. LILO sets it for you at boot time.

The Linux FAQ (see Appendix A) provides more information on LILO, including
how to use LILO to boot with OS/2's Boot Manager.

4.3   Shutting Down

Shutting down a Linux system is a bit tricky. Remember that you should never just
turn off the power or hit the reset switch while the system is running. The kernel
keeps track of disk I/O in memory buffers. If you reboot the system without giving
the kernel the chance to write its buffers to disk, you can corrupt your filesystems.

Other precautions are taken at shutdown time as well. All processes are sent a
signal, which allows them to die gracefully (writing and closing all files, and so on).
Filesystems are unmounted for safety. If you wish, the system can also alert users
that the system is going down and give them a chance to log off.

The easiest way to shutdown is with the shutdown command. The format of
the command is

> shutdown ⟨time⟩ ⟨warning-message⟩

The ⟨time⟩ argument is the time to shutdown the system (in the format hh:mm:ss),
and ⟨warning-message⟩ is a message displayed on all user's terminals before shutdown. Alternately, you can specify the ⟨time⟩ as "now", to shutdown immediately.
The -r option may be given to shutdown to reboot the system after shutting down.

For example, to shutdown the system at 8:00pm, use the command

> # *shutdown -r 20:00*

The command `halt` may be used to force an immediate shutdown, without any warning messages or grace period. `halt` is useful if you're the only one using the system, and want to shut down the system and turn it off.

◇   Don't turn off the power or reboot the system until you see the message:

> `The system is halted`

It is very important that you shutdown the system "cleanly" using the `shutdown` or `halt` commands. Pressing ⌈`ctrl-alt-del`⌉ will be trapped and also cause a `shutdown`.

4.4   Managing Users

Whether or not you have many users on your system, it's important to understand the aspects of user management under Linux. Even if you're the only user, you should presumably have a separate account for yourself (an account other than `root` to do most of your work).

Each person using the system should have his or her own account. It is seldom a good idea to have several people share the same account. Not only is security an issue, but accounts are used to uniquely identify users to the system. You need to be able to keep track of who is doing what.

4.4.1   User management concepts

The system keeps track of a number of pieces of information about each user. They are summarized below.

username   The username is the unique identifier given to every user on the system. Examples of usernames are `larry`, `karl`, and `mdw`. Letters and digits may be used, as well as the characters "_" (underscore) and "." (period). Usernames are usually limited to 8 characters in length.

user ID   The user ID, or UID, is a unique number given to every user on the system. The system usually keeps track of information by UID, not username.

group ID   The group ID, or GID, is the ID of the user's default group. In
                   Section 3.9 we discussed group permissions; each user belongs to
                   one or more groups defined by the system administrator. More
                   about this below.

password   The system also stores the user's encrypted password. The `passwd`
                   command is used to set and change user passwords.

full name   The user's "real name" or "full name" is stored along with the
                   username. For example, the user `schmoj` may have the name "Joe
                   Schmo" in real life.

home directory
                   The home directory is the directory in which the user is initially
                   placed at login time. Every user should have his or her own home
                   directory, usually found under `/home`.

login shell   The user's login shell is the shell which is started for the user at
                   login time. Examples are `/bin/bash` and `/bin/tcsh`.

The file `/etc/passwd` contains this information about users. Each line in the
file contains information about a single user; the format of each line is

```
username:encrypted password:UID:GID:full name:home
directory:login shell
```

An example might be:

```
kiwi:Xv8Q981g71oKK:102:100:Laura Poole:/home/kiwi:/bin/bash
```

As we can see, the first field, "`kiwi`", is the username.

The next field, "`Xv8Q981g71oKK`", is the encrypted password. Passwords are not
stored on the system in any human-readable format. The password is encrypted
using itself as the secret key. In other words, you need to know the password to
decrypt it. This form of encryption is fairly secure.

The third field, "`102`", is the UID. This must be unique for each user. The
fourth field, "`100`", is the GID. This user belongs to the group numbered 100.
Group information, like user information, is stored in the file `/etc/group`. See
Section 4.4.5 for more information.

The fifth field is the user's full name, "`Laura Poole`". The last two fields are
the user's home directory (`/home/kiwi`) and login shell (`/bin/bash`), respectively.

It is not required that the user's home directory be given the same name as the username. It does help identify the directory, however.

4.4.2 Adding users

When adding a user, there are several steps to be taken. First, the user must be given an entry in `/etc/passwd`, with a unique username and UID. The GID, fullname, and other information must be specified. The user's home directory must be created, and the permissions on the directory set so that the user owns the directory. Shell initialization files must be provided in the new home directory and other system-wide configuration must be done (for example, setting up a spool for incoming e-mail for the new user).

While it is not difficult to add users by hand (I do), when you are running a system with many users it is easy to forget something. The easiest way to add users is to use an interactive program which asks you for the required information and updates all of the system files automatically. The name of this program is `adduser`.

4.4.3 Disabling users

If you'd like to temporarily "disable" a user from logging into the system (without deleting the user's account), you can simply prepend an asterisk ("*") to the password field in `/etc/passwd`. For example, changing `kiwi`'s `/etc/passwd` entry to

```
kiwi:*Xv8Q981g71oKK:102:100:Laura Poole:/home/kiwi:/bin/bash
```

will restrict `kiwi` from logging in.

4.4.4 Setting user attributes

After you have created a user, you may need to change attributes for that user, such as home directory or password. The easiest way to do this is to change the values directly in `/etc/passwd`. To set a user's password, use the `passwd` command. For example,

```
# passwd larry
```

will change `larry`'s password. Only root may change other user's password in this manner. Users can change their own passwords with `passwd` as well.

The commands `chfn` and `chsh` will be available to allow users to set their own fullname and login shell attributes.

4.4.5   Groups

As we have mentioned, each user belongs to one or more groups. The only real importance of group relationships pertains to file permissions, as you'll recall from Section 3.9, each file has a "group ownership" and a set of group permissions which defines how users in that group may access the file.

There are several system-defined groups such as `bin`, `mail`, and `sys`. Users should not belong to any of these groups; they are used for system file permissions. Instead, users should belong to an individual group such as `users`. If you want to be cute, you can maintain several groups of users such as `student`, `staff`, and `faculty`.

The file `/etc/group` contains information about groups. The format of each line is

```
group name:password:GID:other members
```

Some example groups might be:

```
root:*:0:
users:*:100:mdw,larry
guest:*:200:
other:*:250:kiwi
```

The first group, `root`, is a special system group reserved for the `root` account. The next group, `users`, is for regular users. It has a GID of 100. The users `mdw` and `larry` are given access to this group. Remember that in `/etc/passwd` each user was given a default GID. However, users may belong to more than one group, by adding their usernames to other group lines in `/etc/group`. The `groups` command lists what groups you are given access to.

The third group, `guest`, is for guest users, and `other` is for "other" users. The user `kiwi` is given access to this group as well.

As you can see, the "password" field of /etc/group is rarely used. It is sometimes used to set a password on group access. This is seldom necessary. To protect
users from changing into priveleged groups, set the password field to "*".

To add groups to your system, just add entries in /etc/group, as no other
configuration needs to be done to add a group. To delete a group, simply delete its
entry in /etc/group.

4.5   Archiving and Compressing Files

Before we can talk about backups, we need to introduce the tools used to archive
files and software on UNIX systems.

4.5.1   Using tar

The tar command is most often used to archive files.

The format of the tar command is

    tar ⟨options⟩ ⟨file1⟩ ⟨file2⟩ ... ⟨fileN⟩

where ⟨options⟩ is the list of commands and options for tar, and ⟨file1⟩ through
⟨fileN⟩ is the list of files to add or extract from the archive.

For example, the command

    # tar cvf backup.tar /etc

would pack all of the files in /etc into the tar archive backup.tar. The first
argument to tar—"cvf"—is the tar "command". "c" tells tar to create a new
archive file. The "v" option forces tar into verbose mode—printing each filename
as it is archived. The "f" option tells tar that the next argument—backup.tar—is
the name of the archive to create. The rest of the arguments to tar are the file and
directory names to add to the archive.

The command

    # tar xvf backup.tar

will extract the tar file backup.tar in the current directory. This can sometimes
be dangerous—when extracting files from a tar file, old files are overwritten.

Furthermore, before extracting tar files it is important to know where the files should be unpacked. For example, let's say you archived the following files: /etc/hosts, /etc/group, and /etc/passwd. If you use the command

> # *tar cvf backup.tar /etc/hosts /etc/group /etc/passwd*

the directory name /etc/ is added to the beginning of each filename. In order to extract the files to the correct location, you would need to use the following commands:

> # *cd /*
> # *tar xvf backup.tar*

because files are extracted with the pathname saved in the archive file.

If, however, you archived the files with the command

> # *cd /etc*
> # *tar cvf hosts group passwd*

the directory name is not saved in the archive file. Therefore, you would need to "cd /etc" before extracting the files. As you can see, how the tar file is created makes a large difference in where you extract it. The command

> # *tar tvf backup.tar*

may be used to display an "index" of the tar file before unpacking it. In this way you can see what directory the filenames in the archive are stored relative to, and can extract the archive from the correct location.

4.5.2   gzip and compress

Unlike archiving programs for MS-DOS, tar does not automatically compress files as it archives them. Therefore, if you are archiving two 1-megabyte files, the resulting tar file will be two megabytes in size. The gzip command may be used to compress a file (the file to compress need not be a tar file). The command

> # *gzip -9 backup.tar*

will compress `backup.tar` and leave you with `backup.tar.gz`, the compressed version of the file. The `-9` switch tells `gzip` to use the highest compression factor.

The `gunzip` command may be used to uncompress a gzipped file. Equivalently, you may use "`gzip -d`".

`gzip` is a relatively new tool in the UNIX community. For many years, the `compress` command was used instead. However, because of several factors[1], `compress` is being phased out.

`compress`ed files end in the extension `.Z`. For example, `backup.tar.Z` is the compressed version of `backup.tar`, while `backup.tar.gz` is the gzipped version[2]. The `uncompress` command is used to expand a `compress`ed file; `gunzip` knows how to handle `compress`ed files as well.

4.5.3 Putting them together

Therefore, to archive a group of files and compress the result, you can use the commands:

    # *tar cvf backup.tar /etc*
    # *gzip -9 backup.tar*

The result will be `backup.tar.gz`. To unpack this file, use the reverse set of commands:

    # *gunzip backup.tar.gz*
    # *tar xvf backup.tar*

Of course always make sure that you are in the correct directory before unpacking a tar file.

You can use some UNIX cleverness to do all of this on one command line, as in the following:

    # *tar cvf - /etc | gzip -9c > backup.tar.gz*

---

[1]These factors include a software patent dispute against the `compress` algorithm and the fact that `gzip` is much more efficient than `compress`.

[2]To add further confusion, for some time the extension `.z` (lowercase "z") was used for gzipped files. The official `gzip` extension is now `.gz`.

Here, we are sending the tar file to "-", which stands for `tar`'s standard output. This is piped to `gzip`, which compresses the incoming tar file, and the result is saved in `backup.tar.gz`. The `-c` option to `gzip` tells `gzip` to send its output to stdout, which is redirected to `backup.tar.gz`.

A single command used to unpack this archive would be:

> # *gunzip -c backup.tar.gz | tar xvf -*

Again, `gunzip` uncompresses the contents of `backup.tar.gz` and sends the resulting tar file to stdout. This is piped to `tar`, which reads "-", this time referring to `tar`'s standard input.

Happily, the `tar` command also includes the `z` option to automatically compress/uncompress files on the fly, using the `gzip` compression algorithm.

For example, the command

> # *tar cvfz backup.tar.gz /etc*

is equivalent to

> # *tar cvf backup.tar /etc*
> # *gzip backup.tar*

Just as the command

> # *tar xvfz backup.tar.Z*

may be used instead of

> # *uncompress backup.tar.Z*
> # *tar xvf backup.tar*

Refer to the man pages for `tar` and `gzip` for more information.

4.6   Using Floppies and Making Backups

Floppies are usually used as backup media. If you don't have a tape drive connected to your system, floppy disks can be used (although they are slower and somewhat less reliable).

You may also use floppies to hold individual filesystems—in this way, you can **mount** the floppy to access the data on it.

4.6.1 Using floppies for backups

The easiest way to make a backup using floppies is with `tar`. The command

> # *tar cvfzM /dev/fd0 /*

will make a complete backup of your system using the floppy drive **/dev/fd0**. The "M" option to `tar` allows the backup to be a multivolume backup; that is, when one floppy is full, `tar` will prompt for the next. The command

> # *tar xvfzM /dev/fd0*

can be used to restore the complete backup. This method can also be used if you have a tape drive (**/dev/rmt0**) connected to your system.

Several other programs exist for making multiple-volume backups; the `backflops` program found on `tsx-11.mit.edu` may come in handy.

Making a complete backup of the system can be time- and resource-consuming. Most system administrators use a incremental backup policy, in which every month a complete backup is taken, and every week only those files which have been modified in the last week are backed up. In this case, if you trash your system in the middle of the month, you can simply restore the last full monthly backup, and then restore the last weekly backups as needed.

The `find` command can be useful in locating files which have changed since a certain date. Several scripts for managing incremental backups can be found on `sunsite.unc.edu`.

4.6.2 Using floppies as filesystems

You can create a filesystem on a floppy just as you would on a hard drive partition. For example, as root

> # */sbin/mke2fs /dev/fd0*

creates a filesystem on the floppy in **/dev/fd0**.

In order to access the floppy, you must **mount** the filesystem contained on it. The command

> # *mount -t ext2 /dev/fd0 /mnt*

will mount the floppy in /dev/fd0 on the directory /mnt. Now, all of the files on the floppy will appear under /mnt on your drive. The "-t ext2" specifies an ext2fs filesystem type. If you created another type of filesystem on the floppy, you'll need to specify its type to the mount command.

The "mount point" (the directory where you're mounting the filesystem) needs to exist when you use the mount command. If it doesn't exist, simply create it with mkdir.

See Section 4.8 for more information on filesystems, mounting, and mount points.

◇   Note that any I/O to the floppy is buffered just as hard disk I/O is. If you change data on the floppy, you may not see the drive light come on until the kernel flushes its I/O buffers. It's important that you not remove a floppy before you unmount it; this can be done with the command

    # *umount /dev/fd0*

Do not simply switch floppies as you would on an MS-DOS system; whenever you change floppies, umount the first one and mount the next.

4.7   Upgrading and Installing New Software

Another duty of the system administrator is upgrading and installing new software.

The Linux community is very dynamic. New kernel releases come out every few weeks, and other software is updated almost as often. Because of this, new Linux users often feel the need to upgrade their systems constantly to keep up the the rapidly changing pace. Not only is this unnecessary, it's a waste of time: to keep up with all of the changes in the Linux world, you would be spending all of your time upgrading and none of your time using the system.

So, when should you upgrade? Some people feel that you should upgrade when a new distribution release is made—for example, when Slackware comes out with a new version. Many Linux users completely reinstall their system with the newest Slackware release every time. This, also, is a waste of time. In general, changes to Slackware releases are small. Downloading and reinstalling 30 disks when only 10% of the software has been actually modified is, of course, pointless.

The best way to upgrade your system is to do it by hand: only upgrade those software packages which you know that you should upgrade. This scares a lot of people: they want to know what to upgrade, and how, and what will break if they don't upgrade. In order to be successful with Linux, it's important to overcome your fears of "doing it yourself"— which is what Linux is all about. In fact, once you have your system working and all software correctly configured, reinstalling with the newest release will no doubt wipe all of your configuration and things will be broken again, just as they were when you first installed your system. Setting yourself back in this manner is unnecessary—all that is needed is some know-how about upgrading your system, and how to do it right.

You'll find that when you upgrade one component of your system, other things should not break. For example, most of the software on my system is left over from an ancient 0.96 MCC Interim installation. Yet, I run the newest version of the kernel and libraries with this software with no problem. For the most part, senselessly upgrading to "keep up with the trend" is not important at all. This isn't MS-DOS or Microsoft Windows. There is no important reason to run the newest version of all of the software. If you find that you would like or need features in a new version, then upgrade. If not, then don't. In other words, only upgrade what you have to, and when you have to. Don't just upgrade for the sake of upgrading. That will waste a lot of time and effort trying to keep up.

The most important software to upgrade on your system is the kernel, the libraries, and the `gcc` compiler. These are the three essential parts of your system, and in some cases they all depend on each other for everything to work successfully. Most of the other software on your system does not need to be upgraded periodically.

4.7.1 Upgrading the kernel

Upgrading the kernel is simply a matter of getting the sources and compiling them yourself. You must compile the kernel yourself in order to enable or disable certain features, as well as to ensure that the kernel will be optimized to run on your machine. The process is quite painless.

The kernel sources may be retrieved from any of the Linux FTP sites (see Section B for a list). On `sunsite.unc.edu`, for instance, the kernel sources are found in `/pub/Linux/kernel`. Kernel versions are numbered using a version number and a patchlevel. For example, kernel version 0.99 patchlevel 11 is usually written as `0.99.pl11`, or just `0.99.11`.

The kernel sources are released as a gzipped tar file[3]. For example, the file

---

[3]Often, a patch file is also released for the current kernel version which allows you to patch your current kernel sources from the last patchlevel to the current one (using the program `patch`).

containing the 0.99.pl11 kernel sources is `linux-0.99.11.tar.gz`.

Unpack this tar file from the directory `/usr/src`; it creates the directory `/usr/src/linux` which contains the kernel sources. You should delete or rename your existing `/usr/src/linux` before unpacking the new version.

Once the sources are unpacked, you need to make sure that two symbolic links in `/usr/include` are correct. To create these links, use the commands

> \# *ln -sf /usr/src/linux/include/linux /usr/include/linux*
> \# *ln -sf /usr/src/linux/include/asm /usr/include/asm*

Once you have created these links once, there is no reason to create them again when you install the next version of the kernel sources. (See Section 3.10 for more about symbolic links.)

Note that in order to compile the kernel, you must have the `gcc` and `g++` C and C++ compilers installed on your system. You may need to have the most recent versions of these compilers: see Section 4.7.3, below, for more information.

To compile the kernel, first `cd` to `/usr/src/linux`. Run the command `make config`. This command will prompt you for a number of configuration options, such as what filesystem types you wish to include in the new kernel.

Next, edit `/usr/src/linux/Makefile`. Be sure that the definition for ROOT_DEV is correct—it defines the device used as the root filesystem at boot time. The usual definition is

> ROOT_DEV = CURRENT

Unless you are changing your root filesystem device, there is no reason to change this.

Next, run the command `make dep` to fix all of the source dependencies. This is a very important step.

Finally, you're ready to compile the kernel. The command `make Image` will compile the kernel and leave the new kernel image in the file `/usr/src/linux/Image`. Alternately, the command `make zImage` will compile a compressed kernel image, which uncompresses itself at boot time and uses less drive space.

Once you have the kernel compiled, you need to either copy it to a boot floppy (with a command such as "`cp Image /dev/fd0`") or install it using LILO to boot from your hard drive. See Section 4.2.2 for more information.

In most cases, however, it's usually easier to install the entire new version of the kernel sources.

4.7.2   Upgrading the libraries

As mentioned before, most of the software on the system is compiled to use shared libraries, which contain common subroutines shared among different programs.

If you see the message

```
Incompatible library version
```

when attempting to run a program, then you need to upgrade to the version of the libraries which the program requires. Libraries are back-compatible; that is, a program compiled to use an older version of the libraries should work with the new version of the libraries installed. However, the reverse is not true.

The newest version of the libraries can be found on the Linux FTP sites. On `sunsite.unc.edu`, they are located in `/pub/Linux/GCC`. The "release" files there should explain what files you need to download and how to install them. Briefly, you should get the files `image-`*version*`.tar.gz` and `inc-`*version*`.tar.gz` where *version* is the version of the libraries to install, such as `4.4.1`. These are gzipped tar files; the `image` file contains the library images to install in `/lib` and `/usr/lib`. The `inc` file contains include files to install in `/usr/include`

The `release-`*version*`.tar.gz` should explain the installation procedure in detail (the exact instructions vary for each release). In general you need to install the library `.a` and `.sa` files in `/usr/lib`. These are the libraries used at compilation time.

In addition, the shared library image files, `libc.so.`*version* are installed in `/lib`. These are the shared library images loaded at runtime by programs using the libraries. Each library has a symbolic link using the major version number of the library in `/lib`.

For example, the `libc` library version 4.4.1 has a major version number of 4. The file containing the library is `libc.so.4.4.1`. A symbolic link of the name `libc.so.4` is also in `/lib` pointing to this file. You need to change this symbolic link when upgrading the libraries. For example, when upgrading from `libc.so.4.4` to `libc.so.4.4.1`, you need to change the symbolic link to point to the new version.

◇   It is very important that you change the symbolic link in one step, as given below. If you somehow delete the symbolic link `libc.so.4`, then programs which depend on the link (including basic utilities like `ls` and `cat`) will stop working. Use the following command to update the symbolic link `libc.so.4` to point to the file `libc.so.4.4.1`:

```
# ln -sf /lib/libc.so.4.4.1 /lib/libc.so.4
```

You also need to change the symbolic link libm.so.*version* in the same manner. If you are upgrading to a different version of the libraries substitute to appropriate filenames above. The library release notice should explain the details. (See Section 3.10 for more information about symbolic links.)

4.7.3   Upgrading gcc

The gcc C and C++ compiler is used to compile software on your system, most importantly the kernel. The newest version of gcc is found on the Linux FTP sites. On sunsite.unc.edu, it is found in the directory /pub/Linux/GCC (along with the libraries). There should be a **release** file for the gcc distribution detailing what files you need to download and how to install them.

4.7.4   Upgrading other software

Upgrading other software is usually just a matter of downloading the appropriate files and installing them. Most software for Linux is distributed at gzipped tar files, including either sources or binaries or both. If binaries are not included in the release, you may need to compile them yourself; usually, this means typing make in the directory where the sources are held.

Reading the USENET newsgroup comp.os.linux.announce for announcements of new software releases is the easiest way to find out about new software. Whenever you are looking for software on an FTP site, downloading the ls-lR index file from the FTP site and using grep to find the files in question is the easiest way to locate software. If you have archie available to you, it can be of assistance as well[4]. See Appendix A for more details.

One handy source of Linux software is the Slackware distribution disk images. Each disk contains a number of .tgz files which are simply gzipped tar files. Instead of downloading the disks, you can download the desired .tgz files from the Slackware directories on the FTP site and install them directly. If you run the Slackware distribution, the setup command can be used to automatically load and install a complete series of disks.

---

[4]If you don't have archie, you can telnet to an archie server such as archie.rutgers.edu, login as "archie" and use the command "help"

Again, it's usually not a good idea to upgrade by reinstalling with the newest version of Slackware, or another distribution. If you reinstall in this way, you will no doubt wreck your current installation, including user directories and all of your customized configuration. The best way to upgrade software is piecewise; that is, if there is a program that you use often that has a new version, upgrade it. Otherwise, don't bother. Rule of thumb: If it ain't broke, don't fix it. If your current software works, there's no reason to upgrade.

4.8 Managing Filesystems

Another task of the system administrator is taking care of filesystems. Most of this job entails periodically checking the filesystems for damage or corrupted files; many systems automatically check the filesystems at boot time.

4.8.1 Mounting filesystems

First, a few concepts about filesystems. Before a filesystem is accessible to the system, it must be **mounted** on some directory. For example, if you have a filesystem on a floppy, you must mount it under some directory, say /mnt, in order to access the files on it (see Section 4.6.2). After mounting the filesystem, all of the files in the filesystem appear in that directory. After unmounting the filesystem, the directory (in this case, /mnt) will be empty.

The same is true of filesystems on the hard drive. The system automatically mounts filesystems on your hard drive for you at bootup time. The so-called "root filesystem" is mounted on the directory /. If you have a separate filesystem for /usr, for example, it is mounted on /usr. If you only have a root filesystem, all files (including those in /usr) exist on that filesystem.

The command **mount** is used to mount a filesystem. The command

```
mount -av
```

is executed from the file /etc/rc.d/rc.S (which is the system initialization file executed at boot time; see Section 4.10.1). The mount -av command obtains information on filesystems and mount points from the file /etc/fstab. An example fstab file appears below.

```
# device      directory     type     options
```

```
/dev/hda2       /                ext2     defaults
/dev/hda3       /usr             ext2     defaults
/dev/hda4       none             swap     sw
/proc           /proc            proc     none
```

The first field is the device—the name of the partition to mount. The second
field is the mount point. The third field is the filesystem type—such as ext2 (for
ext2fs) or minix (for Minix filesystems). Table 4.1 lists the various filesystem
types available for Linux.[5] Not all of these filesystem types may be available on
your system; your kernel must have support for them compiled in. See Section 4.7
for information on building the kernel.

Filesystem	Type name	Comment
Second Extended Filesystem	ext2	Most common Linux filesystem.
Extended Filesystem	ext	Superseded by ext2.
Minix Filesystem	minix	Original Minix filesystem; rarely used.
Xia Filesystem	xiafs	Like ext2, but rarely used.
UMSDOS Filesystem	umsdos	Used to install Linux on an MS-DOS partition.
Network Filesystem	ufs	Used to access remote file systems.
MS-DOS Filesystem	msdos	Used to access MS-DOS files.
BSD UFS Filesystem	ufs	Read only access to SunOS, FreeBSD and NEXTSTEP.
SMB Filesystem	smb	Server Message Buffer Support For Windows For Workgroups and NT.
NCP Filesystem	ncf	Netware Core Protocol file server support (over IPX).
/proc Filesystem	proc	Provides process information for ps, etc.
ISO 9660 Filesystem	iso9660	Format used by most CD-ROMs.
Xenix Filesystem	xenix	Used to access files from Xenix.
System V Filesystem	sysv	Used to access files from System V variants for the x86.
Coherent Filesystem	coherent	Used to access files from Coherent.
HPFS Filesystem	hpfs	Read-only access for HPFS partitions (OS/2, NT).
Amiga FFS Filesystem	affs	Amiga Fast File System Support

Table 4.1: Linux Filesystem Types

---

[5]This table is current as of kernel version 2.0.7.

The last field of the `fstab` file contains `mount` options—usually, this is set to "`defaults`".

As you can see, swap partitions are included in `/etc/fstab` as well. They have a mount directory of `none`, and type `swap`. The `swapon -a` command, executed from `/etc/rc` as well, is used to enable swapping on all swap devices listed in `/etc/fstab`.

The `fstab` file contains one special entry—for the `/proc` filesystem. As mentioned in Section 3.11.1, the `/proc` filesystem is used to store information about system processes, available memory, and so on. If `/proc` is not mounted, commands such as `ps` will not work.

◇   The `mount` command may only be used by root. This is to ensure security on the system; you wouldn't want regular users mounting and unmounting filesystems on a whim. There are several software packages available which allow regular users to mount and unmount filesystems (floppies in particular) without compromising system security.

The `mount -av` command actually mounts all filesystems other than the root filesystem (in the table above, `/dev/hda2`). The root filesystem is automatically mounted at boot time by the kernel.

Instead of using `mount -av`, you can mount a filesystem by hand. The command

> # *mount -t ext2 /dev/hda3 /usr*

is equivalent to mounting the filesystem with the entry `/dev/hda3` in the `fstab` example file above.

In general, you should never have to mount or unmount filesystems by hand. The `mount -av` command in `/etc/rc` takes care of mounting the filesystems at boot time. Filesystems are automatically unmounted by the `shutdown` or `halt` commands before bringing the system down.

4.8.2   Checking filesystems

It is usually a good idea to check your filesystems for damage or corrupt files every now and then. Slackware Linux automatically checks it's filesystems at boot time (with the appropriate commands in `/etc/rc.d/rc.S`).

For example, the command

> # *e2fsck -av /dev/hda2*

will check the ext2fs filesystem on **/dev/hda2** and automatically correct any errors.

It is usually a good idea to unmount a filesystem before checking it. For example, the command

> # *umount /dev/hda2*

will unmount the filesystem on **/dev/hda2**, after which you can check it. The one exception is that you cannot unmount the root filesystem. In order to check the root filesystem when it's unmounted, you should use a maintenance boot/root diskette (see Section 4.11.1). You also cannot unmount a filesystem if any of the files in it are "busy"—that is, being used by a running process. For example, you cannot unmount a filesystem if any user's current working directory is on that filesystem. You will receive a "**Device busy**" error if you attempt to unmount a filesystem which is in use.

Other filesystem types use different forms of the **e2fsck** command, such as **efsck** and **xfsck**. On Slackware Linux, you can simply use the command **fsck**, which will determine the filesystem type and execute the appropriate command.

◇   It is important that you reboot your system immediately after checking a mounted filesystem if any corrections were made to that filesystem. (However, in general, you shouldn't check filesystems while they are mounted.) For example, if **e2fsck** reports that it corrected any errors with the filesystem, you should immediately **shutdown -r** in order to reboot the system. This is to allow the system to re-sync its information about the filesystem when **e2fsck** modifies it.

The **/proc** filesystem never needs to be checked in this manner. **/proc** is a memory filesystem, managed directly by the kernel.

4.9   Using a swap file

Instead of reserving an individual partition for swap space, you can use a file. However, to do so you'll need install the Linux software and get everything going *before* you create the swap file.

If you have a Linux system installed, you can use the following commands to create a swap file. Below, we're going to create a swap file of size 8208 blocks (about 8 megs).

> # *dd if=/dev/zero of=/swap bs=1024 count=8208*

This command creates the swap file itself. Replace the "`count=`" with the size of the swap file in blocks.

> # *mkswap /swap 8208*

This command will initialize the swapfile; again, replace the name and size of the swapfile with the appropriate values.

> # */etc/sync*
> # *swapon /swap*

Now we are swapping on the file `/swap` which we have created, after syncing, which ensures that the file has been written to disk.

The one major drawback to using a swapfile in this manner is that all access to the swap file is done through the filesystem. This means that the blocks which make up the swap file may not be contiguous. Therefore, performance may not be as great as using a swap partition, for which blocks are always contiguous and I/O requests are done directly to the device.

Another drawback in using a swapfile is the chance to corrupt your filesystem data—when using large swap files, there is the chance that you can corrupt your filesystem if something goes wrong. Keeping your filesystems and swap partitions separate will prevent this from happening.

Using a swap file can be very useful if you have a temporary need for more swap space. For example, if you're compiling a large program and would like to speed things up somewhat, you can temporarily create a swap file and use it in addition to your regular swap space.

To get rid of a swap file, first use **swapoff**, as in

> # *swapoff /swap*

And you can safely delete the file.

> # *rm /swap*

Remember that each swap file (or partition) may be as large as 16 megabytes, but you may use up to 8 swap files or partitions on your system.

4.10   Miscellaneous Tasks

Believe it or not, there are a number of housekeeping tasks for the system administrator which don't fall into any major category.

4.10.1   System startup files

When the system boots, a number of scripts are executed automatically by the
system before any user logs in. Here is a description of what happens.

At bootup time, the kernel spawns the process `/sbin/init`. init is a program
which reads its configuration file, `/etc/inittab`, and spawns other processes based
on the contents of this file. One of the important processes started from `inittab`
is the `/sbin/agetty` process started on each Virtual Console. The `agetty` process
grabs the VC for use, and starts a `login` process on the VC. This allows you to
login on each VC; if `/etc/inittab` does not contain a `agetty` process for a certain
VC, you will not be able to login on that VC.

Another process executed from `/etc/inittab` is `/etc/rc.d/rc.S`, the main
system initialization file. This file is a simple shell script which executes any initialization commands needed at boot time, such as mounting the filesystems and
initializing swap space. The `rc.S` file calls many of the files you will find in the
`/etc/rc.d` directory, which is where most of the start up scripts are kept. See the
chart of rc files and their uses in Chapter 3.

4.10.2   Setting the hostname

In a networked environment, the hostname is used to uniquely identify a particular
machine, while in a standalone environment the hostname just gives the system
personality and charm. It's like naming a pet: you can always address to your dog
as "The dog," but it's much more interesting to assign the dog a name such as Spot
or Woofie.

Setting the system's hostname is a simple matter of using the `hostname` command. If you are on a network, your hostname should be the full hostname of your
machine, such as `goober.norelco.com`. If you are not on a network of any kind,
you can choose an arbitrary host and domain name, such as `loomer.vpizza.com`,
`shoop.nowhere.edu`, or `floof.org`.

When setting the hostname, the hostname must appear in the file `/etc/hosts`, which assigns an IP address to each host. Even if your machine is not on a network, you should include your own hostname in `/etc/hosts`.

For example, if you are not on a TCP/IP network, and your hostname is `floof.org`, simply include the following line in `/etc/hosts`:

```
127.0.0.1       floof.org localhost
```

This assigns your hostname, `floof.org`, to the loopback address 127.0.0.1 (used if you're not on a network). The `localhost` alias is also assigned to this address.

If you are on a TCP/IP network, however, your real IP address and hostname should appear in `/etc/hosts`. For example, if your hostname is `goober.norelco.com`, and your IP address is 128.253.154.32, add the following line to `/etc/hosts`:

```
128.253.154.32      goober.norelco.com
```

If your hostname does not appear in `/etc/hosts`, you will not be able to set it.

To set your hostname, simply edit the /etc/HOSTNAME command. Your hostname will be automatically set when your Slackware Linux system is restarted.

The following line appears in the standard Slackware Linux /etc/rc.d/rc.M file:

```
/bin/hostname `cat /etc/HOSTNAME | cut -f1 -d .`
```

This line processes the `/etc/HOSTNAME` file by clipping off the host part of the completely qualified name. So if your `/etc/HOSTNAME` file contains a line like the below:

```
relay2.kgb.ru
```

then only the string "relay2" will actually be passed to hostname.

Another way to set your hostname in Slackware Linux is to user the built-in program '`/sbin/netconfig`'. Netconfig is a menu-based, easy to use TCP/IP suite configuration tool that is described in chapter five.

4.11   What To Do In An Emergency

On some occasions, the system administrator will be faced with the problem of
recovering from a complete disaster, such as forgetting the root password or trashing
filesystems. The best advice is, *don't panic.* Everyone makes stupid mistakes—
that's the best way to learn about system administration: the hard way.

Linux is not an unstable version of UNIX. In fact, I have had fewer problems
with system hangs than with commercial versions of UNIX on many platforms.
Linux also benefits from a strong complement of wizards who can help you get out
of a bind.

The first step in investigating any problem is to attempt to fix it yourself. Poke
around, see how things work. Too much of the time, a system administrator will
post a desperate plea for help before looking into the problem at all. Most of the
time, you'll find that fixing problems yourself is actually very easy. It is the path
to guruhood.

There are very few cases where reinstalling the system from scratch is necessary.
Many new users accidentally delete some essential system file, and immediately
reach for the installation disks. This is not a good idea. Before taking such drastic
measures, investigate the problem and ask others to help fix things up. In almost
all cases, you can recover your system from a maintenance diskette.

4.11.1   Recovering using a maintenance diskette

One indispensable tool for the system administrator is the so called "boot/root
disk"—a floppy which can be booted for a complete Linux system, independent
of your hard drive. Boot/root disks are actually very simple—you create a root
filesystem on the floppy, place all of the necessary utilities on it, and install LILO
and a bootable kernel on the floppy. Another technique is to use one floppy for the
kernel and another for the root filesystem. In any case, the result is the same: you
are running a Linux system completely from floppy.

The canonical example of a boot/root disk is the Slackware rescue disk[6]. These
diskettes contain a bootable kernel and a root filesystem, all on floppy. It comes in
very handy when doing system maintenance.

Using the rescue disk is very simple. Just boot the disk on your system, and

---

[6]See Section ?? for information on downloading these from the Internet. For this procedure,
you don't need to download the entire Slackware release—only the boot and root diskettes.

login as `root` (usually no password). In order to access the files on your hard drive, you will need to mount your filesystems by hand. For example, the command

>   # mount -t ext2 /dev/hda2 /mnt

will mount an ext2fs filesystem on `/dev/hda2` under `/mnt`. Remember that `/` is now on the rescue disk itself; you need to mount your hard drive filesystems under some directory in order to access the files. Therefore, `/etc/passwd` on your hard drive is now `/mnt/etc/passwd` if you mount your root filesystem on `/mnt`.

4.11.2   Fixing the root password

If you forget your root password, no problem. Just boot the rescue disk, mount your root filesystem on `/mnt`, and blank out the password field for `root` in `/mnt/etc/passwd`, as so:

>   root::0:0:root:/:/bin/sh

Now `root` has no password; when you reboot from the hard drive you should be able to login as `root` and reset the password using `passwd`.

Aren't you glad you learned how to use `vi`? On your rescue disk, other editors such as Emacs aren't available, but `vi` is.

4.11.3   Fixing trashed filesystems

If you somehow trash your filesystems, you can run `e2fsck` (if you use the ext2fs filesystem type, that is) to correct any damaged data on the filesystems from floppy. Other filesystem types use different forms of the `fsck` command; see Section 4.8 for details.

When checking your filesystems from floppy, it's best for the filesystems to not be mounted.

One common cause of filesystem damage is superblock corruption. The *superblock* is the "header" of the filesystem that contains information on the filesystem status, size, free blocks, and so forth. If you corrupt your superblock (for example, by accidentally writing data directly to the filesystem's partition), the system may not recognize the filesystem at all. Any attempt to mount the filesystem could fail, and `e2fsck` won't be able to fix the problem.

Happily, the *ext2fs* filesystem type saves copies of the superblock at "block group" boundaries on the drive—usually, every 8K blocks. In order to tell `e2fsck` to use a copy of the superblock, you can use a command such as

> # *e2fsck -b 8193 ⟨partition⟩*

where ⟨*partition*⟩ is the partition on which the filesystem resides. The `-b 8193` option tells `e2fsck` to use the copy of the superblock stored at block 8193 in the filesystem.

4.11.4   Recovering lost files

If you accidentally deleted important files on your system, there's no way to "undelete" them. However, you can copy the relevant files from the floppy to your hard drive. For example, if you deleted `/bin/login` on your system (which allows you to login), simply boot the rescue floppy, mount the root filesystem on `/mnt`, and use the command

> # *cp -a /bin/login /mnt/bin/login*

The `-a` option tells `cp` to preserve the permissions on the file(s) being copied.

Of course, if the files you deleted weren't essential system files which have counterparts on the rescue floppy copy them from the cdrom.

4.11.5   Fixing trashed libraries

If you accidentally trashed your libraries or symbolic links in `/lib`, more than likely commands which depended on those libraries will no longer run (see Section 4.7.2). The easiest solution is to boot your rescue floppy, mount your root filesystem, and fix the libraries in `/mnt/lib`.

Chapter 5

Advanced Features

This chapter will introduce you to some of the more interesting features of Linux. This assumes that you have at least basic UNIX experience, and understand the information contained in the previous chapters.

The most important aspect of Linux that distinguishes it from other implementations of UNIX is its open design and philosophy. Linux was not developed by a small team of programmers headed by a marketing committee with a single goal in mind. It was developed by an ever-increasing group of hackers, putting what they wanted into a homebrew UNIX system. The types of software and diversity of design in the Linux world is large. Some people dislike this lack of uniformity and conformity—however, some call it one of the strongest qualities of Linux.

5.1   The X Window System

The X Window System is a large and powerful (and somewhat complex) graphics environment for UNIX systems. The original X Window System code was developed at MIT; commercial vendors have since made X the industry standard for UNIX platforms. Virtually every UNIX workstation in the world runs some variant of the X Window system.

A free port of the MIT X Window System version 11, release 6 (X11R6) for 80386/80486/Pentium UNIX systems has been developed by a team of programmers

originally headed by David Wexelblat[1]. The release, known as XFree86[2], is available
for System V/386, 386BSD, and other x86 UNIX implementations, including Linux.
It includes all of the required binaries, support files, libraries, and tools.

Configuring and using the X Window System is far beyond the scope of this
book. You are encouraged to read *The X Window System: A User's Guide*—see
Appendix A for information on this book. In this section, we'll give a step-by-
step description of how to install and configure XFree86 for Linux, but you will
have to fill in some of the details yourself by reading the documentation released
with XFree86 itself. (This documentation is discussed below.) The Linux *XFree86
HOWTO* is another good source of information.

5.1.1   Hardware requirements

As of XFree86 version 3.1.2, July 1996, the following video chipsets are supported. The documentation included with your video adaptor should specify the
chipset used. If you are in the market for a new video card, or are buying a new
machine that comes with a video card, have the vendor find out exactly what the
make, model, and chipset of the video card is. This may require the vendor to
call technical support on your behalf; in general vendors will be happy to do this.
Many PC hardware vendors will state that the video card is a "standard SVGA
card" which "should work" on your system. Explain that your software (mention
Slackware Linux and XFree86!) does not support all video chipsets and that you
must have detailed information.

You can also determine your video card chipset by running the `SuperProbe`
program included with the XFree86 distribution. This is covered in more detail
below.

Video chipsets supported by XFree86 3.1.2:

- 8514/A (and true clones)

- Advance Logic: ALG2101, ALG2228, ALG2301, ALG2302, ALG2308,
  ALG2401

- ARK Logic: ARK1000PV, ARK2000PV

- ATI: Mach8, Mach32, Mach64, 18800, 18800-1, 28800-2, 28800-4, 28800-5,
  28800-6, 68800-3, 68800-6, 68800AX, 68800LX, 88800CX, 88800GX

---

[1]David may be reached on the Internet at `dwex@XFree86.org`.

[2]XFree86 is a trademark of The XFree86 Project, Inc.

- Chips & Technology: 65520, 65530, 65540, 65545

- Cirrus: CLGD5420, CLGD5422, CLGD5424, CLGD5426, CLGD5428, CLGD5429, CLGD5430, CLGD5434, CLGD5420, CLGD5422, CLGD5424, CLGD5426, CLGD5428, CLGD5429, CLGD5430, CLGD5434, CLGD6205, CLGD6215, CLGD6225, CLGD6235, CLGD6410, CLGD6412, CLGD6420, CLGD6440

- Compaq: AVGA

- Genoa: GVGA

- IBM: XGA-2

- IIT: AGX-014, AGX-015, AGX-016

- MX: MX68000, MX680010

- NCR: 77C22, 77C22E, 77C22E+

- OAK: OTI067, OTI077, OTI087

- RealTek: RTG3106

- S3: 86C911, 86C924, 86C801, 86C805, 86C805i, 86C928, 86C864, 86C964, 86C732, 86C764, 86C868, 86C968

- Tseng: ET4000/W32, ET4000/W32i, ET4000/W32p, ET3000, ET4000AX.

- Trident: TVGA8800CS, TVGA8900B, TVGA8900C, TVGA8900CL, TVGA9000, TVGA9000i, TVGA9100B, TVGA9200CX, TVGA9320, TVGA9400CX, TVGA9420

- Video 7/Headland Technologies: HT216-32

- Weitek: P9000

- Western Digital Paradise: PVGA1

- Western Digital: WD90C31, WD90C33, WD90C24A, WD90C00, WD90C10, WD90C11, WD90C24, WD90C24A, WD90C30, WD90C31, WD90C33

All of the above are supported in both 256 color and monochrome modes, with the exception of the Avance Logic, MX and Video 7 chipsets, which are only supported in 256 color mode. If your video card has enough DRAM installed, many of the above chipsets are supported in 16 and 32 bits-per-pixel mode (specifically, some Mach32, P9000, S3 and Cirrus boards). The usual configuration is 8 bits per pixel (that is, 256 colors).

The monochrome server also supports generic VGA cards, the Hercules monochrome card, the Hyundai HGC1280, Sigma LaserView, and Apollo monochrome cards. On the Compaq AVGA, only 64k of video memory is supported for the monochrome server, and the GVGA has not been tested with more than 64k.

This list will undoubtedly expand as time passes. The release notes for the current version of XFree86 should contain the complete list of supported video chipsets.

One problem faced by the XFree86 developers is that some video card manufacturers use non-standard mechanisms for determining clock frequencies used to drive the card. Some of these manufacturers either don't release specifications describing how to program the card, or they require developers to sign a non-disclosure statement to obtain the information. This would obviously restrict the free distribution of the XFree86 software, something that the XFree86 development team is not willing to do. For a long time, this has been a problem with certain video cards manufactured by Diamond, but as of release 3.1 of XFree86, Diamond has started to work with the development team to release free drivers for these cards.

The suggested setup for XFree86 under Linux is a 486 machine with at least 8 megabytes of RAM, and a video card with a chipset listed above. For optimal performance, we suggest using an accelerated card, such as an S3-chipset card. You should check the documentation for XFree86 and verify that your particular card is supported before taking the plunge and purchasing expensive hardware. Benchmark ratings comparisons for various video cards under XFree86 are posted routinely to the USENET newsgroups `comp.windows.x.i386unix` and `comp.os.linux.misc`.

As a side note, my personal Linux system is a 486DX2-66, 20 megabytes of RAM, and is equipped with a VLB S3-864 chipset card with 2 megabytes of DRAM. I have run X benchmarks on this machine as well as on Sun Sparc IPX workstations. The Linux system is roughly 7 times faster than the Sparc IPX (for the curious, XFree86-3.1 under Linux, with this video card, runs at around 171,000 xstones; the Sparc IPX at around 24,000). In general, XFree86 on a Linux system with an accelerated SVGA card will give you much greater performance than that found on commercial UNIX workstations (which usually employ simple framebuffers for graphics).

Your machine will need at least 4 megabytes of physical RAM, and 16 megabytes of virtual RAM (for example, 8 megs physical and 8 megs swap). Remember that the more physical RAM that you have, the less that the system will swap to and from disk when memory is low. Because swapping is inherently slow (disks are very slow compared to memory), having 8 megabytes of RAM or more is necessary to run XFree86 comfortably. A system with 4 megabytes of physical RAM could run *much* (up to 10 times) more slowly than one with 8 megs or more.

5.1.2 Installing XFree86

The Linux binary distribution of XFree86 can be found on a number of FTP sites. On `sunsite.unc.edu`, it is found in the directory `/pub/Linux/X11`. (As of the time of this writing, the current version is 3.1; newer versions are released periodically).

It's quite likely that you obtained XFree86 as part of a Linux distribution, in which case downloading the software separately is not necessary.

If you are downloading XFree86 directly, This table lists the files in the XFree86-3.1 distribution.

One of the following servers is required:

File	Description
`XF86-3.1-8514.tar.gz`	Server for 8514-based boards.
`XF86-3.1-AGX.tar.gz`	Server for AGX-based boards.
`XF86-3.1-Mach32.tar.gz`	Server for Mach32-based boards.
`XF86-3.1-Mach8.tar.gz`	Server for Mach8-based boards.
`XF86-3.1-Mono.tar.gz`	Server for monochrome video modes.
`XF86-3.1-P9000.tar.gz`	Server for P9000-based boards.
`XF86-3.1-S3.tar.gz`	Server for S3-based boards.
`XF86-3.1-SVGA.tar.gz`	Server for Super VGA-based boards.
`XF86-3.1-VGA16.tar.gz`	Server for VGA/EGA-based boards.
`XF86-3.1-W32.tar.gz`	Server for ET4000/W32-based boards.

All of the following files are required:

File	Description
`XF86-3.1-bin.tar.gz`	The rest of the X11R6 binaries.
`XF86-3.1-cfg.tar.gz`	Config files for `xdm`, `xinit` and `fs`.
`XF86-3.1-doc.tar.gz`	Documentation and manpages.
`XF86-3.1-inc.tar.gz`	Include files.
`XF86-3.1-lib.tar.gz`	Shared X libraries and support files.
`XF86-3.1-fnt.tar.gz`	Basic fonts.

The following files are optional:

File	Description
XF86-3.1-ctrb.tar.gz	Selected contrib programs.
XF86-3.1-extra.tar.gz	Extra XFree86 servers and binaries.
XF86-3.1-lkit.tar.gz	Server linkkit for customization.
XF86-3.1-fnt75.tar.gz	75-dpi screen fonts.
XF86-3.1-fnt100.tar.gz	100-dpi screen fonts.
XF86-3.1-fntbig.tar.gz	Large Kanji and other fonts.
XF86-3.1-fntscl.tar.gz	Scaled fonts (Speedo, Type1).
XF86-3.1-man.tar.gz	Manual pages.
XF86-3.1-pex.tar.gz	PEX binaries, includes and libraries.
XF86-3.1-slib.tar.gz	Static X libraries and support files.
XF86-3.1-usrbin.tar.gz	Daemons which reside in /usr/bin.
XF86-3.1-xdmshdw.tar.gz	Shadow password version of xdm.

The XFree86 directory should contain README files and installation notes for the current version.

All that is required to install XFree86 is to obtain the above files, create the directory /usr/X11R6 (as root), and unpack the files from /usr/X11R6 with a command such as:

```
# gzip –dc XF86-3.1-bin.tar.gz | tar xfB –
```

Remember that these tar files are packed relative to /usr/X11R6, so it's important to unpack the files there.

After unpacking the files, you first need to link the file /usr/X11R6/bin/X to the server that you're using. For example, if you wish to use the SVGA color server, /usr/bin/X11/X should be linked to /usr/X11R6/bin/XF86_SVGA. If you wish to use the monochrome server instead, relink this file to XF86_MONO with the command

```
# ln –sf /usr/X11R6/bin/XF86_MONO  /usr/X11R6/bin/X
```

The same holds true if you are using one of the other servers.

If you aren't sure which server to use, or don't know your video card chipset, you can run the SuperProbe program found in /usr/X11R6/bin (included in the XF86-3.1-bin listed above). This program will attempt to determine your video chipset type and other information; write down its output for later reference.

You need to make sure that /usr/X11R6/bin is on your path. This can be done by editing your system default /etc/profile or /etc/csh.login (based on the shell that you, or other users on your system, use). Or you can simply add the directory to your personal path by modifying /etc/.bashrc or /etc/.cshrc, based on your shell.

You also need to make sure that **/usr/X11R6/lib** can be located by ld.so, the runtime linker. To do this, add the line

```
/usr/X11R6/lib
```

to the file /etc/ld.so.conf, and run /sbin/ldconfig, as root.

5.1.3 Configuring XFree86

Setting up XFree86 is not difficult in most cases. However, if you happen to be using hardware for which drivers are under development, or wish to obtain the best performance or resolution from an accelerated graphics card, configuring XFree86 can be somewhat time-consuming.

In this section we will describe how to create and edit the XF86Config file, which configures the XFree86 server. In many cases it is best to start out with a "basic" XFree86 configuration, one which uses a low resolution, such as 640x480, which should be supported on all video cards and monitor types. Once you have XFree86 working at a lower, standard resolution, you can tweak the configuration to exploit the capabilities of your video hardware. The idea is that you want to know that XFree86 works at all on your system, and that something isn't wrong with your installation, before attempting the sometimes difficult task of setting up XFree86 for real use.

In addition to the information listed here, you should read the following documentation:

- The XFree86 documentation in **/usr/X11R6/lib/X11/doc** (contained within the **XFree86-3.1-doc** package). You should especially see the file README.Config, which is an XFree86 configuration tutorial.

- Several video chipsets have separate **README** files in the above directory (such as README.Cirrus and README.S3). Read one of these if applicable.

- The man page for **XFree86**.

- The man page for **XF86Config**.

- The man page for the particular server that you are using (such as XF86_SVGA or XF86_S3).

The main XFree86 configuration file is /usr/X11R6/lib/X11/XF86Config. This file contains information on your mouse, video card parameters, and so on. The file XF86Config.eg is provided with the XFree86 distribution as an example. Copy this file to XF86Config and edit it as a starting point.

The XF86Config man page explains the format of this file in detail. Read this man page now, if you have not done so already.

We are going to present a sample XF86Config file, piece by piece. This file may not look exactly like the sample file included in the XFree86 distribution, but the structure is the same.

◇   Note that the XF86Config file format may change with each version of XFree86; this information is only valid for XFree86 version 3.1.

◇   Also, you should not simply copy the configuration file listed here to your own system and attempt to use it. Attempting to use a configuration file which does not correspond to your hardware could drive the monitor at a frequency which is too high for it; there have been reports of monitors (especially fixed-frequency monitors) being damaged or destroyed by using an incorrectly configured XF86Config file. The bottom line is this: Make absolutely sure that your XF86Config file corresponds to your hardware before you attempt to use it.

Each section of the XF86Config file is surrounded by the pair of lines Section "⟨section-name⟩"...EndSection. The first part of the XF86Config file is Files, which looks like this:

```
    Section "Files"
        RgbPath      "/usr/X11R6/lib/X11/rgb"
        FontPath     "/usr/X11R6/lib/X11/fonts/misc/"
        FontPath     "/usr/X11R6/lib/X11/fonts/75dpi/"
    EndSection
```

The RgbPath line sets the path to the X11R6 RGB color database, and each FontPath line sets the path to a directory containing X11 fonts. In general you shouldn't have to modify these lines; just be sure that there is a FontPath entry for each font type that you have installed (that is, for each directory in /usr/X11R6/lib/X11/fonts).

The next section is ServerFlags, which specifies several global flags for the server. In general this section is empty.

```
Section "ServerFlags"
# Uncomment this to cause a core dump at the spot where a signal is
# received.  This may leave the console in an unusable state, but may
# provide a better stack trace in the core dump to aid in debugging
#    NoTrapSignals

# Uncomment this to disable the <Crtl><Alt><BS> server abort sequence
#    DontZap
EndSection
```

Here, we have all lines within the section commented out.

The next section is **Keyboard**. This should be fairly intuitive.

```
Section "Keyboard"
    Protocol    "Standard"
    AutoRepeat  500 5
    ServerNumLock
EndSection
```

Other options are available as well—see the **XF86Config** file if you wish to modify the keyboard configuration. The above should work for most systems.

The next section is **Pointer** which specifies parameters for the mouse device.

```
Section "Pointer"

    Protocol    "MouseSystems"
    Device      "/dev/mouse"

# Baudrate and SampleRate are only for some Logitech mice
#    BaudRate   9600
#    SampleRate 150

# Emulate3Buttons is an option for 2-button Microsoft mice
#    Emulate3Buttons

# ChordMiddle is an option for some 3-button Logitech mice
#    ChordMiddle

EndSection
```

The only options that you should concern yourself with now are **Protocol** and **Device**. **Protocol** specifies the mouse *protocol* that your mouse uses (not the make or brand of mouse). Valid types for `Protocol` (under Linux—there are other options available for other operating systems) are:

- BusMouse

- Logitech

- Microsoft

- MMSeries

- Mouseman

- MouseSystems

- PS/2

- MMHitTab

BusMouse should be used for the Logitech busmouse. Note that older Logitech mice should use `Logitech`, but newer Logitech mice use either `Microsoft` or `Mouseman` protocols. This is a case in which the protocol doesn't necessarily have anything to do with the make of the mouse.

`Device` specifies the device file where the mouse can be accessed. On most Linux systems, this is `/dev/mouse`. `/dev/mouse` is usually a link to the appropriate serial port (such as `/dev/cua0`) for serial mice, or to the appropriate busmouse device for busmice. At any rate, be sure that the device file listed in `Device` exists.

The next section is `Monitor`, which specifies the characteristics of your monitor. As with other sections in the `XF86Config` file, there may be more than one `Monitor` section. This is useful if you have multiple monitors connected to a system, or use the same `XF86Config` file under multiple hardware configurations. In general, though, you will need a single `Monitor` section.

```
Section "Monitor"

    Identifier  "CTX 5468 NI"

    # These values are for a CTX 5468NI only! Don't attempt to use
    # them with your monitor (unless you have this model)

    Bandwidth   60
    HorizSync   30-38,47-50
```

```
VertRefresh  50-90

# Modes: Name        dotclock  horiz                 vert

ModeLine "640x480"  25        640 664 760 800       480 491 493 525
ModeLine "800x600"  36        800 824 896 1024      600 601 603 625
ModeLine "1024x768" 65        1024 1088 1200 1328   768 783 789 818

EndSection
```

The `Identifier` line is used to give an arbitrary name to the `Monitor` entry. This can be any string; you will use it to refer to the `Monitor` entry later in the `XF86Config` file.

they are listed below.

`HorizSync` specifies the valid horizontal sync frequencies for your monitor, in kHz. If you have a multisync monitor, this can be a range of values (or several comma-separated ranges), as seen above. If you have a fixed-frequency monitor, this will be a list of discrete values, such as:

```
HorizSync    31.5, 35.2, 37.9, 35.5, 48.95
```

Your monitor manual should list these values in the technical specifications section. If you do not have this information available, you should either contact the manufacturer or vendor of your monitor to obtain it. There are other sources of information, as well;

`VertRefresh` specifies the valid vertical refresh rates (or vertical synchronization frequencies) for your monitor, in Hz. Like `HorizSync` this can be a range or a list of discrete values; your monitor manual should list them.

`HorizSync` and `VertRefresh` are used only to double-check that the monitor resolutions that you specify are in valid ranges. This is to reduce the chance that you will damage your monitor by attempting to drive it at a frequency for which it was not designed.

The `ModeLine` directive is used to specify a single resolution mode for your monitor. The format of `ModeLine` is

```
ModeLine ⟨name⟩ ⟨clock⟩ ⟨horiz-values⟩ ⟨vert-values⟩
```

⟨name⟩ is an arbitrary string, which you will use to refer to the resolution mode later in the file. ⟨dot-clock⟩ is the driving clock frequency, or "dot clock" associated with the resolution mode. A dot clock is usually specified in MHz, and is the rate at which the video card must send pixels to the monitor at this resolution. ⟨*horiz-values*⟩ and ⟨*vert-values*⟩ are four numbers each which specify when the electron gun of the monitor should fire, and when the horizontal and vertical sync pulses fire during a sweep.

How can you determine the `ModeLine` values for your monitor? The file `VideoModes.doc`, included with the XFree86 distribution, describes in detail how to determine these values for each resolution mode that your monitor supports. First of all, ⟨*clock*⟩ must correspond to one of the dot clock values that your video card can produce. Later in the `XF86Config` file you will specify these clocks; you can only use video modes which have a ⟨*clock*⟩ value supported by your video card.

There are two files included in the XFree86 distribution which may include `ModeLine` data for your monitor. These files are `modeDB.txt` and `Monitors`, both of which are found in `/usr/X11R6/lib/X11/doc`.

You should start with `ModeLine` values for the VESA standard monitor timings, which most monitors support. `modeDB.txt` includes timing values for VESA standard resolutions. In that file, you will see entries such as

```
# 640x480@60Hz Non-Interlaced mode
# Horizontal Sync = 31.5kHz
# Timing: H=(0.95us, 3.81us, 1.59us), V=(0.35ms, 0.064ms, 1.02ms)
#
# name          clock   horizontal timing     vertical timing      flags
  "640x480"     25.175  640  664  760  800    480  491  493  525
```

This is a VESA standard timing for a 640x480 video mode. It uses a dot clock of 25.175, which your video card must support to use this mode (more on this later). To include this entry in the `XF86Config` file, you'd use the line

```
ModeLine "640x480" 25.175  640 664 760 800   480 491 493 525
```

Note that the ⟨*name*⟩ argument to `ModeLine` (in this case `"640x480"`) is an arbitrary string—the convention is to name the mode after the resolution, but ⟨*name*⟩ can technically be anything descriptive which describes the mode to you.

For each `ModeLine` used the server will check that the specifications for the mode fall within the range of values specified with `Bandwidth`, `HorizSync` and `VertRefresh`. If they do not, the server will complain when you attempt to start up X (more on this later). For one thing, the dot clock used by the mode should not be greater than the value used for `Bandwidth`. (However, in many cases it is safe to use modes with a slightly higher bandwidth than your monitor can support.)

If the VESA standard timings do not work for you (you'll know after trying to use them later) then the files `modeDB.txt` and `Monitors` include specific mode values for many monitor types. You can create `ModeLine` entries from the values found in those two files as well. Be sure to only use values for the specific model of monitor that you have. Note that many 14 and 15-inch monitors cannot support higher resolution modes, and often resolutions of 1024x768 at low dot clocks. This means that if you can't find high resolution modes for your monitor in these files, then your monitor probably does not support those resolution modes.

If you are completely at a loss, and can't find working `ModeLine` values for your monitor, you can follow the instructions in the `VideoModes.doc` file included in the XFree86 distribution to generate `ModeLine` values from the specifications listed in your monitor's manual. While your mileage will certainly vary when attempting to generate `ModeLine` values by hand, this is a good place to look if you can't find the values that you need. `VideoModes.doc` also describes the format of the `ModeLine` directive and other aspects of the XFree86 server in gory detail.

Lastly, if you do obtain `ModeLine` values which are almost, but not quite, right, then it may be possible to simply modify the values slightly to obtain the desired result. For example, if while running XFree86 the image on the monitor is shifted slightly, or seems to "roll", you can follow the instructions in the `VideoModes.doc` file to try to fix these values. Also, be sure to check the knobs and controls on the monitor itself! In many cases it is necessary to change the horizontal or vertical size of the display after starting up XFree86 in order for the image to be centered and be of the appropriate size. Having these controls on the front of the monitor can certainly make life easier.

◇ You shouldn't use monitor timing values or `ModeLine` values for monitors other than the model that you own. If you attempt to drive the monitor at a frequency for which it was not designed, you can damage or even destroy it.

The next section of the `XF86Config` file is `Device`, which specifies parameters for your video card. Here is an example.

```
Section "Device"
        Identifier "#9 GXE 64"

        # Nothing yet; we fill in these values later.

EndSection
```

This section defines properties for a particular video card. `Identifier` is an arbitrary string describing the card; you will use this string to refer to the card later.

Initially, you don't need to include anything in the `Device` section, except for `Identifier`. This is because we will be using the X server itself to probe for the properties of the video card, and entering them into the `Device` section later. The XFree86 server is capable of probing for the video chipset, clocks, RAMDAC, and amount of video RAM on the board.

Before we do this, however, we need to finish writing the `XF86Config` file. The next section is `Screen`, which specifies the monitor/video card combination to use for a particular server.

```
Section "Screen"
    Driver      "Accel"
    Device      "#9 GXE 64"
    Monitor     "CTX 5468 NI"
    Subsection "Display"
        Depth      16
        Modes      "1024x768" "800x600" "640x480"
        ViewPort   0 0
        Virtual    1024 768
    EndSubsection
EndSection
```

The `Driver` line specifies the X server that you will be using. The value values for `Driver` are:

- `Accel`: For the XF86_S3, XF86_Mach32, XF86_Mach8, XF86_8514, XF86_P9000, XF86_AGX, and XF86_W32 servers;

- `SVGA`: For the XF86_SVGA server;

- `VGA16`: For the XF86_VGA16 server;

- `VGA2`: For the XF86_Mono server;

- `Mono`: For the non-VGA monochrome drivers in the XF86_Mono and XF86_VGA16 servers.

You should be sure that `/usr/X11R6/bin/X` is a symbolic link to the server that you are using.

The `Device` line specifies the `Identifier` of the `Device` section corresponding to the video card to use for this server. Above, we created a `Device` section with the line

```
Identifier "#9 GXE 64"
```

Therefore, we use `"#9 GXE 64"` on the `Device` line here.

Similarly, the `Monitor` line specifies the name of the `Monitor` section to be used with this server. Here, `"CTX 5468 NI"` is the `Identifier` used in the `Monitor` section described above.

`Subsection "Display"` defines several properties of the XFree86 server corresponding to your monitor/video card combination. The `XF86Config` file describes all of these options in detail; most of them are icing on the cake and not necessary to get the system working.

The options that you should know about are:

- `Depth`. Defines the number of color planes—the number of bits per pixel. Usually, `Depth` is set to 8. For the `VGA16` server, you would use a depth of 4, and for the monochrome server a depth of 1. If you are using an accelerated video card with enough memory to support more bits per pixel, you can set `Depth` to 16, 24, or 32. If you have problems with depths higher than 8, set it back to 8 and attempt to debug the problem later.

- `Modes`. This is the list of video mode names which have been defined using the `ModeLine` directive in the `Monitor` section. In the above section, we used `ModeLines` named `"1024x768"`, `"800x600"`, and `"640x48"0`. Therefore, we use a `Modes` line of

```
Modes    "1024x768" "800x600" "640x480"
```

The first mode listed on this line will be the default when XFree86 starts up. After XFree86 is running, you can switch between the modes listed here using the keys `ctrl`-`alt`-`numeric +` and `ctrl`-`alt`-`numeric -`.

It might be best, when initially configuring XFree86, to use lower resolution video modes, such as 640x480, which tend to work on most systems. Once you have the basic configuration working you can modify `XF86Config` to support higher resolutions.

- `Virtual`. Sets the virtual desktop size. XFree86 has the ability to use any additional memory on your video card to extend the size of your desktop.

When you move the mouse pointer to the edge of the display, the desktop will scroll, bringing the additional space into view. Therefore, even if you are running at a lower video resolution such as 800x600, you can set `Virtual` to the total resolution which your video card can support (a 1-megabyte video card can support 1024x768 at a depth of 8 bits per pixel; a 2-megabyte card 1280x1024 at depth 8, or 1024x768 at depth 16). Of course, the entire area will not be visible at once, but it can still be used.

The `Virtual` feature is a nice way to utilize the memory of your video card, but it is rather limited. If you want to use a true virtual desktop, we suggest using `fvwm`, or a similar window manager, instead. `fvwm` allows you to have rather large virtual desktops (implemented by hiding windows, and so forth, instead of actually storing the entire desktop in video memory at once). See the man pages for `fvwm` for more details about this; most Linux systems use `fvwm` by default.

- ViewPort. If you are using the `Virtual` option described above, `ViewPort` sets the coordinates of the upper-left-hand corner of the virtual desktop when XFree86 starts up. `Virtual 0 0` is often used; if this is unspecified then the desktop is centered on the virtual desktop display (which may be undesirable to you).

Many other options for this section exist; see the `XF86Config` man page for a complete description. In practice these other options are not necessary to get XFree86 initially working.

5.1.4   Filling in video card information

Your `XF86Config` file is now ready to go, with the exception of complete information on the video card. What we're going to do is use the X server to probe for the rest of this information, and fill it into `XF86Config`.

Instead of probing for this information with the X server, the `XF86Config` values for many cards are listed in the files `modeDB.txt`, `AccelCards`, and `Devices`. These files are all found in `/usr/X11R6/lib/X11/doc`. In addition, there are various `README` files for certain chipsets. You should look in these files for information on your video card, and use that information (the clock values, chipset type, and any options) in the `XF86Config` file. If any information is missing, you can probe for it as described here.

In these examples we will demonstrate configuration for a #9 GXE 64 video card, which uses the **XF86_S3** chipset. This card happens to be the one which the author uses, but the discussion here applies to any video card.

The first thing to do is to determine the video chipset used on the card. Running **SuperProbe** (found in `/usr/X11R6/bin`) will tell you this information, but you need to know the chipset name as it is known to the X server.

To do this, run the command

```
X -showconfig
```

This will give the chipset names known to your X server. (The man pages for each X server list these as well.) For example, with the accelerated **XF86_S3** server, we obtain:

```
XFree86 Version 3.1 / X Window System
(protocol Version 11, revision 0, vendor release 6000)
Operating System: Linux
Configured drivers:
  S3: accelerated server for S3 graphics adaptors (Patchlevel 0)
      mmio_928, s3_generic
```

The valid chipset names for this server are **mmio_928** and **s3_generic**. The XF86_S3 man page describes these chipsets and which videocards use them. In the case of the #9 GXE 64 video card, **mmio_928** is appropriate.

If you don't know which chipset to use, the X server can probe it for you. To do this, run the command

```
X -probeonly > /tmp/x.out 2>&1
```

if you use **bash** as your shell. If you use **csh**, try:

```
X -probeonly &> /tmp/x.out
```

You should run this command while the system is unloaded, that is, while no other activity is occurring on the system. This command will also probe for your video card dot clocks (as seen below), and system load can throw off this calculation.

The output from the above (in `/tmp/x.out` should contain lines such as the following:

```
XFree86 Version 3.1 / X Window System
(protocol Version 11, revision 0, vendor release 6000)
Operating System: Linux
Configured drivers:
  S3: accelerated server for S3 graphics adaptors (Patchlevel 0)
        mmio_928, s3_generic
```
Several lines deleted...
```
(--) S3: card type: 386/486 localbus
(--) S3: chipset:   864 rev. 0
(--) S3: chipset driver: mmio_928
```

Here, we see that the two valid chipsets for this server (in this case, XF86_S3) are
mmio_928 and s3_generic. The server probed for and found a video card using the
mmio_928 chipset.

In the Device section of the XF86Config file, add a Chipset line, containing the
name of the chipset as determined above. For example,

```
Section "Device"
        # We already had Identifier here...
        Identifier "#9 GXE 64"
        # Add this line:
        Chipset "mmio_928"
EndSection
```

Now we need to determine the driving clock frequencies used by the video card.
A driving clock frequency, or dot clock, is simply a rate at which the video card
can send pixels to the monitor. As we have seen, each monitor resolution has a
dot clock associated with it. Now we need to determine which dot clocks are made
available by the video card.

First you should look into the files (modeDB.txt, and so forth) mentioned above
and see if your card's clocks are listed there. The dot clocks will usually be a list of
8 or 16 values, all of which are in MHz. For example, when looking at modeDB.txt
we see an entry for the Cardinal ET4000 video board, which looks like this:

```
# chip    ram    virtual    clocks              default-mode  flags
  ET4000   1024   1024 768   25  28  38  36  40  45  32   0    "1024x768"
```

As we can see, the dot clocks for this card are 25, 28, 38, 36, 40, 45, 32, and 0 MHz.

In the `Devices` section of the `XF86Config` file, you should add a `Clocks` line containing the list of dot clocks for your card. For example, for the clocks above, we would add the line

```
Clocks 25 28 38 36 40 45 32 0
```

to the `Devices` section of the file, after `Chipset`. Note that the order of the clocks is important! Don't resort the list of clocks or remove duplicates.

If you cannot find the dot clocks associated with your card, the X server can probe for these as well. Using the `X -probeonly` command described above, the output should contain lines which look like the following:

```
(--) S3: clocks:  25.18  28.32  38.02  36.15  40.33  45.32  32.00  00.00
```

We could then add a `Clocks` line containing all of these values, as printed. You can use more than one `Clocks` line in `XF86Config` should all of the values (sometimes there are more than 8 clock values printed) not fit onto one line. Again, be sure to keep the list of clocks in order as they are printed.

Be sure that there is no `Clocks` line (or that it is commented out) in the `Devices` section of the file when using `X -probeonly` to probe for the clocks. If there is a `Clocks` line present, the server will *not* probe for the clocks—it will use the values given in `XF86Config`.

Note that some accelerated video boards use a programmable clock chip. (See the `XF86_Accel` man page for details; this generally applies to S3, AGX, and XGA-2 boards.) This chip essentially allows the X server to tell the card which dot clocks to use. If this is the case, then you may not find a list of dot clocks for the card in any of the above files. Or, the list of dot clocks printed when using `X -probeonly` will only contain one or two discrete clock values, with the rest being duplicates or zero.

For boards which use a programmable clock chip, you would use a `ClockChip` line, instead of a `Clocks` line, in your `XF86Config` file. `ClockChip` gives the name of the clock chip as used by the video card; the man pages for each server describe what these are. For example, in the file `README.S3`, we see that several S3-864 video cards use an "ICD2061A" clock chip, and that we should use the line

```
ClockChip "icd2061a"
```

instead of `Clocks` in the `XF86Config` file. As with `Clocks`, this line should go in
the `Devices` section, after `Chipset`.

Similarly, some accelerated cards require you to specify the RAMDAC chip type
in the `XF86Config` file, using a `Ramdac` line. The `XF86_Accel` man page describes
this option. Usually, the X server will correctly probe for the RAMDAC.

Some video card types require you to specify several options in the `Devices`
section of `XF86Config`. These options will be described in the man page for your
server, as well as in the various files (such as `README.cirrus` or `README.S3`. These
options are enabled using the `Option` line. For example, the #9 GXE 64 card
requires two options:

```
Option "number_nine"
Option "dac_8_bit"
```

Usually, the X server will work without these options, but they are necessary
to obtain the best performance. There are too many such options to list here,
and they each depend on the particular video card being used. If you must
use one of these options, fear not—the X server man pages and various files in
`/usr/X11R6/lib/X11/doc` will tell you what they are.

So, when you're finished, you should end up with a `Devices` section which looks
something like this:

```
Section "Device"
        # Device section for the #9 GXE 64 only !
        Identifier "#9 GXE 64"
        Chipset "mmio_928"
        ClockChip "icd2061a"
        Option "number_nine"
        Option "dac_8_bit"
EndSection
```

Most video cards will require a `Clocks` line, instead of `ClockChip`, as described
above. The above `Device` entry is only valid for a particular video card, the #9
GXE 64. It is given here only as an example.

There are other options that you can include in the `Devices` entry. Check the
X server man pages for the gritty details, but the above should suffice for most
systems.

5.1.5   Running XFree86

With your `XF86Config` file configured, you're ready to fire up the X server and give it a spin. First, be sure that `/usr/X11R6/bin` is on your path.

The command to start up XFree86 is

```
startx
```

This is a front-end to `xinit` (in case you're used to using `xinit` on other UNIX systems).

This command will start the X server and run the commands found in the file `.xinitrc` in your home directory. `.xinitrc` is just a shell script containing X clients to run. If this file does not exist, the system default `/usr/X11R6/lib/X11/xinit/xinitrc` will be used.

A standard `.xinitrc` file looks like this:

```
#!/bin/sh

xterm -fn 7x13bold -geometry 80x32+10+50 &
xterm -fn 9x15bold -geometry 80x34+30-10 &
oclock -geometry 70x70-7+7 &
xsetroot -solid midnightblue &

exec twm
```

This script will start up two `xterm` clients, an `oclock`, and set the root window (background) color to `midnightblue`. It will then start up `twm`, the window manager. Note that `twm` is executed with the shell's `exec` statement; this causes the `xinit` process to be replaced with `twm`. Once the `twm` process exits, the X server will shut down. You can cause `twm` to exit by using the root menus: depress mouse button 1 on the desktop background—this will display a pop up menu which will allow you to `Exit Twm`.

Be sure that the last command in `.xinitrc` is started with `exec`, and that it is not placed into the background (no ampersand on the end of the line). Otherwise the X server will shut down as soon as it has started the clients in the `.xinitrc` file.

Alternately, you can exit X by pressing `ctrl`-`alt`-`backspace` in combination. This will kill the X server directly, exiting the window system.

The above is a very, very simple desktop configuration. Many wonderful programs and configurations are available with a bit of work on your `.xinitrc` file. For example, the `fvwm` window manager will provide a virtual desktop, and you can customize colors, fonts, window sizes and positions, and so forth to your heart's content. Although the X Window System might appear to be simplistic at first, it is extremely powerful once you customize it for yourself.

If you are new to the X Window System environment, we strongly suggest picking up a book such as *The X Window System: A User's Guide*. Using and configuring X is far too in-depth to cover here. See the man pages for `xterm`, `oclock`, and `twm` for clues on getting started.

5.1.6   Running into trouble

Often, something will not be quite right when you initially fire up the X server. This is almost always caused by a problem in your `XF86Config` file. Usually, the monitor timing values are off, or the video card dot clocks set incorrectly. If your display seems to roll, or the edges are fuzzy, this is a clear indication that the monitor timing values or dot clocks are wrong. Also be sure that you are correctly specifying your video card chipset, as well as other options for the `Device` section of `XF86Config`. Be absolutely certain that you are using the right X server and that `/usr/X11R6/bin/X` is a symbolic link to this server.

If all else fails, try to start X "bare"; that is, use a command such as:

```
X > /tmp/x.out 2>&1
```

You can then kill the X server (using the `ctrl` `alt` `backspace` key combination) and examine the contents of `/tmp/x.out`. The X server will report any warnings or errors—for example, if your video card doesn't have a dot clock corresponding to a mode supported by your monitor.

The file `VideoModes.doc` included in the XFree86 distribution contains many hints for tweaking the values in your `XF86Config` file.

Remember that you can use `ctrl` `alt` `numeric +` and `ctrl` `alt` `numeric -` to switch between the video modes listed on the `Modes` line of the `Screen` section of `XF86Config`. If the highest resolution mode doesn't look right, try switching to lower resolutions. This will let you know, at least, that those parts of your X configuration are working correctly.

Also, check the vertical and horizontal size/hold knobs on your monitor. In many cases it is necessary to adjust these when starting up X. For example, if the display seems to be shifted slightly to one side, you can usually correct this using the monitor controls.

The USENET newsgroup `comp.windows.x.i386unix` is devoted to discussions about XFree86. It might be a good idea to watch that newsgroup for postings relating to your video configuration—you might run across someone with the same problems as your own.

5.2   Accessing MS-DOS Files

If, for some twisted and bizarre reason, you would have need to access files from MS-DOS, it's quite easily done under Linux.

The usual way to access MS-DOS files is to mount an MS-DOS partition or floppy under Linux, allowing you to access the files directly through the filesystem. For example, if you have an MS-DOS floppy in `/dev/fd0`, the command

        # *mount -t msdos /dev/fd0 /mnt*

will mount it under `/mnt`. See Section 4.6.2 for more information on mounting floppies.

You can also mount an MS-DOS partition of your hard drive for access under Linux. If you have an MS-DOS partition on `/dev/hda1`, the command

        # *mount -t msdos /dev/hda1 /mnt*

will mount it. Be sure to `umount` the partition when you're done using it. You can have your MS-DOS partitions automatically mounted at boot time if you include entries for them in `/etc/fstab`; see Section 4.8 for details. For example, the following line in `/etc/fstab` will mount an MS-DOS partition on `/dev/hda1` on the directory `/dos`.

        /dev/hda1   /dos   msdos   defaults

The `Mtools` software may also be used to access MS-DOS files. For example, the commands `mcd`, `mdir`, and `mcopy` all behave as their MS-DOS counterparts. If you installed `Mtools`, there should be man pages available for these commands.

Accessing MS-DOS files is one thing; running MS-DOS programs from Linux is another. There is an MS-DOS Emulator under development for Linux. It can be retrieved from a number of locations, including the various Linux FTP sites (see Appendix B for details). The MS-DOS Emulator is reportedly powerful enough to run a number of applications, including WordPerfect, from Linux. However, Linux and MS-DOS are vastly different operating systems. The power of any MS-DOS emulator under UNIX is somewhat limited.

In addition, work is underway on a Microsoft Windows emulator to run under X Windows. Watch the newsgroups and FTP sites for more information.

5.3   Networking with TCP/IP

Linux supports a full implementation of the TCP/IP (Transport Control Protocol/Internet Protocol) networking protocols. TCP/IP has become the most successful mechanism for networking computers worldwide. With Linux and an Ethernet card, you can network your machine to a local area network, or (with the proper network connections), to the Internet—the worldwide TCP/IP network.

Hooking up a small LAN of UNIX machines is easy. It simply requires an Ethernet controller in each machine and the appropriate Ethernet cables and other hardware. Or, if your business or university provides access to the Internet, you can easily add your Linux machine to this network.

The current implementation of TCP/IP and related protocols for Linux is called "NET-2". This has no relationship to the so-called NET-2 release of BSD UNIX; instead, "NET-2" in this context means the second implementation of TCP/IP for Linux.

Linux NET-2 also supports SLIP—Serial Line Internet Protocol. SLIP allows you to have dialup Internet access using a modem. If your business or university provides SLIP access, you can dial in to the SLIP server and put your machine on the Internet over the phone line. Alternately, if your Linux machine also has Ethernet access to the Internet, you can set up your Linux box as a SLIP server.

For complete information on setting up TCP/IP under Linux, we encourage you to read the Linux NET-2 HOWTO, available via anonymous FTP from sunsite.unc.edu. The NET-2 HOWTO is a complete guide to configuring TCP/IP, including Ethernet and SLIP connections, under Linux. The Linux Ethernet HOWTO is a related document that describes configuration of various Ethernet card drivers for Linux. The *Linux Network Administrator's Guide*, from the Linux

Documentation Project, is also available. See Appendix A for more information on these documents.

Also of interest is the book *TCP/IP Network Administration*, by Craig Hunt. It contains complete information on using and configuring TCP/IP on UNIX systems.

5.3.1 Hardware Requirements

You can use Linux TCP/IP without any networking hardware at all—configuring "loopback" mode allows you to talk to yourself. This is necessary for some applications and games which use the "loopback" network device.

However, if you want to use Linux with an Ethernet TCP/IP network, you will need one of the following Ethernet cards: 3Com 3C503, 3C505, 3C507, 3C509/3C509B (ISA) / 3C579 (EISA); AMD LANCE (79C960) / PCnet-ISA/PCI (AT1500, HP J2405A, NE1500/NE2100); AT&T GIS WaveLAN; Allied Telesis AT1700; Ansel Communications AC3200 EISA; Apricot Xen-II; Cabletron E21xx; DEC DE425 (EISA) / DE434/DE435 (PCI); DEC DEPCA and EtherWORKS; HP PCLAN (27245 and 27xxx series); HP PCLAN PLUS (27247B and 27252A); HP 10/100VG PCLAN (ISA/EISA/PCI); Intel EtherExpress and EtherExpress Pro; NE2000/NE1000 (be careful with clones); New Media Ethernet; Racal-Interlan NI5210 (i82586 Ethernet chip); Racal-Interlan NI6510 (am7990 lance chip) - doesn't work with more than 16 megs RAM; PureData PDUC8028, PDI8023; SEEQ 8005; SMC Ultra; Schneider & Koch G16; Western Digital WD80x3; Zenith Z-Note / IBM ThinkPad 300 built-in adapter; AT-Lan-Tec/RealTek parallel port adapter; D-Link DE600/DE620 parallel port adapter.

See the Linux Ethernet HOWTO for a more complete discussion of Linux Ethernet hardware compatibility.

Linux also supports SLIP and PPP, which allows you to use a modem to access the Internet over the phone line. In this case, you'll need a modem compatible with your SLIP server—most servers require a 14.4bps V.32bis modem.

5.3.2 Configuring TCP/IP on your system

In this section we're going to discuss how to configure an Ethernet TCP/IP connection on your system. Note that this method should work for many systems, but certainly not all. This discussion should be enough to get you on the right path to configuring the network parameters of your machine, but there are numerous caveats and fine details not mentioned here. We direct you to the *Linux Network Administrators' Guide* and the NET-2-HOWTO for more information.[3]

First of all, we assume that you have a Linux system that has the TCP/IP software installed. This includes basic clients such as `telnet` and `ftp`, system administration commands such as `ifconfig` and `route` (found in `/sbin`), and networking configuration files (such as `/etc/hosts`). The other Linux-related networking documents described above explain how to go about installing the Linux networking software if you do not have it already.

We also assume that your kernel has been configured and compiled with TCP/IP support enabled. See Section 4.7 for information on compiling your kernel. To enable networking, you must answer "yes" to the appropriate questions during the `make config` step, and rebuild the kernel.

Once this has been done, you must modify a number of configuration files used by NET-2. For the most part this is a simple procedure. The various TCP/IP configuration files and support programs can be found in `/etc` and `/sbin` respectively.

The following information applies primarily to Ethernet connections. If you're planning to use SLIP, read this section to understand the concepts, and follow the SLIP-specific instructions in the following section, if you're planing to use PPP, follow the instructions in the PPP section.

5.3.2.1   Your network configuration

Before you can configure TCP/IP, you need to determine the following information about your network setup. In most cases, your local network administrator can provide you with this information.

- IP address. This is the unique machine address in dotted-decimal format. An example is 128.253.153.54. Your network administrator will provide you with this number.

  If you're only configuring loopback mode (i.e. no SLIP, no ethernet card, just TCP/IP connections to your own machine) then your IP address is 127.0.0.1.

- Your network mask ("netmask"). This is a dotted quad, similar to the IP address, which determines which portion of the IP address specifies the sub-network number, and which portion specifies the host on that subnet. (If

---

[3]Some of this information is adapted from the NET-2-HOWTO by Terry Dawson and Matt Welsh.

you're shaky on these TCP/IP networking terms, we suggest reading some introductory material on network administration.) The network mask is a pattern of bits, which when overlayed onto an address on your network, will tell you which subnet that address lives on. This is very important for routing, and if you find, for example, that you can happily talk to people outside your network, but not to some people within your network, there is a good chance that you have an incorrect mask specified.

Your network administrators will have chosen the netmask when the network was designed, and therefore they should be able to supply you with the correct mask to use. Most networks are class C subnetworks which use 255.255.255.0 as their netmask. Other Class B networks use 255.255.0.0. The NET-2 code will automatically select a mask that assumes no subnetting as a default if you do not specify one.

This applies as well to the loopback port. Since the loopback port's address is always 127.0.0.1, the netmask for this port is always 255.0.0.0. You can either specify this explicitly or rely on the default mask.

- Your network address. This is your IP address masked bitwise-ANDed the netmask. For example, if your netmask is 255.255.255.0, and your IP address is 128.253.154.32, your network address is 128.253.154.0. With a netmask of 255.255.0.0, this would be 128.253.0.0.

If you're only using loopback, you don't have a network address.

- Your broadcast address. The broadcast address is used to broadcast packets to every machine on your subnet. Therefore, if the host number of machines on your subnet is given by the last byte of the IP address (netmask 255.255.255.0), your broadcast address will be your network address ORed with 0.0.0.255.

For example, if your IP address is 128.253.154.32, and your netmask is 255.255.255.0, your broadcast address is 128.253.154.255.

Note that for historical reasons, some networks are setup to use the network address as the broadcast address, if you have any doubt, check with your network administrators. (In many cases, it will suffice to duplicate the network configuration of other machines on your subnet, substituting your own IP address, of course.)

If you're only using loopback, you don't have a broadcast address.

- Your gateway address. This is the address of the machine which is your "gateway" to the outside world (i.e. machines not on your subnet). In many cases the gateway machine has an IP address identical to yours but with a ".1"

as its host address; e.g., if your IP address is 128.253.154.32, your gateway
might be 128.253.154.1. Your network admins will provide you with the IP
address of your gateway.

In fact, you may have multiple gateways. A *gateway* is simply a machine that
lives on two different networks (has IP addresses on different subnets), and
routes packets between them. Many networks have a single gateway to "the
outside world" (the network directly adjacent to your own), but in some cases
you will have multiple gateways—one for each adjacent network.

If you're only using loopback, you don't have a gateway address. The same is
true if your network is isolated from all others.

- Your nameserver address. Most machines on the net have a name server
  which translates hostnames into IP addresses for them. Your network admins
  will tell you the address of your name server. You can also run a server on
  your own machine by running **named**, in which case the nameserver address is
  127.0.0.1. Unless you absolutely *must* run your own name server, we suggest
  using the one provided to you on the network (if any). Configuration of **named**
  is another issue altogether; our priority at this point is to get you talking to
  the network. You can deal with name resolution issues later.

  If you're only using loopback, you don't have a nameserver address.

SLIP or PPP users: You may or may not require any of the above information,
except for a nameserver address. When using SLIP or PPP, your IP address is usually determined in one of two ways: Either (a) you have a "static" IP address, which
is the same every time you connect to the network, or (b) you have a "dynamic" IP
address, which is allocated from a pool available addresses when you connect to the
server. In the following section on SLIP or PPP configuration covers this in more
detail.

NET-2 supports full routing, multiple routes, subnetworking , the whole nine
yards. The above describes most basic TCP/IP configurations. Yours may be quite
different: when in doubt, consult your local network gurus and check out the man
pages for **route** and **ifconfig**. Configuring TCP/IP networks is very much beyond
the scope of this book; the above should be enough to get most people started.

5.3.2.2   About the netconfig utility

Slackware includes a built in script 'netconfig' that can be found in the /sbin
directory. This script will help the novice user in easily setting up all the TCP/IP

configuration files that are mentioned in section called Configuring TCP/IP on your
system. The script will prompt you for basic configuration All of the

5.3.2.3 The networking `rc` files

`rc` files are systemwide configuration scripts executed at boot time by `init`, which
start up all of the basic system daemons (such as `sendmail`, `cron`, etc.) and configure things such as the network parameters, system hostname, and so on. `rc` files
are found in the directory `/etc/rc.d`.

Here, we're going to describe the `rc` files used to configure TCP/IP. There are
two of them: `rc.inet1` and `rc.inet2`. `rc.inet1` is used to configure the basic
network parameters (such as IP addresses and routing information) and `rc.inet2`
fires up the TCP/IP daemons (`telnetd`, `ftpd`, and so forth).

`rc.inet1` configures the basic network interface. This includes your IP and
network address, and the routing table information for your network. The routing tables are used to route outgoing (and incoming) network datagrams to other
machines. On most simple configurations, you have three routes: One for sending
packets to your own machine, another for sending packets to other machines on
your network, and another for sending packets to machines outside of your network (through the gateway machine). Two programs are used to configure these
parameters: `ifconfig` and `route`. Both of these are found in `/sbin`.

`ifconfig` is used for configuring the network device interface with the parameters that it requires to function, such as the IP address, network mask, broadcast
address and the like. `route` is used to create and modify entries in the routing
table.

For most configurations, an `rc.inet1` file that looks like the following should
work. You will, of course, have to edit this for your own system. Do *not* use the
sample IP and network addresses listed here for your own system; they correspond
to an actual machine on the Internet.

```
#!/bin/sh
# This is /etc/rc.d/rc.inet1 -- Configure the TCP/IP interfaces

# First, configure the loopback device

HOSTNAME=`hostname`

/etc/ifconfig lo 127.0.0.1 # uses default netmask 255.0.0.0
```

```
/etc/route add 127.0.0.1 # a route to point to the loopback
                         # device


# Next, configure the ethernet device. If you're only using loopback or
# SLIP, comment out the rest of these lines.


# Edit for your setup.
IPADDR="128.253.154.32"      # REPLACE with YOUR IP address
NETMASK="255.255.255.0"      # REPLACE with YOUR netmask
NETWORK="128.253.154.0"      # REPLACE with YOUR network address
BROADCAST="128.253.154.255"  # REPLACE with YOUR broadcast
                             # address, if you have one. If not,
                             # leave blank and edit below.
GATEWAY="128.253.154.1"      # REPLACE with YOUR gateway address!


/etc/ifconfig eth0 ${IPADDR} netmask ${NETMASK} broadcast ${BROADCAST}


# If you don't have a broadcast address, change the above line to just:
# /etc/ifconfig eth0 ${IPADDR} netmask ${NETMASK}


/etc/route add ${NETWORK}


# The following is only necessary if you have a gateway; that is, your
# network is connected to the outside world.
/etc/route add default gw ${GATEWAY} metric 1


# End of Ethernet Configuration
```

Again, you may have to tweak this file somewhat to get it to work. The above should be sufficient for the majority of simple network configurations, but certainly not all.

rc.inet2 starts up various servers used by the TCP/IP suite. The most important of these is inetd. inetd sits in the background and listens to various network ports. When a machine tries to make a connection to a certain port (for example, the incoming telnet port), inetd forks off a copy of the appropriate daemon for that port (in the case of the telnet port, inetd starts in.telnetd). This is simpler than running many separate, standalone daemons (e.g., individual copies of telnetd, ftpd, and so forth)—inetd starts up the daemons only when they are needed.

syslogd is the system logging daemon—it accumulates log messages from various applications and stores them into log files based on the configuration information in `/etc/syslogd.conf`. `routed` is a server used to maintain dynamic routing information. When your system attempts to send packets to another network, it may require additional routing table entries in order to do so. `routed` takes care of manipulating the routing table without the need for user intervention.

Our example `rc.inet2`, below, only starts up the bare minimum of servers. There are many other servers as well—many of which have to do with NFS configuration. When attempting to setup TCP/IP on your system, it's usually best to start with a minimal configuration and add more complex pieces (such as NFS) when you have things working.

Note that in the below file, we assume that all of the network daemons are held in `/usr/sbin`. As usual, edit this for your own configuration.

```
#! /bin/sh
# Sample /etc/rc.d/rc.inet2

# Start syslogd
if [ -f /usr/sbin/syslogd ]
then
        /usr/sbin/syslogd
fi


# Start inetd
if [ -f /usr/sbin/inetd ]
then
        /usr/sbin/inetd
fi


# Start routed
if [ -f /usr/sbin/routed ]
then
        /usr/sbin/routed -q
fi


# Done!
```

Among the various additional servers that you may want to start in `rc.inet2` is `named`. `named` is a name server—it is responsible for translating (local) IP addresses to names, and vice versa. If you don't have a nameserver elsewhere on the network, or want to provide local machine names to other machines in your domain, it may be necessary to run **named**. (For most configurations it is not necessary, however.) **named** configuration is somewhat complex and requires planning; we refer interested readers to a good book on TCP/IP network administration.

5.3.2.4   /etc/hosts

/etc/hosts contains a list of IP addresses and the hostnames that they correspond to. In general, **/etc/hosts** only contains entries for your local machine, and perhaps other "important" machines (such as your nameserver or gateway). Your local name server will provide address-to-name mappings for other machines on the network, transparently.

For example, if your machine is **loomer.vpizza.com** with the IP address 128.253.154.32, your **/etc/hosts** would look like:

```
127.0.0.1               localhost
128.253.154.32          loomer.vpizza.com loomer
```

If you're only using loopback, the only line in **/etc/hosts** should be for 127.0.0.1, with both **localhost** and your hostname after it.

5.3.2.5   /etc/networks

The **/etc/networks** file lists the names and addresses of your own, and other, networks. It is used by the **route** command, and allows you to specify a network by name, should you so desire.

Every network you wish to add a route to using the **route** command (generally called from **rc.inet1**—see above) *must* have an entry in **/etc/networks**.

As an example,

```
default 0.0.0.0 # default route    - mandatory
loopnet 127.0.0.0 # loopback network - mandatory
mynet 128.253.154.0 # Modify for your own network address
```

5.3.2.6   /etc/host.conf

This file is used to specify how your system will resolve hostnames. It should contain the two lines:

```
order hosts,bind
multi on
```

These lines tell the resolve libraries to first check the /etc/hosts file for any names to lookup, and then ask the nameserver (if one is present). The multi entry allows you to have multiple IP addresses for a given machine name in /etc/hosts.

5.3.2.7 /etc/resolv.conf

This file configures the name resolver, specifying the address of your name server (if any) and your domain name. Your domain name is your fully-qualified hostname (if you're a registered machine on the Internet, for example), with the hostname chopped off. That is, if your full hostname is loomer.vpizza.com, your domain name is just vpizza.com.

For example, if your machine is goober.norelco.com, and has a nameserver at the address 128.253.154.5, your /etc/resolv.conf would look like:

```
domain      norelco.com
nameserver  127.253.154.5
```

You can specify more than one nameserver—each must have a nameserver line of its own in resolv.conf.

5.3.2.8 Setting your hostname

You should set your system hostname with the hostname command. This is usually called from /etc/rc.d/rc.M.. For example, if your (full) hostname is loomer.vpizza.com, edit the appropriate rc file to execute the command:

```
/bin/hostname loomer.vpizza.com
```

Note: This is automatically configured by the netconfig command.

5.3.2.9 Trying it out

Once you have all of these files set up, you should be able to reboot your new kernel and attempt to use the network. There are many places where things can go wrong, so it's a good idea to test individual aspects of the network configuration (e.g., it's probably not a good idea to test your network configuration by firing up Mosaic over a network-based X connection).

You can use the `netstat` command to display your routing tables; this is usually the source of the most trouble. The `netstat` man page describes the exact syntax of this command in detail. In order to test network connectivity, we suggest using a client such as `telnet` to connect to machines both on your local subnetwork and external networks. This will help to narrow down the source of the problem. (For example, if you're unable to connect to local machines, but can connect to machines on other networks, more than likely there is a problem with your netmask and routing table configuration). You can also invoke the `route` command directly (as `root`) to play with the entries in your routing table.

You should also test network connectivity by specifying IP addresses directly, instead of hostnames. For example, if you have problems with the command

> $ *telnet shoop.vpizza.com*

the cause may be incorrect nameserver configuration. Try using the actual IP address of the machine in question; if that works, then you know that your basic network setup is (more than likely) correct, and the problem lies in your specification of the name server address.

Debugging network configurations can be a difficult task, and we can't begin to cover it here. If you are unable to get help from a local guru we strongly suggest reading the *Linux Network Administrators' Guide* from the LDP.

5.3.3   SLIP Configuration

SLIP (Serial Line Internet Protocol) allows you to use TCP/IP over a serial line, be that a phone line, with a dialup modem, or a leased asynchronous line of some sort. Of course, to use SLIP you'll need access to a dial-in SLIP server in your area. Many universities and businesses provide SLIP access for a modest fee.

There are two major SLIP-related programs available—`/sbin/dip` and `/usr/sbin/slattach`. Both of these programs are used to initiate a SLIP connection over a serial device. It is *necessary* to use one of these programs in order to enable SLIP—it will not suffice to dial up the SLIP server (with a communications program such as `kermit`) and issue `ifconfig` and `route` commands. This is because `dip` and `slattach` issue a special *ioctl()* system call to seize control of the serial device to be used as a SLIP interface.

`dip` can be used to dial up a SLIP server, do some handshaking to login to the server (exchanging your username and password, for example) and then initate the SLIP connection over the open serial line. `slattach`, on the other hand, does very little other than grab the serial device for use by SLIP. It is useful if you have a permanent line to your SLIP server and no modem dialup or handshaking is necessary to initiate the connection. Most dialup SLIP users should use `dip`, on the other hand.

`dip` can also be used to configure your Linux system as a SLIP server, where other machines can dial into your own and connect to the network through a secondary Ethernet connection on your machine. See the documentation and man pages for `dip` for more information on this procedure.

SLIP is quite unlike Ethernet, in that there are only two machines on the "network"—the SLIP host (that's you) and the SLIP server. For this reason, SLIP is often referred to as a "point-to-point" connection. A generalization of this idea, known as PPP (Point to Point Protocol) has also been implemented for Linux (see the PPP section).

When you initiate a connection to a SLIP server, the SLIP server will give you an IP address based on (usually) one of two methods. Some SLIP servers allocate "static" IP addresses—in which case your IP address will be the same every time you connect to the server. However, many SLIP servers allocate IP addresses dynamically—in which case you receive a different IP address each time you connect. In general, the SLIP server will print the values of your IP and gateway addresses when you connect. `dip` is capable of reading these values from the output of the SLIP server login session and using them to configure the SLIP device.

Essentially, configuring a SLIP connection is just like configuring for loopback or ethernet. The main differences are discussed below. Read the previous section on configuring the basic TCP/IP files, and apply the changes described below.

5.3.3.1 Static IP address SLIP connections using `dip`

If you are using a static-allocation SLIP server, you may want to include entries for your IP address and hostname in `/etc/hosts`. Also, configure these files listed in the above section: `rc.inet2`, `host.conf`, and `resolv.conf`.

Also, configure `rc.inet1`, as described above. However, you only want to execute `ifconfig` and `route` commands for the loopback device. If you use `dip` to connect to the SLIP server, it will execute the appropriate `ifconfig` and `route` commands for the SLIP device for you. (If you're using `slattach`, on the other hand, you *will* need to include `ifconfig/route` commands in `rc.inet1` for the SLIP device—see below.)

`dip` *should* configure your routing tables appropriately for the SLIP connection when you connect. In some cases, however, `dip`'s behavior may not be correct for your configuration, and you'll have to run `ifconfig` or `route` commands by hand after connecting to the server with `dip` (this is most easily done from within a shell script that runs `dip` and immediately executes the appropriate configuration commands). Your gateway is, in most cases, the address of the SLIP server. You may know this address before hand, or the gateway address will be printed by the SLIP server when you connect. Your `dip` chat script (described below) can obtain this information from the SLIP server.

`ifconfig` may require use of the `pointopoint` argument, if `dip` doesn't configure the interface correctly. For example, if your SLIP server address is 128.253.154.2, and your IP address is 128.253.154.32, you may need to run the command

```
ifconfig sl0 128.253.154.32 pointopoint 128.253.154.2
```

as `root`, after connecting with `dip`. The man pages for `ifconfig` will come in handy.

Note that SLIP device names used with the `ifconfig` and `route` commands are `sl0`, `sl1` and so on (as opposed to `eth0`, `eth1`, etc. for Ethernet devices).

In Section 5.3.4, below, we explain how to configure `dip` to connect to the SLIP server.

5.3.3.2   Static IP address SLIP connections using `slattach`

If you have a leased line or cable running directly to your SLIP server, then there is no need to use `dip` to initiate a connection. `slattach` can be used to configure the SLIP device instead.

In this case, your `/etc/rc.d/rc.inet1` file should look something like the following:

```
#!/bin/sh
IPADDR="128.253.154.32"            # Replace with your IP address
REMADDR="128.253.154.2" # Replace with your SLIP server address

# Modify the following for the appropriate serial device for the SLIP
# connection:
```

```
slattach -p cslip -s 19200 /dev/ttyS0
/usr/sbin/ifconfig sl0 $IPADDR pointopoint $REMADDR up
/usr/sbin/route add default gw $REMADDR
```

slattach allocates the first unallocated SLIP device (sl0, sl1, etc.) to the serial line specified.

Note that the first parameter to slattach is the SLIP protocol to use. At present the only valid values are slip and cslip. slip is regular SLIP, as you would expect, and cslip is SLIP with datagram header compression. In most cases you should use cslip; however, if you seem to be having problems with this, try slip.

If you have more than one SLIP interface then you will have routing considerations to make. You will have to decide what routes to add, and those decisions can only be made on the basis of the actual layout of your network connections. A book on TCP/IP network configuration, as well as the man pages to route, will be of use.

5.3.3.3 Dynamic IP address SLIP connections using dip

If your SLIP server allocates an IP address dynamically, then you certainly don't know your address in advance—therefore, you can't include an entry for it in /etc/hosts. (You should, however, include an entry for your host with the loopback address, 127.0.0.1.)

Many SLIP servers print your IP address (as well as the server's address) when you connect. For example, one type of SLIP server prints a string such as,

```
Your IP address is 128.253.154.44.
Server address is 128.253.154.2.
```

dip can capture these numbers from the output of the server and use them to configure the SLIP device.

See Section 5.3.3.1, above, for information on configuring your various TCP/IP files for use with SLIP. Below, we explain how to configure dip to connect to the SLIP server.

5.3.4 Using dip

dip can simplify the process of connecting to a SLIP server, logging in, and config-

uring the SLIP device. Unless you have a leased line running to your SLIP server,
dip is the way to go.

To use dip, you'll need to write a "chat script" which contains a list of commands
used to communicate with the SLIP server at login time. These commands can
automatically send your username/password to the server, as well as get information
on your IP address from the server.

Here is an example dip chat script, for use with a dynamic IP address server.
For static servers, you will need to set the variables $local and $remote to the
values of your local IP address and server IP address, respectively, at the top of the
script. See the dip man page for details.

```
main:
    # Set Maximum Transfer Unit. This is the maximum size of packets
    # transmitted on the SLIP device. Many SLIP servers use either 1500 or
    # 1006; check with your network admins when in doubt.
    get $mtu 1500

    # Make the SLIP route the default route on your system.
    default

    # Set the desired serial port and speed.
    port cua03
    speed 38400

    # Reset the modem and terminal line. If this causes trouble for you,
    # comment it out.
    reset

    # Prepare for dialing. Replace the following with your
    # modem initialization string.
    send ATT&C1&D2\\N3&Q5%M3%C1N1W1L1S48=7\r
    wait OK 2
    if $errlvl != 0 goto error
    # Dial the SLIP server
    dial 2546000
    if $errlvl != 0 goto error
    wait CONNECT 60
    if $errlvl != 0 goto error

    # We are connected.  Login to the system.
login:
```

```
    sleep 3
    send \r\n\r\n
    # Wait for the login prompt
    wait login: 10
    if $errlvl != 0 goto error

    # Send your username
    send USERNAME\n

    # Wait for password prompt
    wait ord: 5
    if $errlvl != 0 goto error

    # Send password.
    send PASSWORD\n

    # Wait for SLIP server ready prompt
    wait annex: 30
    if $errlvl != 0 goto error

    # Send commands to SLIP server to initate connection.
    send slip\n
    wait Annex 30

    # Get the remote IP address from the SLIP server. The 'get...remote'
    # command reads text in the form xxx.xxx.xxx.xxx, and assigns it
    # to the variable given as the second argument (here, $remote).
    get $remote remote
    if $errlvl != 0 goto error
    wait Your 30

    # Get local IP address from SLIP server, assign to variable $local.
    get $local remote
    if $errlvl != 0 goto error

    # Fire up the SLIP connection
done:
    print CONNECTED to $remote at $rmtip
    print GATEWAY address $rmtip
    print LOCAL address $local
    mode SLIP
    goto exit
```

```
error:
  print SLIP to $remote failed.

exit:
```

dip automatically executes ifconfig and route commands based on the values of the variables $local and $remote. Here, those variables are assigned using the get...remote command, which obtains text from the SLIP server and assigns it to the named variable.

If the ifconfig and route commands that dip runs for you don't work, you can either run the correct commands in a shell script after executing dip, or modify the source for dip itself. Running dip with the -v option will print debugging information while the connection is being set up, which should help you to determine where things might be going awry.

Now, in order to run dip and open the SLIP connection, you can use a command such as:

```
/sbin/dip -v /etc/dip/mychat 2>&1
```

Where the various dip files, and the chat script (mychat.dip), are stored in /etc/dip.

The above discussion should be enough to get you well on your way to talking to the network, either via Ethernet or SLIP. Again, we strongly suggest looking into a book on TCP/IP network configuration, especially if your network has any special routing considerations, other than those mentioned here.

5.4   Networking with UUCP

UUCP (UNIX-to-UNIX Copy) is an older mechanism used to transfer information between UNIX systems. Using UUCP, UNIX systems dial each other up (using a modem) and transfer mail messages, news articles, files, and so on. If you don't have TCP/IP or SLIP access, you can use UUCP to communicate with the world. Most of the mail and news software (see Sections 5.5 and 5.6) can be configured to use UUCP to transfer information to other machines. In fact, if there is an Internet site nearby, you can arrange to have Internet mail sent to your Linux machine via UUCP from that site.

The *Linux Network Administrator's Guide* contains complete information on configuring and using UUCP under Linux. Also, the Linux UUCP HOWTO, available via anonymous FTP from `sunsite.unc.edu`, should be of help. Another source of information on UUCP is the book *Managing UUCP and USENET*, by Tim O'Reilly and Grace Todino. See Appendix A for more information.

5.5 Electronic Mail

Like most UNIX systems, Linux provides a number of software packages for using electronic mail. E-mail on your system can either be local (that is, you only mail other users on your system), or networked (that is, you mail, using either TCP/IP or UUCP, users on other machines on a network). E-mail software usually consists of two parts: a *mailer* and a *transport*. The mailer is the user-level software which is used to actually compose and read e-mail messages. Popular mailers include `elm`, `pine` and `mailx`. The transport is the low-level software which actually takes care of delivering the mail, either locally or remotely. The user never sees the transport software; they only interact with the mailer. However, as the system administrator, it is important to understand the concepts behind the transport software and how to configure it.

`Sendmail`, one of the most powerful mail transports, is the standard mail transport implementation on Slackware Linux systems. Customizing and configuring it manually is a complicated process. You can use the setup program during and after installing your system to simplify this process as long as you are planning on using a standard mail setup.

The Linux Mail HOWTO gives more information on the available mail software for Linux and how to configure it on your system. If you plan to send mail remotely, you'll need to understand either TCP/IP or UUCP, depending on how your machine is networked (see Sections 5.3 and 5.4). The UUCP and TCP/IP documents listed in Appendix A should be of help there.

Most of the Linux mail software can be retrieved via anonymous FTP from `sunsite.unc.edu` in the directory `/pub/Linux/system/Mail`.

5.6 News and USENET

Linux also provides a number of facilities for managing electronic news. You may choose to set up a local news server on your system, which will allow users to post "articles" to various "newsgroups" on the system... a lively form of discussion. However, if you have access to a TCP/IP or UUCP network, then you will be able to participate in USENET—a worldwide network news service.

There are two parts to the news software—the *server* and the *client*. The news server is the software which controls the newsgroups and handles delivering articles to other machines (if you are on a network). The news client, or *newsreader*, is the software which connects to the server to allow users to read and post news.

There are several forms of news servers available for Linux. They all follow the same basic protocols and design. The two primary versions are "C News" and "INN". There are many types of newsreaders, as well, such as `rn` and `tin`. The choice of newsreader is more or less a matter of taste; all newsreaders should work equally well with different versions of the server software. That is, the newsreader is independent of the server software, and vice versa.

If you only want to run news locally (that is, not as part of USENET), then you will need to run a server on your system, as well as install a newsreader for the users. The news server will store the articles in a directory such as `/usr/spool/news`, and the newsreader will be compiled to look in this directory for news articles.

However, if you wish to run news over the network, there are several options open to you. TCP/IP network-based news uses a protocol known as NNTP (Network News Transmission Protocol). NNTP allows a newsreader to read news over the network, on a remote machine. NNTP also allows news servers to send articles to each other over the network—this is the software upon which USENET is based. Most businesses and universities have one or more NNTP servers set up to handle all of the USENET news for that site. Every other machine at the site runs an NNTP-based newsreader to read and post news over the network via the NNTP server. This means that only the NNTP server actually stores the news articles on disk.

Here are some possible scenarios for news configuration.

- You run news locally. That is, you have no network connection, or no desire to run news over the network. In this case, you need to run C News or INN on your machine, and install a newsreader to read the news locally.

- You have access to a TCP/IP network and an NNTP server. If your organization has an NNTP news server set up, you can read and post news from your Linux machine by simply installing an NNTP-based newsreader. (Most newsreaders available can be configured to run locally or use NNTP). In this case, you do not need to install a news server or store news articles on your system. The newsreader will take care of reading and posting news over the network. Of course, you will need to have TCP/IP configured and have access to the network (see Section 5.3).

- You have access to a TCP/IP network but have no NNTP server. In this case, you can run an NNTP news server on your Linux system. You can install either a local or an NNTP-based newsreader, and the server will store news articles on your system. In addition, you can configure the server to communicate with other NNTP news servers to transfer news articles.

- You want to transfer news using UUCP. If you have UUCP access (see Section 5.4), you can participate in USENET as well. You will need to install a (local) news server and a news reader. In addition, you will need to configure your UUCP software to periodically transfer news articles to another nearby UUCP machine (known as your "news feed"). UUCP does not use NNTP to transfer news; simply, UUCP provides its own mechanism for transferring news articles.

The one down side of most news server and newsreader software is that it must be compiled by hand. Most of the news software does not use configuration files; instead, configuration options are determined at compile time.

Most of the "news" software is included with the core Slackware TCP/IP networking system (group N). Additional news software can be found on sunsite.unc.edu an its mirrors in the directory `/pub/Linux/system/Mail`.

For more information, refer to the Linux News HOWTO from `sunsite.unc.edu` in `/pub/Linux/docs/HOWTO`. Also, the LDP's *Linux Network Administrator's Guide* contains complete information on configuring news software for Linux. The book *Managing UUCP and Usenet*, by Tim O'Reilly and Grace Todino, is an excellent guide to setting up UUCP and news software. Also of interest is the USENET document "How to become a USENET site," available from `ftp.uu.net`, in the directory `/usenet/news.announce.newusers`.

Chapter 6

Installing Linux PPP

6.1 Introduction

Copyright

The copyright of this document is retained by the author. Permission is granted to distribute the document by electronic means and on CDs provided that it is kept entirely in its original format. Permission is also granted to print a copy of this document for personal use.

The republishing of this document in part or in whole without the permission of the copyright holder by any means other than as noted above is prohibited.

Distribution

This document will be posted to comp.os.linux.answers as new versions of the document are produced.It is also available in HTML format at:-

* `http://sunsite.unc.edu/mdw/linux.html#howto` Linux Howto Index

Other formats (SGML, ASCII, PostScript, DVI) are available from `ftp://sunsite.unc.edu/pub/Linux/docs/HOWTO/other-formats` As sunsite.unc.edu carries a very heavy load, please use an appropriate mirror site closest to you.

Acknowledgements

A growing number of people have provided me with assistance in preparing this document. Special thanks go to Al Longyear for the guidance on PPP itself (if there

are mistakes here, they are mine not his), Greg Hankins (maintainer of the Linux
Howto system) and Daniel Berinson for assistance with the linuxdoc-sgml package
when it started to choke on my text (3 days before a publication dead line, no less!)
and Debi Tackett (of MaximumAccess.com) for many helpful suggestions on style,
content order, logic and clarity of explanations.

Finally, to the many people who have contacted me by email offering comments
- my thanks. As with all HOWTO authors, the satisfaction of helping is all the
payment we receive and it is enough. By writing this HOWTO I am repaying in a
small way the debt I - and all other Linux users - owe to the people who write and
maintain our OS of choice.

PPP (the Point to Point Protocol) is a mechanism for creating and running IP
(the Internet Protocol) and other network protocols over a serial link - be that a
direct serial connection (using a null-modem cable), over a telnet established link
or a link made using modems and telephone lines. Using PPP, you can connect
your Linux PC to a PPP server and access the resources of the network to which
the server is connected (almost) as if you were directly connected to that network.

You can also set up your Linux PC as a PPP server, so that other computers can
dial into your computer and access the resources on your local PC and/or network.

As PPP is a peer-to-peer system, you can also use PPP on two Linux PCs to
link together two networks (or a local network to the Internet).

One major difference between PPP and an Ethernet connection is of course
speed - a standard Ethernet connection operates at 10 Mbs (million bits per second)
maximum theoretical throughput, whereas a modem operates at speeds up to 33.6
kbps (thousand bits per second). Also, depending on the type of PPP connection,
there may be some limitations in usage of some applications and services.

6.1.1   Clients and Servers

PPP is strictly a peer to peer protocol; there is (technically) no difference between
the machine that dials in and the machine that is dialed into. However, for clarity's
sake, it is useful to think in terms of **servers** and **clients**.

When you dial into a site to establish a PPP connection, you are a **client**. The
machine to which you connect is the **server**.

When you are setting up a Linux box to receive and handle dial in PPP connections, you are setting up a PPP **server**.

Any Linux PC can be both a PPP server and client - even simultaneously if you have more than one serial port (and modem if necessary). As stated above, there is no real difference between clients and servers as far as PPP is concerned, once the connection is made.

This document refers to the machine that initiates the call (that "dials in") as the **CLIENT**, whilst the machine that answers the telephone, checks the authentication of the dial in request (using user ids, passwords and possibly other mechanisms) is referred to as the **SERVER**.

The use of PPP as a client to link one or more machines at a location into the Internet is probably, the one in which most people are interested - that is using their PC as a client.

The procedure described in this document will allow you to establish and automate your Internet connection.

This document will also give you guidance in setting up your Linux PC as a PPP **server** and in linking two LANs together (with full routing) using PPP (this is frequently characterized as establishing a WAN - wide area network - link).

6.1.2 Differences between Linux distributions

There are many different Linux distributions and they all have their own idiosyncrasies and ways of doing things.

In particular, there are two different ways a Linux (and Unix) computer actually starts up, configures its interfaces and so forth.

These are **BSD style system initialization** and **System V system initialization**. If you dip into some of the Unix news groups, you will find occasional religious wars between proponents of these two systems. If that sort of thing amuses you, have fun burning bandwidth and join in!

Possibly the two most widely used distributions are

- Slackware
  which uses BSD style system initialization

- Red Hat (and its sibling Caldera)
  which uses SysV system initialization

BSD style initialization keeps its initialization files in /etc/... and these files are:-

```
/etc/rc
/etc/rc.local
/etc/rc.serial
```

System V initialization keeps its initialization files in /etc/rc.d/... and a number of subdirectories under there:-

```
drwxr-xr-x  2 root    root      1024 Jul  6 15:12 init.d
-rwxr-xr-x  1 root    root      1776 Feb  9 05:01 rc
-rwxr-xr-x  1 root    root       820 Jan  2  1996 rc.local
-rwxr-xr-x  1 root    root      2567 Jul  5 20:30 rc.sysinit
drwxr-xr-x  2 root    root      1024 Jul  6 15:12 rc0.d
drwxr-xr-x  2 root    root      1024 Jul  6 15:12 rc1.d
drwxr-xr-x  2 root    root      1024 Jul  6 15:12 rc2.d
drwxr-xr-x  2 root    root      1024 Jul 18 18:07 rc3.d
drwxr-xr-x  2 root    root      1024 May 27  1995 rc4.d
drwxr-xr-x  2 root    root      1024 Jul  6 15:12 rc5.d
drwxr-xr-x  2 root    root      1024 Jul  6 15:12 rc6.d
```

If you are trying to track down where your Ethernet interface and associated network routes are actually configured, you will need to track through these files to actually find where the actual commands are that do this.

On some installations (for example Red Hat and Caldera), there is a X Windows configured PPP dial up system. This HOWTO does not cover these distribution specific tools. If you are having problems with them, contact the distributors directly!

6.2 IP Numbers

Every device that connects to the Internet must have its own, unique IP number. These are assigned centrally by a designated authority for each country.

If you are connecting a local area network (LAN) to the Internet, **YOU MUST** use an IP number from your own assigned network range for all the computers and devices you have on your LAN. You **MUST NOT** pick IP numbers out of the air and use these whilst connecting to another LAN (let alone the Internet). At worst this will simply not work at all and could cause total havoc as your 'stolen'

IP number starts interfering with the communications of another computer that is already using the IP number you have picked out of the air.

Please note that the IP numbers used throughout this document (with some exceptions) are from the 'unconnected network numbers' series that are reserved for use by networks that are not (ever) connected to the Internet.

There are IP numbers that are specifically dedicated to LANs that do not connect to the Internet. The IP number sequences are:-

- One A Class Address
  10.0.0.0 - 10.255.255.255

- 16 B Class Addresses
  172.16.0.0 - 172.31.255.255

- 256 C Class Addresses
  192.168.0.0 - 192.168.255.255

If you have a LAN for which you have **not** been allocated IP numbers by the responsible authority in your country, you should use one of the network numbers from the above sequences for your machines.

These numbers should **never** be used on the Internet. However, they can be used for the local Ethernet on a machine that is connecting to the Internet. This is because IP numbers are actually allocated to a network interface, not to a computer. So whilst your Ethernet interface may use 10.0.0.1 (for example), when you hook onto the Internet using PPP, your PPP interface will be given another (and valid) IP number by the server. Your PC will have Internet connectivity, but the other computers on your LAN will not.

However, using Linux and the IP masquerade capabilities of the ipfwadm software, you can connect the rest of your LAN to the Internet (with some restriction of services).

For more information on how to do this see the IP Masquerade mini-HOWTO at http://sunsite.unc.edu/mdw/HOWTO/mini/IP-Masquerade Linux IP Masquerade mini HOWTO

For most users, who are connecting a single machine to an Internet service provider via PPP, obtaining an IP number (or more accurately, a network number) will not be necessary.

If you wish to connect a small LAN to the Internet, many Internet Service Providers (ISPs) can provide you with a dedicated subnet (a specific sequence of IP numbers) from their existing IP address space.

For users, who are connecting a single PC to the Internet via an ISP, most providers use **dynamic** IP number assignment. That is, as part of the connection process, the PPP service you contact will tell your machine what IP number to use for the PPP interface during the current session.

With dynamic IP numbers, you are **not** given the same IP number each time you connect. This has implications for server type applications on your Linux machine such as sendmail, ftpd, httpd and so forth. The limitations of service due to dynamic IP number assignment (and ways to work around these, where possible) are discussed later in the document.

6.3   Aim of this Document

6.3.1   Setting up a PPP Client

This document provides guidance to people who wish to use Linux and PPP to dial into a PPP server and set up an IP connection using PPP. It assumes that PPP has been compiled and installed on your Linux machine (but does briefly cover reconfiguring/recompiling your kernel to include PPP support).

6.3.1.1   Using DIP - don't, use CHAT instead

Whilst DIP (the standard way of creating a SLIP connection) can be used to forge a PPP connection, DIP scripts are generally quite complex. For this reason, this document does NOT cover using DIP to forge a PPP connection.

Instead, this document describes the standard Linux PPP software (chat/pppd).

6.3.2   Setting up a PPP server

This document provides guidance on how to configure your Linux PC as a PPP server (allowing other people to dial into your Linux PC and establish a PPP connection).

You should note that there are a myriad of ways of setting up Linux as a PPP server. This document (currently) gives one method - that used by the author to set up several small PPP server (each of 16 modems).

This method is known to work well. However, it is not necessarily the best method. If other users have particularly clever PPP server setups, please feel free to email information on them to the author of this HOWTO.

6.3.3 Linking two LANs or a LAN to the Internet using PPP

This document provides (basic) information on linking two LANs or a LAN to the Internet using PPP.

6.3.4 This document at present does NOT cover...

- Connecting and configuring a modem to Linux (in detail)
  See the Serial-HOWTO

- Using DIP to make PPP connections
  Use chat instead...

- Using socks or IP Masquerade
  There are perfectly good documents already covering these two packages.

6.4 Software versions covered

This HOWTO assumes that you are using a Linux 1.2.x kernel with the PPP 2.1.2 software or Linux 1.3.X/2.0.x and PPP 2.2

It is possible to use PPP 2.2.0 with kernel 1.2.13. However, to do so requires kernel patches. This document does **NOT** cover this mix of software.

Also, you should particularly not that you cannot use the PPP 2.1.2 software with Linux kernel version 2.0.X.

Please note that this document does **NOT** cover problems arising from the use of loadable modules for Linux kernel 2.0.x. Please see the kerneld mini-HOWTO and the kernel/module 2.0.x documentation (in the Linux 2.0.x source tree at `/usr/src/linux/Documentation/...`).

As this document is designed to assist new users, it is highly recommended that you use a version of Linux and the appropriate PPP version that are known to be stable together.

6.5   Other Useful/Important Documents

Users are advised to read :-

- the documentation that comes with the PPP package
  (Look in /usr/doc...)

- the pppd and chat man pages
  (use man chat and man pppd to explore these)

- the Linux Network Administration Guide (NAG)
  http://sunsite.unc.edu/mdw/LDP-books/nag-1.0/nag.html   The
  Network Administrators' Guide

- the Net-2/3 HOWTO
  http://sunsite.unc.edu/mdw/HOWTO/NET-2-HOWTO.html Linux NET-2/3-
  HOWTO

- Linux kernel documentation in /usr/src/linux/Documentation

- The excellent Unix/Linux books published by O'Reilly and Associates.
  (http://www.ora.com/ O'Reilly and Associates On-Line Catalogue). If you
  are new to Unix/Linux, **run** (don't walk) to your nearest computer book shop
  and invest in a number of these immediately!

The   best   general   starting   point   for   Linux   documentation is http://sunsite.unc.edu/mdw/ The Linux Documentation Project
Home Page

Whilst you can use this document to create your PPP link without reading any
of these documents, you will have a far better understanding of what is going on if
you do so! You will also be able to address problems yourself (or at least ask more
intelligent questions on the comp.os.linux... newsgroups).

These documents (as well as various others, including the relevant RFCs) provide
additional and more detailed explanation than is possible in this HOWTO.

If you are connecting a LAN to the Internet using PPP, you will need to know a
reasonable amount about TCP/IP networking. In addition to the documents above,
you will find the O'Reilly books "TCP/IP Network Administration" and "Building
Internet Firewalls" of considerable benefit!

6.5.1   Useful Linux Mailing Lists

There are many Linux mailing lists that operate as a means of communication between users of many levels of ability. By all means subscribe to those that interest you and contribute your expertise and views.

A word to the wise: some lists are specifically aimed at "high powered" users and/or specific topics. Whilst no-one will complain if you 'lurk' (subscribe but don't post messages), you are likely to earn heated comments (if not outright flames) if you post 'newbie' questions to inappropriate lists! This is not because guru level users hate new users, but because these lists are there to handle the specific issues at particular levels of difficulty.

By all means join the lists that offer open subscription, but keep you comments relevant to the subject of the list!

A good starting point for Linux mailing lists is
`http://summer.snu.ac.kr/ djshin/linux/mail-list/index.shtml`
Linux Mailing List Directory

6.6   Configuring your Linux Kernel

In order to use PPP, your Linux kernel must be compiled to include PPP support. Obtain the Linux source code for your kernel if you do not already have this - it belongs in `/usr/src/linux` on Linux's standard file system.

Check out this directory - many Linux distributions install the source tree (the files and subdirectories) as part of their installation process.

Linux kernel sources can be obtained by ftp from `sunsite.unc.edu` or its mirror sites.

6.6.1   Installing the Linux Kernel source

The following are brief instructions for obtaining and installing the Linux kernel sources. Full information can be obtained from
`http://sunsite.unc.edu/mdw/HOWTO/Kernel-HOWTO.html` The Linux Kernel HOWTO.

In order to install and compile the Linux kernel, you need to be logged in as root.

1. Change to the `/usr/src` directory
   `cd /usr/src`

2. Check in `/usr/src/linux` to see if you already have the sources installed.

3. If you don't have the sources, get them from
   `ftp://sunsite.unc.edu/pub/Linux/kernel/v2.0` Linux kernel source directory. If you are looking for earlier versions of the kernel (such as 1.2.X), these are kept in `ftp://sunsite.unc.edu/pub/Linux/kernel/old` Old Linux kernel source directory.

4. Choose the appropriate kernel - usually the most recent one available is what you are looking for. Retrieve this and put the source tar file in `/usr/src`.

   Note: a 'tar' file is an archive - possibly compressed, as are the Linux kernel source tar files - containing many files in a number of directories. It is the Linux equivalent of a DOS zip file.

5. If you already have the Linux sources installed but are upgrading to a new kernel, you must remove the old sources. Use the command
   `rm -rf /usr/src/linux`

6. Now uncompress and extract the sources using the command
   `tar xzf linux-2.0.6.tar.gz`

7. Now, `cd /usr/src/linux` and read the README file. This contains an excellent explanation of how to go about configuring and compiling a new kernel. Read this file (it's a good idea to print it out and have a copy handy whilst you are compiling until you have done this enough times to know your way around).

6.6.2   Knowing your hardware

You MUST know what cards/devices you have inside your PC if you are going to recompile your kernel!!! For some devices (such as sound cards) you will also need to know various settings (such as IRQ's, I/O addresses and such).

6.6.3   Kernel compilation - the Linux 1.2.13 kernel

To start the configuration process, follow the instructions in the README file to properly install the sources. You start the kernel configuration process with

```
make config
```

In order to use PPP, you must configure the kernel to include PPP support (PPP requires BOTH pppd AND kernel support for PPP).

```
PPP (point-to-point) support (CONFIG_PPP) [n] y
```

Answer the other make config questions according to the hardware in your PC and the features of the Linux operating system you want. Then continue to follow the README to compile and install your new kernel.

The 1.2.13 kernel creates only 4 PPP devices. For multi- port serial cards, you will need to edit the kernel PPP sources to obtain more ports. (See the README.linux file that comes as part of the PPP-2.1.2 distribution for full details of the simple edits you need to make).

Note: the 1.2.13 configuration dialogue does NOT allow you to go backwards - so if you make a mistake in answering one of the questions in the `make config` dialogue, exit by typing CTRL C and start again.

6.6.4   Kernel compilation - the Linux 1.3.x and 2.0.x kernels

For Linux 2.0.x, you can use a similar process as for Linux 1.2.13. Again, follow the instructions in the README file to properly install the sources. You start the kernel configuration process with

```
make config
```

However, you also have the choice of

```
make menuconfig
```

This provides a menu based configuration system with online help that allows you to jump around in the configuration process.

There is also a highly recommended X windows based configuration interface

```
make xconfig
```

You can compile PPP support directly into your kernel or as a loadable module. If you only use PPP some of the time that your Linux machine is operating, then compiling PPP support as a loadable module is recommended. Using 'kerneld', your kernel will automatically load the module(s) required to provide PPP support when you start your PPP link process. This saves valuable memory space: no part of the kernel can be swapped out of memory, but loadable modules are automatically removed if they are not in use.

To do this, you need to enable loadable module support:-

```
Enable loadable module support (CONFIG_MODULES) [Y/n/?] y
```

To add PPP kernel support, answer the following question:-

```
PPP (point-to-point) support (CONFIG_PPP) [M/n/y/?]
```

For a PPP loadable module, answer **M**, otherwise for PPP compiled in as part of the kernel, answer **Y**.

Unlike kernel 1.2.13, kernel 2.0.x creates PPP devices on the fly as needed and it is not necessary to hack the sources to increase available PPP device numbers at all.

6.6.5   General kernel config considerations

If you are setting up your Linux PC as a PPP server, you must compile in IP forwarding support. This is also necessary if you want to use Linux to link to LANs together or your LAN to the Internet.

If you are linking a LAN to the Internet (or linking together two LANs), you should be concerned about security. Adding support for IP firewalls to the kernel is probably a MUST!

You will also need this if you want to use IP masquerade to connect a LAN that uses any of the above mentioned 'unconnected' IP network numbers.

Once you have installed and rebooted your new kernel, you can start configuring and testing your PPP link(s).

6.7 Getting the Information you need about the PPP service

Before you can establish a PPP connection with a server, you need to obtain the following information (from the sysadmin/user support people of the PPP server):-

- The telephone number(s) to dial for the service
  If you are behind a PABX, you also need the PABX number that gives you an outside dial tone - this is frequently digit zero (0) or nine (9).

- Does the server use DYNAMIC or STATIC IP numbers?
  If the server uses STATIC IP numbers, then you need to know what IP number to use for your end of the PPP connection.
  Most Internet Service Providers use DYNAMIC IP numbers. As mentioned above, this has some implications in terms of the services you can use.

- If you are using static IP numbers, ask for the network mask your ISP uses as well.

- What are the IP numbers of the ISPs Domain Name Servers?
  There should be at least two although only one is needed.

- Does the server require the use of PAP/CHAP?
  If this is the case you need to know the "id" and "secret" you are to use in connecting. (These are probably your username and password).

- Does the server automatically start PPP or do you need to issue any commands to start PPP on the server once you are logged in?
  If you must issue a command to start PPP, what is it?

Carefully note down this information - you are going to use it!

6.7.1 Testing your Modem Connection for outgoing calls

You should make sure that your modem is correctly set up and that you know which serial port it is connected to.

Remember:-

- DOS com1: = Linux /dev/cua0 (and /dev/ttyS0)

- DOS com2: = Linux /dev/cua1 (and /dev/ttyS1)
  et cetera

Using you terminal communications package (such as minicom), dial into the
PPP server you want to connect to with a PPP session.

(Note: at this stage we are **NOT** trying to make a PPP connection - just
establishing that we have the right phone number and also to find out **exactly**
what the server sends to us in order to get logged in and start PPP).

During this process, either capture (log to a file) the entire login process or
carefully (very carefully) write down exactly what prompts the remote server gives
to let you know it is time to enter your user name and password (and any other
commands needed to establish the PPP connection).

It is worth dialing in at least twice - some servers change their prompts (e.g.
with the time!) every time you log in. The two critical prompts your Linux box
needs to be able to identify every time you dial in are:-

- the prompt that requests you to enter your user name;

- the prompt that requests you to enter your password;

If you have to issue a command to start PPP on the server, you will also need
to find out the prompt the server gives you once you are logged in.

If your server automatically starts PPP, once you have logged in, you will start to
see garbage on your screen - this is the PPP server sending your machine information
to start up and configure the PPP connection.

This should look something like this :-

```
~y}#.!}!}!} }8}!}$}%U}"}&} } } } }%}& ...}'}"}(}"} .~~y}
```

(and it just keeps on coming!)

At this point, you can hang up your modem (usually, type +++ quickly and
then issue the ATHO command once your modem responds with OK).

On some systems PPP must be explicitly started on the server. This is usually
because the server has been set up to allow PPP logins and shell logins using the
same username/password pair. If this is the case, issue this command once you have
logged in. Again, you will see the garbage as the server end of the PPP connection
starts up - so you can now hang up.

If you do NOT see the garbage on your screen when the server starts up PPP, it is quite likely (though not certain) that you have done something wrong.

Notwithstanding this, some PPP servers are set up to be passive - they send nothing until the client (your computer) starts the PPP process from your end.

However, the majority of servers are active and you should see the garbage.

If you can't get your modem to work, read your modem manual, the man pages for your communications software and the Serial HOWTO! Once you have this sorted out, carry on as above.

6.8 A note about serial ports and speed capabilities

If you are using a high speed (external) modem (14,400 Baud or above), your serial port needs to be capable of handling the throughput that such a modem is capable of producing, particularly when the modems are compressing the data.

This requires your serial port to use a modern UART (Universal Asynchronous Receiver Transmitter) such as a 16550(A). If you are using an old machine (or old serial card), it is quite possible that your serial port has only an 8250 UART, which will cause you considerable problems when used with a high speed modem.

Use the command

```
setserial -a /dev/ttySx
```

to get Linux to report to you the type of UART you have. If you do not have a 16550A type UART, invest in a new serial card (available for under $50).

Note: the first versions of the 16550 UART chip had an error. This was rapidly discovered and a revision of the chip was released - the 16550A UART. A relatively small number of the faulty chips did however get into circulation. It is unlikely that you will encounter one of these but you should look for a response that says 16550A, particularly on serial cards of some vintage.

6.9 Configuring your modem

You will need to configure your modem correctly for PPP - to do this **READ YOUR MODEM MANUAL**! Most modems come with a **factory default**

setting that selects the options required for PPP. The minimum configuration specifies:-

- Hardware flow control (RTS/CTS) (&K3 on many Hayes modems)

Other settings (in standard Hayes commands) you should investigate are:-

- E1 Command Echo ON (required for chat to operate)

- Q0 Report result codes (required for chat to operate)

- S0=0 Auto Answer OFF (unless you want your modem to answer the phone)

- &C1 Carrier Detect ON only after connect

- &S0 Data Set Ready (DSR) always ON

- (depends) Data Terminal Ready

It is also worth while investigating how the modem's serial interface between your computer and modem operates. Most modern modems allow you to run the serial interface at a FIXED speed whilst allowing the telephone line interface to change its speed to the highest speed it and the remote modem can both handle.

This is known as split speed operation. If your modem supports this, lock the modem's serial interface to its highest available speed (usually 115,200 baud but maybe 38,400 baud for 14,400 baud modems).

Use your communications software (e.g. minicom) to find out about your modem configuration and set it to what is required for PPP. Many modems report their current settings in response to AT&V, but you should consult your modem manual. If you completely mess up the settings, you can return to sanity (usually) by issuing an AT&F - return to factory settings. (For most modem modems I have encountered, the factory settings include all you need for PPP - but you should check).

Save your modem configuration in non-volatile RAM (usually the modem command AT&W will do this - but check in your modem manual).

With the correct modem configuration already in the modem, resetting the modem will activate this. Arranging things this way considerably simplifies the chat script necessary for the PPP connection.

6.9.1 Note on Serial Flow Control

When data is traveling on serial communication lines, it can happen that data arrives faster than a computer can handle it (the computer may be busy doing something else - remember, Linux is a multi-user, multi- tasking operating system). In order to ensure that data is not lost (data does not over run in the input buffer and hence get lost), some method of controlling the flow of data is necessary.

There are two ways of doing this on serial lines:-

- Using hardware signals (Clear To Send/Request to Send - CTS/RTS)

- Using software signals (control S and control Q).

Whilst the latter may be fine for a terminal (text) link, data on a PPP link uses all 8 bits - and it is quite probable that somewhere in the data there will be data bytes that translate as control S and control Q. So, if a modem is set up to use software flow control, things can rapidly go berserk!

For PPP (which uses 8 bits of data) hardware flow control is vital.

6.10 Using PPP and root privileges

Because PPP needs to set up networking devices, change the kernel routing table and so forth, it requires root privileges to do this.

If users other than root are to set up PPP connections, the pppd program should be setuid root :-

```
-r-sr-xr-x   1 root     root        95225 Jul 11 00:27 /usr/sbin/pppd
```

If /usr/sbin/pppd is not set up this way, then **as root** issue the command:-

```
chmod u+s /usr/sbin/pppd
```

What this does is make pppd run with root privileges **even** if the binary is run by an ordinary user. This allows a normal user to run pppd with the necessary privileges to set up the network interfaces and the kernel routing table.

Programs that run 'set uid root' are potential security holes and you should be extremely cautious about making programs 'suid root'. A number of programs (including pppd) have been carefully written to minimise the danger of running suid root, so you should be safe with this one (but no guarantees).

Depending on how you want your system to operate - specifically if you want ANY user on your system to be able to initiate a PPP link, you should make your ppp-on/off scripts world read/execute. (This is probably fine if your PC is used ONLY by you).

However, if you do NOT want just anyone to be able to start up a PPP connection (for example, your children have accounts on your Linux PC and you do not want them hooking into the Internet without your supervision), you will need to establish a PPP group (edit /etc/group) and :-

- Make the ppp-on/off scripts owned by user root and group PPP

- Make the ppp-on/off scripts read/executable by group PPP

```
-rwxr-x---   1 root    PPP   587 Mar 14  1995 /usr/sbin/ppp-on
-rwxr-x---   1 root    PPP   631 Mar 14  1995 /usr/sbin/ppp-off
```

- Make the other access rights for ppp-on/off nill.

- add the users who will be firing up PPP to the PPP group in /etc/group

Even if you do this, ordinary users will STILL not be able to shut down the link under software control! Running the `ppp-off` script requires root privileges. However, any user can just turn off the modem!

On my home PC, I do **NOT** make pppd suid root. In order to start the ppp link I must then become root - and know the password! This provides me with the ability to supervise my son's access to the Internet!

6.11   Setting up the PPP connection files

You now need to be logged in as root to create the directories and edit the files needed to set up PPP, even if you want PPP to be accessible to all users.

PPP uses a number of files to connect and set up a ppp connection. These differ in name and location between PPP 2.1.2 and 2.2.

For PPP 2.1.2 the files are:-

```
/usr/sbin/pppd              # the ppp binary
/usr/sbin/ppp-on            # the dialer/connection script
/usr/sbin/ppp-off           # the disconnection script
/etc/ppp/options            # the options pppd uses for all
                            connections
/etc/ppp/options.ttyXX  # the option specific to a connection on
                            this port
```

For PPP 2.2 the files are:-

```
/usr/sbin/pppd                    # the ppp binary
/etc/ppp/scripts/ppp-on           # the dialer/connection script
/etc/ppp/scripts/ppp-on-dialer    # part 1 of the dialer script
/etc/ppp/scripts/ppp-off          # the actual chat script itself
/etc/ppp/options                  # the options pppd uses for
                                  all connections
/etc/ppp/options.ttyXX  # the option specific to a connection
                            on this port
```

As you can see, in your /etc directory there should be a ppp directory:-

```
drwxrwxr-x   2 root      root        1024 Oct  9 11:01 ppp
```

If it does not exist - create it.

If the directory already existed, it should contain a template options file called **options.tpl**. This file is included below.

Print it out as it contains an explanation of all the PPP options (these are useful to read in conjunction with the pppd man pages). Whilst you can use this file as the basis of your /etc/ppp/options file, it is probably better to create your own options file that does not include all the comments in the template - it will be much shorter and easier to read/maintain.

If you have multiple serial lines/modems (typically the case for PPP servers), create a general /etc/ppp/options file containing the options that are common for all the serial ports on which you are supporting dial in and set up individual option files for each serial line on which you will be establishing a PPP connection with the individual settings required for each port.

These are named options.ttyx1<, options.ttyx2 and so forth (where x is the appropriate letter for your serial ports).

However, for a single PPP connection, you can happily use the
/etc/ppp/options file. Alternatively, you can put all the options as arguments
in the pppd command itself.

It is easier to maintain a setup that uses /etc/ppp/options.ttySx files. If you
use PPP to connect to a number of different sites, you can create option files for
each site in /etc/ppp/options.site and then specify the option file as a parameter
to the PPP command as you connect.

6.11.1   The supplied options.tpl file

Some distributions of PPP seem to have lost the options.tpl file, so here is the complete file. I suggest that you do NOT edit this file to create your /etc/ppp/options
file(s). Rather, copy this to a new file and then edit that. If you mess up your edits,
you can then go back to the original ands start again.

```
# /etc/ppp/options -*- sh -*- general options for pppd
# created 13-Jul-1995 jmk
# autodate: 01-Aug-1995
# autotime: 19:45


# Use the executable or shell command specified to set up the
# serial line.  This script would typically use the "chat" program
# to dial the modem and start the remote ppp session.
#connect "echo You need to install a connect command."


# Run the executable or shell command specified after pppd
# has terminated the link.  This script could, for example, issue
# commands to the modem to cause it to hang up if hardware
# modem control signals were not available.
#disconnect "chat -- \d+++\d\c OK ath0 OK"


# async character map -- 32-bit hex; each bit is a character
# that needs to be escaped for pppd to receive it.  0x00000001
# represents '\x01', and 0x80000000 represents '\x1f'.
#asyncmap 0


# Require the peer to authenticate itself before allowing network
# packets to be sent or received.
```

```
#auth

# Use hardware flow control (i.e. RTS/CTS) to control the flow
# of data on the serial port.
#crtscts

# Use software flow control (i.e. XON/XOFF) to control the flow
# of data on the serial port.
#xonxoff

# Add a default route to the system routing tables, using the
# peer as the gateway, when IPCP negotiation is successfully
# completed.  This entry is removed when the PPP
# connection is broken.
#defaultroute

# Specifies that certain characters should be escaped on
# transmission (regardless of whether the peer requests
# them to be escaped with its async control character map).
# The characters to be escaped are specified as a list of
# hex numbers separated by commas.  Note that almost
# any character can be specified for the escape option,
# unlike the asyncmap option which only allows control
# characters to be specified.  The characters which may
# not be escaped are those with hex values 0x20 - 0x3f
# or 0x5e.
#escape 11,13,ff

# Don't use the modem control lines.
#local

# Specifies that pppd should use a UUCP-style lock on
# the serial device to ensure exclusive access to the
# device.
#lock

# Use the modem control lines.  On Ultrix, this option
# implies hardware flow control, as for the crtscts option.
# (This option is not fully implemented.)
```

```
#modem

# Set the MRU [Maximum Receive Unit] value to <n>
# for negotiation.  pppd will ask the peer to send
# packets of no more than <n> bytes. The minimum
# MRU value is 128.  The default MRU value is
# 1500.  A value of 296 is recommended for slow
# links (40 bytes for TCP/IP header + 256
# bytes of data).
#mru 542

# Set the interface netmask to <n>, a 32 bit netmask in
# "decimal dot" notation (e.g. 255.255.255.0).
#netmask 255.255.255.0

# Disables the default behaviour when no local IP
# address is specified, which is to determine (if
# possible) the local IP address from the hostname.
# With this option, the peer will have to supply the
# local IP address during IPCP negotiation (unless
# it specified explicitly on the command line or in an
# options file).
#noipdefault

# Enables the "passive" option in the LCP.  With this
# option, pppd will attempt to initiate a connection; if no
# reply is received from the peer, pppd will then just
# wait passively for a valid LCP packet from the peer
# (instead of exiting, as it does without this option).
#passive

# With this option, pppd will not transmit LCP packets
# to initiate a connection until a valid LCP packet is
# received from the peer (as for the "passive" option
#with old versions of pppd).
#silent

# Don't request or allow negotiation of any options for
# LCP and IPCP (use default values).
```

```
#-all

# Disable Address/Control compression
# negotiation (use default, i.e. address/control
# field disabled).
#-ac

# Disable asyncmap negotiation (use the default
# asyncmap, i.e. escape all control characters).
#-am

# Don't fork to become a background process
# (otherwise pppd will do so if a serial device is
# specified).
#-detach

# Disable IP address negotiation (with this option, the
# remote IP address must be specified with an option
# on the command line or in an options file).
#-ip

# Disable magic number negotiation.  With this option,
# pppd cannot detect a looped-back line.
#-mn

# Disable MRU [Maximum Receive Unit] negotiation (use
# default, i.e. 1500).
#-mru

# Disable protocol field compression negotiation (use
# default, i.e. protocol field compression disabled).
#-pc

# Require the peer to authenticate itself using PAP.
#+pap

# Don't agree to authenticate using PAP.
#-pap
```

```
# Require the peer to authenticate itself using CHAP
# [Cryptographic Handshake Authentication Protocol]
# authentication.
#+chap

# Don't agree to authenticate using CHAP.
#-chap

# Disable negotiation of Van Jacobson style IP header
#compression (use default, i.e. no compression).
#-vj

# Increase debugging level (same as -d).  If this option is
# given, pppd will log the contents of all control packets
# sent or received in a readable form.  The packets are
# logged through syslog with facility daemon and level
# debug. This information can be directed to a file by
# setting up /etc/syslog.conf appropriately (see
# syslog.conf(5)).  (If pppd is compiled with extra
# debugging enabled, it will log messages using
# facility local2 instead of daemon).
#debug

# Append the domain name <d> to the local host name for
# authentication purposes.  For example, if gethostname() returns
# the name porsche, but the fully qualified domain name is
# porsche.Quotron.COM, you would use the domain option to set
# the domain name to Quotron.COM.
#domain <d>

# Enable debugging code in the kernel-level PPP driver.  The
# argument n is a number which is the sum of the following values:
# 1 to enable general debug messages, 2 to request that the
# contents of received packets be printed, and 4 to request that
# the contents of transmitted packets be printed.
#kdebug n

# Set the MTU [Maximum Transmit Unit] value to <n>. Unless the
# peer requests a smaller value via MRU negotiation, pppd will
```

```
# request that the kernel networking code send data packets of no
# more than n bytes through the PPP network interface.
#mtu <n>

# Set the name of the local system for authentication purposes
# to <n>.
#name <n>

# Set the user name to use for authenticating this machine with
# the peer using PAP to <u>.
#user <u>

# Enforce the use of the hostname as the name of the local system
# for authentication purposes (overrides the name option).
#usehostname

# Set the assumed name of the remote system for authentication
# purposes to <n>.
#remotename <n>

# Add an entry to this system's ARP [Address Resolution Protocol]
# table with the IP address of the peer and the Ethernet address of
# this system.
#proxyarp

# Use the system password database for authenticating the peer
# using PAP.
#login

# If this option is given, pppd will send an LCP echo-request
# frame to the peer every n seconds. Under Linux, the echo-request
# is sent when no packets have been received from the peer for n
# seconds. Normally the peer should respond to the echo-request
# by sending an echo-reply. This option can be used with the
# lcp-echo-failure option to detect that the peer is no longer
# connected. lcp-echo-interval <n>

# If this option is given, pppd will presume the peer to be dead
# if n LCP echo-requests are sent without receiving a valid LCP
```

```
# echo-reply. If this happens, pppd will terminate the connection.
# Use of this option requires a non-zero value for the lcp-echo-
# interval parameter. This option can be used to enable pppd to
# terminate after the physical connection has been broken (e.g.,
# the modem has hung up) in situations where no hardware
# modem control lines are available. lcp-echo-failure <n>

# Set the LCP restart interval (retransmission timeout) to
# <n> seconds (default 3).
#lcp-restart <n>

# Set the maximum number of LCP terminate-request transmissions
# to <n>  (default 3).
#lcp-max-terminate <n>

# Set the maximum number of LCP configure-request transmissions
# to <n> (default 10).
#lcp-max-configure <n>

# Set the maximum number of LCP configure-NAKs returned before
# starting to send configure-Rejects instead to <n> (default 10).
#lcp-max-failure <n>

# Set the IPCP restart interval (retransmission timeout) to <n>
# seconds (default 3).
#ipcp-restart <n>

# Set the maximum number of IPCP terminate-request transmissions
# to <n> (default 3).
#ipcp-max-terminate <n>

# Set the maximum number of IPCP configure-request transmissions
# to <n> (default 10).
#ipcp-max-configure <n>

# Set the maximum number of IPCP configure-NAKs returned before
# starting to send configure-Rejects instead to <n> (default 10).
#ipcp-max-failure <n>
```

```
# Set the PAP restart interval (retransmission timeout) to <n>
# seconds (default 3).
#pap-restart <n>

# Set the maximum number of PAP authenticate-request transmissions
# to <n> (default 10).
#pap-max-authreq <n>

# Set the CHAP restart interval (retransmission timeout for
# challenges) to <n> seconds (default 3).
#chap-restart <n>

# Set the maximum number of CHAP challenge transmissions to <n>
# (default 10).
#chap-max-challenge

# If this option is given, pppd will rechallenge the peer every <n>
# seconds.
#chap-interval <n>

# With this option, pppd will accept the peer's idea of our local IP
# address, even if the local IP address was specified in an option.
#ipcp-accept-local

# With this option, pppd will accept the peer's idea of its (remote)
# IP address, even if the remote IP address was specified in an
# option. ipcp-accept-remote
```

6.11.2 What options should I use?

Well, as in all things that depends (sigh).

Provided here are two basic versions of the options file that cover the most common cases.

However, if it does NOT work, READ THE TEMPLATE FILE (/etc/ppp/options.tpl) **and** the pppd man pages **and** speak to the sysadmin/user support people who run the server into which you are connecting.

6.11.2.1   /etc/ppp/options (NO PAP/CHAP)

The following should work for connections that do not require PAP/CHAP authentication.

```
# /etc/ppp/options (NO PAP/CHAP)
#
# If you are using a STATIC IP number, edit the 0.0.0.0 part of the
# following line to your static IP number.
0.0.0.0:
#
# use the modem control lines
modem
# use uucp style locks to ensure exclusive access to the serial
# device
lock
# use hardware flow control
crtscts
# create a default route for this connection in the routing table
defaultroute
# do NOT set up any "escaped" control sequences
asyncmap 0
# use a maximum transmission packet size of 552 bytes
mtu 552
# use a maximum receive packet size of 552 bytes
mru 552
#
#-------END OF SAMPLE /etc/ppp/options (no PAP/CHAP)
```

6.11.2.2   /etc/ppp/options (using PAP/CHAP)

If the server to which you are connecting requires PAP or CHAP authentication,
to the above options file, add the following lines

```
#
# force pppd to use your ISP username as your 'host name' during the
# authentication process
name <your ISP username>        # you need to edit this line
```

```
#
# If you need to force PAP or CHAP authentication on the server,
# uncomment the appropriate one of the following lines.
#+chap
#+pap
#
# If you are using ENCRYPTED secrets in the /etc/ppp/pap-secrets
# file, then uncomment the following line.
#+papcrypt
```

6.12 Setting up your /etc/resolv.conf file

Whilst we humans like to give names to things, computers really like numbers. On a TCP/IP network (which is what the Internet is), we call machines by a particular name - and every machine lives in a particular `dquot;domaindquot;`. For example, my Linux workstation is called **archenland** and it resides in the **hedland.edu.au** domain. Its human readable address is thus archenland.hedland.edu.au. In order for this machine to be findable by other computers on the Internet, it is actually known by its IP number.

Translating (resolving) machine (and domain) names into the numbers actually used on the Internet is the business of machines that offer the Domain Name Service.

When you make a PPP connection, you need to tell your Linux machine where it can get host name to IP number (address resolution) information so that **you** can use the machine names but your **computer** can translate these to the IP numbers it needs to work.

One way is to enter every host that you want to talk to into the /etc/hosts file (which is in reality totally impossible if you are connecting to the Internet); another is to use the machine IP numbers as opposed to the names (an impossible memory task for all but the smallest LANs).

The best way is to set up Linux so that it knows where to go to get this name to number information - automatically. This service is provided by the Domain Name Server system. All that is necessary is to enter the IP numbers in your /etc/resolv.conf file.

Your PPP server sysadmin/user support people should provide you with two DNS IP numbers (only one is necessary - but two gives some redundancy in the event of failure).

Your /etc/resolv.conf should look something like :-

```
domain your.isp.domain.name
nameserver 10.25.0.1
nameserver 10.25.1.2
```

Edit this file (creating it if necessary) to represent the information that your ISP has provided. It should have ownership and permissions as follows :-

```
 -rw-r--r--    1 root      root          73 Feb 19 01:46 /etc/resolv.conf
```

If you have already set up a /etc/resolv.conf because you are on a LAN, simply add the IP numbers of the PPP DNS servers to your existing file.

6.13   The PAP/CHAP secrets file

If you are using pap or chap authentication, then you also need to create the secrets file. These are:

```
/etc/ppp/pap-secrets /etc/pp/chap-secrets
```

The first point to note about PAP and CHAP is that they are designed to authenticate **computer systems** not **users**.

"Huh? What's the difference?" I hear you ask.

Well now, once your computer has made its PPP connection to the server, **ANY** user on your system can use that connection - not just you. This is why you can set up a WAN (wide area network) link that joins two LANs (local area networks) using PPP.

That being said, your ISP will probably have given you a username and password to allow you to connect to their system and thence the Internet. Your ISP is not interested in your computer's name at all, so you will probably need to use the username at your ISP as the name for your computer.

This is done using the **name username** option to pppd. So, if you are to use the username given you by your ISP, add the line

```
name your_username_at_your_ISP
```

to your `/etc/ppp/options` file.

Technically, you should really use `user our_username_at_your_ISP` for PAP, but pppd is sufficiently intelligent to interpret `name` as `user` if it is required to use PAP. The advantage of using the `name` option is that this is also valid for CHAP.

As PAP/CHAP are for authenticating **computers**, technically you need also to specify a remote computer name. However, as most people only have one ISP, you can use a wild card (*) for the remote host name in the secrets file.

It is also worth noting that many ISPs operate multiple modem banks connected to different terminal servers - each with a different name, but ACCESSED from a single (rotary) dial in number. It can therefore be quite difficult in some circumstances to know ahead of time what the name of the remote computer is!

6.13.1   The PAP secrets file

The `/etc/ppp/pap-secrets` file looks like

```
# Secrets for authentication using PAP
# client        server      secret      acceptable local IP addresses
```

The four fields are white space delimited.

Suppose your ISP gave you a username of `fred` and a password of `flintstone` you would set the `name fred` option in `/etc/ppp/options.ttySx` and set up your `/etc/ppp/pap-secrets` file as follows

```
# Secrets for authentication using PAP
# client        server  secret          acceptable local IP addresses
fred            *       flintstone
```

This says for the local machine name `fred` (which we have told pppd to use even though it is not our local machine name) and for **ANY** server, use the password (secret) of `flintstone`.

Note that we do not need to specify a local IP address, unless we are required to FORCE a particular local, static IP address.

If you have several machines to which you connect using PAP, either arrange to have different usernames on each machine or find out the remote machine name to which you will be connecting. This will allow you to add lines to your `pap-secrets` file - provided you correctly set the `name` option for each separate machine to which you connect.

6.13.2   The CHAP secrets file

The current pppd version requires that you have mutual authentication methods - that is you must allow for both your machine to authenticate the remote server **AND** the remote server to authenticate your machine.

So, if your machine is `fred` and the remote is `barney`, your machine would set `name fred remotename barney` and the remote machine would set `name barney remotename fred` in their respective /etc/ppp/options.ttySx files.

The /etc/chap-secrets file for fred would look like

```
# Secrets for authentication using CHAP
# client        server  secret          acceptable local IP addresses
fred            barney  flintstone
```

and for barney

```
# Secrets for authentication using CHAP
# client        server  secret          acceptable local IP addresses
barney          fred    flintstone
```

6.14   Setting up the PPP connection manually

Now that you have created your /etc/ppp/options and /etc/resolv.conf files (and, if necessary, the /etc/ppp/pap|chap-secrets file), you can test the settings by manually establishing a PPP connection. (Once we have the manual connection working, we will automate the process).

To do this, your communications software must be capable of quitting WITHOUT resetting the modem. Minicom can do this - ALT Q (or in older version of minicom CTRL A Q)

Make sure you are logged in as root.

Fire up you communications software (such as minicom), dial into the PPP server and log in as normal. If you need to issue a command to start up PPP on the server, do so. You will now see the garbage you saw before.

If you are using pap/chap, then merely connecting to the remote system should start ppp on the remote and you will see the garbage without logging in (although this may not happen for some servers).

Now quit the communications software without resetting the modem (ALT Q or CTL A Q in minicom) and at the Linux prompt (as root) type

```
pppd -d -detach /dev/cuaX &
```

The -d option turns on debugging - the ppp connection start up "conversation" will be logged to your system log - which is useful if you are having trouble.

Naturally, you should use cua0 or cua1 etc - the actual port to which your modem is connected, **NOT** cuaX!

Your modem lights should now flash as the PPP connection is established. It will take a short while for the PPP connection to be made.

At this point you can look at the PPP interface, by issuing the command

```
ifconfig
```

In addition to any Ethernet and loop back devices you have, you should see something like :-

```
ppp0    Link encap:Point-Point Protocol
        inet addr:10.144.153.104  P-t-P:10.144.153.51
        Mask:255.255.255.0
        UP POINTOPOINT RUNNING  MTU:552  Metric:1
        RX packets:0 errors:0 dropped:0 overruns:0
        TX packets:0 errors:0 dropped:0 overruns:0
```

Where

- inet addr:10.144.153.10 is the IP number of your end of the link.

- P-t-P:10.144.153.5 is the SERVER's IP number.

(Naturally, ifconfig will not report these IP numbers, but the ones used by your PPP server.)

Note: ifconfig also tells you that the link is UP and RUNNING!

If you get something like

```
ppp0      Link encap:Point-Point Protocol
          inet addr:0.0.0.0  P-t-P:0.0.0.0  Mask:0.0.0.0
          POINTOPOINT  MTU:1500  Metric:1
          RX packets:0 errors:0 dropped:0 overruns:0
          TX packets:0 errors:0 dropped:0 overruns:0
```

Your PPP connection has not been made...see the later section on debugging!

You should also be able to see a route to the the remote host (and beyond). To do this, issue the command

```
    route -n>
```

You should se something like:-

```
Kernel routing table
Destination    Gateway      Genmask       Flags MSS   Window Use Iface
10.144.153.3   *        255.255.255.255 UH   1500   0       1 ppp0
127.0.0.0      *        255.0.0.0       U    3584   0      11 lo
10.0.0.0       *        255.0.0.0       U    1500   0      35 eth0
default        10.144.153.3    *  UG         1500   0       5 ppp0
```

Of particular importance here, notice we have TWO entries pointing to our ppp interface.

The first is a HOST route (indicated by the H flag) and that allows us to see the host to which we are connected to - but no further.

The second is the **default** route - this is the route that tells our Linux PC to send any packets NOT destined for the local Ethernet(s) - to which we have specific network routes - to the PPP server itself. The PPP server then is responsible for routing our packets out onto the Internet and routing the return packets back to us.

If you do not see a routing table with two entries, something is wrong (see the debugging section).

Now test the link by 'pinging' the server at its IP number as reported by the ifconfig output, i.e.

```
ping 10.144.153.51
```

You should receive output like

```
PING 10.144.153.51 (10.144.153.51): 56 data bytes
64 bytes from 10.144.153.51: icmp_seq=0 ttl=255 time=328.3 ms
64 bytes from 10.144.153.51: icmp_seq=1 ttl=255 time=190.5 ms
64 bytes from 10.144.153.51: icmp_seq=2 ttl=255 time=187.5 ms
64 bytes from 10.144.153.51: icmp_seq=3 ttl=255 time=170.7 ms
```

This listing will go on for ever - to stop it press CTRL C, at which point you will receive some more information :-

```
--- 10.144.153.51 ping statistics ---
4 packets transmitted, 4 packets received, 0% packet loss
round-trip min/avg/max = 170.7/219.2/328.3 ms
```

So far so good.

Now try pinging a host by name (not the name of the PPP server itself) but a host at another site that you KNOW is probably going to be up and running...). For example

```
ping sunsite.unc.edu
```

This time there will be a bit of a pause as Linux obtains the IP number for the fully qualified host name you have 'ping'ed from the DNS you specified in /etc/resolv.conf - so don't worry (but you will see your modem lights flash). Shortly you will receive output like

```
PING sunsite.unc.edu (152.2.254.81): 56 data bytes
64 bytes from 152.2.254.81: icmp_seq=0 ttl=254 time=190.1 ms
64 bytes from 152.2.254.81: icmp_seq=1 ttl=254 time=180.6 ms
64 bytes from 152.2.254.81: icmp_seq=2 ttl=254 time=169.8 ms
64 bytes from 152.2.254.81: icmp_seq=3 ttl=254 time=170.6 ms
64 bytes from 152.2.254.81: icmp_seq=4 ttl=254 time=170.6 ms
```

Again, stop the output by pressing CTRL C and get the statistics...

```
--- sunsite.unc.edu ping statistics ---
5 packets transmitted, 5 packets received, 0% packet loss
round-trip min/avg/max = 169.8/176.3/190.1 ms
```

If you don't get any response, check in the debugging section of this document.

If everything works, shut down the connection by typing

```
ppp-off
```

After a short pause, the modem should hang itself up.

If that does not work, either turn off your modem or fire up your communications software and interrupt the modem with +++ and then hang up with ATH0 when you receive the modem's OK prompt.

You may also need to clean up the lock file created by pppd

```
rm -f /var/lock/LCK..cuaX
```

6.15   Automating your connections - Creating the connection scripts

A chat script automates the log in and PPP start up so all you have to do (as root or as a member of the ppp group) is issue a single command to fire up your connection.

6.15.1   Connection scripts for Username/Password Authentication

If your ISP does NOT require the use of PAP/CHAP, these are the scripts for you!

If the ppp package installed correctly, you should have two example files. For PPP 2.1.2 they are in /usr/sbin and for PPP 2.2 they are in /etc/ppp/scripts. They are called

for PPP-2.1.2

```
ppp-on
ppp-off
```

and for PPP-2.2

```
ppp-off
ppp-on
ppp-on-dialer
```

Now, if you are using PPP 2.1.2, I strongly urge you to delete the sample files. There are potential problems with these - and don't tell me they work fine - I used them for ages too (and recommended them in the first version of this HOWTO!

For the benefit of PPP 2.1.2 users, here are BETTER template versions, taken from the PPP 2.2 distribution. I suggest you copy and use these scripts **instead of** the old PPP-2.1.2 scripts.

6.15.2 The ppp-on script

This is the first of a PAIR of scripts that actually fire up the connection.

```
#!/bin/sh
#
# Script to initiate a PPP connection. This is the first part of the
# pair of scripts. This is not a secure pair of scripts as the codes
# are visible with the 'ps' command.  However, it is simple.
#
# These are the parameters. Change as needed.
TELEPHONE=555-1212 #The telephone number for the connection
ACCOUNT=george #The account name for logon (as in 'George Burns')
PASSWORD=gracie #The password for this account (and 'Gracie Allen')
LOCAL_IP=0.0.0.0  #Local IP address if known. Dynamic = 0.0.0.0
REMOTE_IP=0.0.0.0  #Remote IP address if desired. Normally 0.0.0.0
NETMASK=255.255.255.0 #The proper netmask if needed
#
# Export them so that they will be available to 'ppp-on-dialer'
export TELEPHONE ACCOUNT PASSWORD
#
# This is the location of the script which dials the phone and logs
# in.  Please use the absolute file name as the $PATH variable is not
# used on the connect option.  (To do so on a 'root' account would be
# a security hole so don't ask.)
```

```
#
DIALER_SCRIPT=/etc/ppp/ppp-on-dialer
#
# Initiate the connection
#
#
exec /usr/sbin/pppd debug /dev/ttySx 38400 \
        $LOCAL_IP:$REMOTE_IP \
        connect $DIALER_SCRIPT
```

Here is the ppp-on-dialer script:-

```
#!/bin/sh
#
# This is part 2 of the ppp-on script. It will perform the connection
# protocol for the desired connection.
#
exec chat -v                                                      \
        TIMEOUT         3                                         \
        ABORT           '\nBUSY\r'                                \
        ABORT           '\nNO ANSWER\r'                           \
        ABORT           '\nRINGING\r\n\r\nRINGING\r'              \
        ''              \rAT                                      \
        'OK-+++\c-OK'   ATH0                                      \
        TIMEOUT         30                                        \
        OK              ATDT$TELEPHONE                            \
        CONNECT         ''                                        \
        ogin:--ogin:    $ACCOUNT                                  \
        assword:        $PASSWORD
```

6.15.3   Editing the supplied PPP startup scripts

As the new scripts come in two parts, we will edit them in turn.

6.15.3.1   The ppp-on script

You will need to edit the script to reflect YOUR user name at your ISP, YOUR
password at your ISP, the telephone number of your ISP.

Each of the lines like `TELEPHONE=` actually set up shell variables that contain the information to the right of the '=' (excluding the comments of course). So edit each of these lines so it is correct for your ISP and connection.

Also, as you are setting the IP number (if you need to) in the **/etc/ppp/options** file, DELETE the line that says

```
$LOCAL_IP:$REMOTE_IP \
```

Also, make sure that the shell variable DIALER_SCRIPT points at the full path and name of the dialer script that you are actually going to use. So, if you have moved this or renamed the script, make sure you edit this line correctly in the **ppp-on** script!

If you have set up your **ppp-on** script correctly and your PPP server uses username/password authentication, you should not need to edit the **ppp-on-dialer** script at all!

Although you can set up your serial port using /etc/rc.serial at boot time, I have found that it is a good idea to explicitly set up the serial port in the ppp-on script. This allows for my using the modem for other purposes (which may reset the serial settings) between times.

Immediately before the line that actually starts pppd, add the line

```
/bin/setserial /dev/cuaX spd_vhi
```

This sets up the serial port to actually set the baud rate to 115,200 baud when a speed of 38,400 baud is requested. This is fine for 28.8k (and faster) baud modems. However, many 14,400 baud modems cannot actually run their serial interface back to the computer at this speed.

Check you modem manual and if the maximum serial speed for your modem is 38,400 use the line

```
/bin/setserial /dev/cuaX spd_normal
```

6.15.3.2 Starting PPP at the server end

Whilst the ppp-on-dialer script is fine for servers that automatically start pppd at the server end once you have logged in, some servers require that you explicitly start PPP on the server.

If you need to issue a command to start up PPP on the server, you DO need to edit the ppp-on-dialer script.

At the END of the script (after the password line) add an additional **expect send** pair - this one would look for your login prompt (beware of characters that have a special meaning in the Bourne shell - such as $ and *or* (open and close square brackets).

Once chat has found the shell prompt, chat must issue the ppp start up command required for your ISPs PPP server.

In my case, my PPP server uses the standard Linux Bash prompt

```
[hartr@kepler hartr]$
```

and requires that I type

```
ppp
```

to start up PPP on the server.

It is a good idea to allow for a bit of error recovery here, so in my case I use

```
    hartr--hartr      ppp
```

This says - if we don't receive the prompt within the timeout, send a carriage return and looks for the prompt again.

Once the prompt is received, then send the string 'ppp'.

Note: don't forget to add a \ to the end of the previous line so chat still thinks the entire chat script is on one line!

Unfortunately, some servers produce a very variable set of prompts! You may need to log in several times using minicom to understand what is going on and pick the stable "expect" strings.

6.15.3.3 The ppp-on-dialer script

This is the second of the scripts that actually brings up our ppp link.

Note: a chat script is normally all on one line. the backslashes are used to allow line continuations across several physical lines (for human readability) and do not form part of the script itself.

However, it is very useful to look at it in detail so that we understand what it is actually (supposed) to be doing!

6.15.4   What a Chat script means...

A chat script is a sequence of "expect string" "send string" pairs. In particular, note that we **ALWAYS** expect **something** before we send something.

If we are to send something **WITHOUT** receiving anything first, we must use an empty expect string (indicated by "") and similarly for expecting something without sending anything! Also, if a string consists of several words, (e.g. NO CARRIER), you must quote the string so that it is seen as a single entity by chat.

The chat line in our template is:-

- `exec chat -v`
  Invoke chat, the -v tells chat to copy ALL its I/O into the system log (usually /var/log/messages).
  Once you are happy that the chat script is working reliably, edit this line to remove the -v to save unnecessary clutter in your syslog.

- `TIMEOUT 3`
  This sets the timeout for the receipt of expected input to three seconds. You may need to increase this to say 5 or 10 seconds if you are using a really slow modem!

- `ABORT '\\nBUSY\\r'`
  If the string BUSY is received, abort the operation.

- `ABORT '\\nNO ANSWER\\r'`
  If the string NO ANSWER is received, abort the operation

- `ABORT '\\nRINGING\\r\\n\\r\\nRINGING\\r'`
  If the (repeated) string RINGING is received, abort the operation.
  This is because someone is ringing your phone line!

- `'' \\rAT`
  Expect nothing from the modem and send the string AT.

- `'OK-+++\\c-OK' ATH0`
  This one is a bit more complicated as it uses some of chat's error recovery capabilities. What is says is...

Expect OK, if it is NOT received (because the modem is not in command mode) then send +++ (the standard Hayes-compatible modem string that returns the modem to command mode) and expect OK; then send ATH0 (the modem hang up string).

This allows your script to cope with the situation of your modem being stuck on-line!

- TIMEOUT 30

  Set the timeout to 30 seconds for the remainder of the script. If you experience trouble with the chat script aborting due to timeouts, increase this to 45 seconds or more.

- OK ATDT$TELEPHONE

  Expect OK (the modem's response to the ATH0 command) and dial the number we want to call.

- CONNECT ''

  Expect CONNECT (which our modem sends when the remote modem answers) and send nothing in reply.

- ogin:--ogin: $ACCOUNT

  Again, we have some error recovery built in here. Expect the login prompt (...ogin:) but if we don't receive it by the timeout, send a return and then look for the login prompt again. When the prompt is received, send the username (stored in the shell variable $ACCOUNT).

- assword: $PASSWORD

  Expect the password prompt and send our password (again, stored in a shell variable).

This chat script has reasonable error recovery capability. Chat has considerably more features than demonstrated here. For more information consult the chat manual page (man 8 chat).

6.15.5   A chat script for PAP/CHAP authenticated connections

If your ISP is using PAP/CHAP, then your chat script is much simpler. All your chat script needs to do is dial the telephone, wait for a connect and then let pppd handle the logging in!

```
#!/bin/sh
#
# This is part 2 of the ppp-on script. It will perform the connection
# protocol for the desired connection.
#
exec chat -v                                                        \
        TIMEOUT          3                                          \
        ABORT            '\nBUSY\r'                                 \
        ABORT            '\nNO ANSWER\r'                            \
        ABORT            '\nRINGING\r\n\r\nRINGING\r'               \
        ''               \rAT                                       \
        'OK-+++\c-OK'    ATHO                                       \
        TIMEOUT          30                                         \
        OK               ATDT$TELEPHONE                             \
        CONNECT          ''                                         \
```

6.15.6   The pppd debug and -f option_ file options

As we have already seen, you can turn on debug information logging with the -d
option to pppd. The 'debug' option is equivalent to this.

As we are establishing a new connection with a new script, leave in the debug
option for now. (Warning: if your disk space is tight, logging pppd exchanges can
rapidly extend your syslog file and run you into trouble - but to do this you must
fail to connect and keep on trying for quite a few minutes).

Once you are happy that all is working properly, then you can remove this
option.

If you have called your ppp options file anything other than /etc/ppp/options
or /etc/ppp/options.ttySx, specify the file name with the -f option to pppd - e.g.

```
exec /usr/sbin/pppd debug -f options.myserver /dev/ttySx 38400 \
```

6.16   Testing your connection script

Open a new root Xterm (if you are in X) or open a new virtual console and log in
as root.

In this new session, issue the command

```
tail -f /var/log/messages
```

(or whatever your system log file is).

In the first window (or virtual console) issue the command

```
ppp-on \&
```

(or whatever name you have called your edited version of /usr/sbin/ppp- on).
If you do not put the script into the background by specifying & at the end of the
command, you will not get your terminal prompt back until ppp exits (when the
link terminates).

Now switch back to the window that is tracking your system log.

You will see something like the following (provided you specified -v to chat and
-d to pppd)....this is the chat script and responses being logged to the system log
file followed by the start up information for pppd :-

```
Oct 21 16:09:58 hwin chat[19868]: abort on (NO CARRIER)
Oct 21 16:09:59 hwin chat[19868]: abort on (BUSY)
Oct 21 16:09:59 hwin chat[19868]: send (ATZ^M)
Oct 21 16:09:59 hwin chat[19868]: expect (OK)
Oct 21 16:10:00 hwin chat[19868]: ATZ^M^M
Oct 21 16:10:00 hwin chat[19868]: OK -- got it
Oct 21 16:10:00 hwin chat[19868]: send (ATDT722298^M)
Oct 21 16:10:00 hwin chat[19868]: expect (CONNECT)
Oct 21 16:10:00 hwin chat[19868]: ^M
Oct 21 16:10:22 hwin chat[19868]: ATDT722298^M^M
Oct 21 16:10:22 hwin chat[19868]: CONNECT -- got it
Oct 21 16:10:22 hwin chat[19868]: send (^M)
Oct 21 16:10:22 hwin chat[19868]: expect (ogin:)
Oct 21 16:10:22 hwin chat[19868]:  57600^M
Oct 21 16:10:23 hwin chat[19868]: ^[[;H^[[2J^M^M
Oct 21 16:10:23 hwin chat[19868]: ^M
Oct 21 16:10:23 hwin chat[19868]: ^M
Oct 21 16:10:23 hwin chat[19868]: ^I^I This is node
kepler.hedland.edu.au^M
Oct 21 16:10:23 hwin chat[19868]: ^I^I^I at Hedland Campus^M
Oct 21 16:10:23 hwin chat[19868]: ^I^I^I Hedland College^M
Oct 21 16:10:23 hwin chat[19868]: ^M
```

```
Oct 21 16:10:23 hwin chat[19868]: ^I^I  Authorised user ONLY are
to use this system^M
Oct 21 16:10:23 hwin chat[19868]: ^M
Oct 21 16:10:23 hwin chat[19868]: ^M
Oct 21 16:10:23 hwin chat[19868]: ^I^I For more information,
contact ComputerSystems^M
Oct 21 16:10:23 hwin chat[19868]: ^I^I^I  on +61 (0)91 72 0400^M
Oct 21 16:10:23 hwin chat[19868]: ^I^I^I^I  or^M
Oct 21 16:10:23 hwin chat[19868]: ^I^I  email:  help@hedunx.
hedland.edu.au^M
Oct 21 16:10:23 hwin chat[19868]: ^M
Oct 21 16:10:23 hwin last message repeated 3 times
Oct 21 16:10:23 hwin chat[19868]: kepler login: -- got it
Oct 21 16:10:23 hwin chat[19868]: send (hartr^M)
Oct 21 16:10:23 hwin chat[19868]: expect (ssword:)
Oct 21 16:10:23 hwin chat[19868]:  hartr^M
Oct 21 16:10:23 hwin chat[19868]: Password: -- got it
Oct 21 16:10:23 hwin chat[19868]: send (??????^M)
Oct 21 16:10:23 hwin chat[19868]: expect (hartr)
Oct 21 16:10:23 hwin chat[19868]:  ^M^M
Oct 21 16:10:24 hwin chat[19868]: Last login: Sat Oct 21 14:55:53 on
ttyC0^M
Oct 21 16:10:24 hwin chat[19868]: ^M
Oct 21 16:10:24 hwin last message repeated 9 times
Oct 21 16:10:24 hwin chat[19868]: ^I^IYou have logged into node
kepler.hedland.edu.au^M
Oct 21 16:10:24 hwin chat[19868]: ^M
Oct 21 16:10:24 hwin chat[19868]:  This is a Compaq Prolinea
486DX2/50 running
Oct 21 16:10:24 hwin chat[19868]: ^M
Oct 21 16:10:24 hwin chat[19868]:  This computer operates as
the main Hedland
Campus communications^M
Oct 21 16:10:24 hwin chat[19868]: ^I  node, providing dial-in terminal
and SLIP access,^M
Oct 21 16:10:24 hwin chat[19868]: ^I^I  Kepler also runs the Hedland
end of^M
Oct 21 16:10:24 hwin chat[19868]: ^I^I the Hedland/Newman
inter-Campus
```

```
WAN link^M
Oct 21 16:10:24 hwin chat[19868]: ^M
Oct 21 16:10:24 hwin chat[19868]: ^M
Oct 21 16:10:24 hwin chat[19868]: [hartr -- got it
Oct 21 16:10:24 hwin chat[19868]: send (ppp^M)
Oct 21 16:10:27 hwin pppd[19872]: pppd 2.1.2 started by root, uid 0
Oct 21 16:10:27 hwin pppd[19873]: Using interface ppp0
Oct 21 16:10:27 hwin pppd[19873]: Connect: ppp0 <--> /dev/cua1
Oct 21 16:10:27 hwin pppd[19873]: fsm_sdata(LCP): Sent code 1, id 1.
Oct 21 16:10:27 hwin pppd[19873]: LCP: sending Configure-Request, id 1
Oct 21 16:10:27 hwin pppd[19873]: fsm_rconfreq(LCP): Rcvd id 1.
Oct 21 16:10:27 hwin pppd[19873]: lcp_reqci: rcvd MRU
Oct 21 16:10:27 hwin pppd[19873]: (1500)
Oct 21 16:10:27 hwin pppd[19873]:  (ACK)
Oct 21 16:10:27 hwin pppd[19873]: lcp_reqci: rcvd ASYNCMAP
Oct 21 16:10:27 hwin pppd[19873]: (0)
Oct 21 16:10:27 hwin pppd[19873]:  (ACK)
Oct 21 16:10:27 hwin pppd[19873]: lcp_reqci: rcvd MAGICNUMBER
Oct 21 16:10:27 hwin pppd[19873]: (a098b898)
Oct 21 16:10:27 hwin pppd[19873]:  (ACK)
Oct 21 16:10:27 hwin pppd[19873]: lcp_reqci: rcvd PCOMPRESSION
Oct 21 16:10:27 hwin pppd[19873]:  (ACK)
Oct 21 16:10:27 hwin pppd[19873]: lcp_reqci: rcvd ACCOMPRESSION
Oct 21 16:10:27 hwin pppd[19873]:  (ACK)
Oct 21 16:10:27 hwin pppd[19873]: lcp_reqci: returning CONFACK.
Oct 21 16:10:27 hwin pppd[19873]: fsm_sdata(LCP): Sent code 2, id 1.
Oct 21 16:10:27 hwin pppd[19873]: fsm_rconfack(LCP): Rcvd id 1.
Oct 21 16:10:27 hwin pppd[19873]: fsm_sdata(IPCP): Sent code 1, id 1.
Oct 21 16:10:27 hwin pppd[19873]: IPCP: sending Configure-Request, id 1
Oct 21 16:10:27 hwin pppd[19873]: fsm_rconfreq(IPCP): Rcvd id 1.
Oct 21 16:10:27 hwin pppd[19873]: ipcp: received ADDR
Oct 21 16:10:27 hwin pppd[19873]: (10.144.153.51)
Oct 21 16:10:27 hwin pppd[19873]:  (ACK)
Oct 21 16:10:27 hwin pppd[19873]: ipcp: received COMPRESSTYPE
Oct 21 16:10:27 hwin pppd[19873]: (45)
Oct 21 16:10:27 hwin pppd[19873]:  (ACK)
Oct 21 16:10:27 hwin pppd[19873]: ipcp: returning Configure-ACK
Oct 21 16:10:28 hwin pppd[19873]: fsm_sdata(IPCP):Sent code 2,id 1.
Oct 21 16:10:30 hwin pppd[19873]: fsm_sdata(IPCP):Sent code 1,id 1.
```

```
Oct 21 16:10:30 hwin pppd[19873]: IPCP:sending ConfigureRequest,id1
Oct 21 16:10:30 hwin pppd[19873]: fsm_rconfreq(IPCP): Rcvd id 255.
Oct 21 16:10:31 hwin pppd[19873]: ipcp: received ADDR
Oct 21 16:10:31 hwin pppd[19873]: (10.144.153.51)
Oct 21 16:10:31 hwin pppd[19873]:  (ACK)
Oct 21 16:10:31 hwin pppd[19873]: ipcp: received COMPRESSTYPE
Oct 21 16:10:31 hwin pppd[19873]: (45)
Oct 21 16:10:31 hwin pppd[19873]:  (ACK)
Oct 21 16:10:31 hwin pppd[19873]: ipcp: returning Configure-ACK
Oct 21 16:10:31 hwin pppd[19873]: fsm_sdata(IPCP):Sent code 2,id 255.
Oct 21 16:10:31 hwin pppd[19873]: fsm_rconfack(IPCP): Rcvd id 1.
Oct 21 16:10:31 hwin pppd[19873]: ipcp: up
Oct 21 16:10:31 hwin pppd[19873]: local  IP address 10.144.153.104
Oct 21 16:10:31 hwin pppd[19873]: remote IP address 10.144.153.51
```

(Note - I am using STATIC IP numbers - hence my machine sent that to the PPP server - you won't see this if you are using DYNAMIC IP numbers.)

This looks OK - so test it out as before with pings to IP numbers and host names.

Fire up you web browser or whatever and go surfing - you are connected!

6.17   Shutting down the PPP link

When you have finished with the PPP link, use the standard ppp-off command to shut it down (remember - you need to be root or a member of the PPP group!).

In your system log you will see something like:-

```
Oct 21 16:10:45 hwin pppd[19873]: Interrupt received: terminating link
Oct 21 16:10:45 hwin pppd[19873]: ipcp: down
Oct 21 16:10:45 hwin pppd[19873]: default route ioctl(SIOCDELRT):
Bad address
Oct 21 16:10:45 hwin pppd[19873]: fsm_sdata(LCP): Sent code 5, id 2.
Oct 21 16:10:46 hwin pppd[19873]: fsm_rtermack(LCP).
Oct 21 16:10:46 hwin pppd[19873]: Connection terminated.
Oct 21 16:10:46 hwin pppd[19873]: Exit.
```

Don't worry about the `SIOCDELRT` - this is just pppd noting that it is terminating and is nothing to worry about.

6.18   Debugging

There are any number of reasons that your connection does not work - chat has failed to complete correctly, you have a dirty line, etc. So check your syslog for indications.

A **VERY** common mistake is that you have mistyped something in your scripts. You need to check these through very carefully - and bear in mind that we humans have a tendency to read what we THINK we have typed - not what is actually there!

Another is to try to use PPP-2.2 with kernel 1.2.X or PPP-2.1.2 with kernel 1.3.X/2.0.X - use the right version of pppd for your kernel!

Now look in the PPP FAQ (which is really a series of questions and answers). This is a very comprehensive document and the answers ARE there! From my own (sad) experience, if the answer to your problems is not there, the problem is NOT ppp's fault! In my case I was using an ELF kernel that I had not upgraded to the appropriate kernel modules. I only wasted about 2 days (and most of one night) cursing what had been a perfect PPP server before the light dawned!

6.18.1   I compiled in PPP but Linux says I don't have it!

You are using kernel 1.3.X/2.0.X and have compiled in module support and then compiled PPP support as a module (and installed the modules) - haven't you?

If you are NOT using kerneld to autoload the required modules, then you must explicitly load the ppp module (and possibly the serial support module too) before you can run PPP!

You can do this by hand - as root, type

```
insmod ppp
```

You may also need to load the serial support module first...

```
insmod slhc
```

However, you should sort out the auto-loading of kernel modules - so go check out the kerneld mini-howto!

6.18.2   I cannot set up a default route

You have a local Ethernet (or another network connection of some kind) with an existing default route already set up.

The section on routing in 'Linking two networks using PPP' covers correctly setting this up (briefly).

Your problem is that you cannot have more than a single default route. A default route is the destination to which all packets are sent that are not covered by a **specific** route. Generally, the default route will point at the route from your computer to the Internet.

Unfortunately, some Linux distributions set up a default route to the local Ethernet interface. You will need to change the system initialization that handles configuring your Ethernet interface and establishes the routing across that interface so that it sets up a specific route to your local Ethernet(s).

See the NET2-Howto and the Linux Network Administrator Guide for this information.

6.19   Linking two networks using PPP

There is basically no difference between linking a single Linux PC to a PPP server and linking two LANs using PPP on a machine on each LAN. Remember, PPP is a **peer to peer** protocol.

However, you **DEFINITELY** need to understand about how routing is established. Read the NET-2 howto and the Linux Network Administrator Guide (NAG). You will also find " TCP/IP Network Administration" (published by O'Reilly and Assoc - ISBN 0-937175-82-X) to be of invaluable assistance.

In order to link two LANs, you **must** be using different IP network numbers (or subnets of the same network number) and you will need to use static IP numbers - or use IP masquerade. If you want to use IP masquerade, see the IP masquerade mini-howto for instructions on setting that up.

6.19.1   Setting up IP numbers

Arrange with the network administrator of the other LAN the IP numbers that will be used for each end of the PPP interface. If you are using static IP numbers, this will also probably require you to dial into a specific telephone number.

Now edit the appropriate /etc/ppp/options[.ttyXX] file - it's a good idea to have a specific modem and port at your end for this connection. This may well require you to change your /etc/ppp/options file too - and create appropriate options.ttyXX files for any other connections too!

Specify the IP numbers for your end of the PPP link in the appropriate options file exactly as shown above for static IP numbers.

6.19.2   Setting up the routing

You must arrange that packets on your local LAN are routed across the interface that the PPP link establishes. This is a two stage process.

First of all, you need to establish a route from the machine running the PPP link to the network(s) at the far end of the link. If the link is to the Internet, this can be handled by a default route established by pppd itself at your end of the connection using the 'defaultroute' option to pppd.

If however, the link is only linking two LANs, then a specific network route must be added. This is done using a 'route' command in the /etc/ppp/ip-up script (see After the link comes up...) for instructions on doing this.

The second thing you need to do is to tell the other computers on your LAN that your Linux computer is actually the 'gateway' for the network(s) at the far end of the ppp link.

Of course, the network administrator at the other end of the link has to do all this too! However, as s/he will be routing packets to your specific networks, a **specific network route** will be required, not a default route (unless the LANs at the far and of the link are linking into you to access the Internet across your connection).

6.19.3   Network security

If you are linking you LAN to the Internet using PPP - or even just to a "foreign" LAN, you need to think about security issues. I strongly urge you to think about setting up a firewall!

6.20 After the link comes up...

Once the PPP link is established, pppd looks for `/etc/ppp/ip-up`. If this script exists and is executable, the PPP daemon executes the script. This allows you to automate any special routing commands that may be necessary and any other actions that you want to occur every time the PPP link is activated.

This is just a shell script and can do anything that a shell script can do (i.e. virtually anything you want).

For example, you can get sendmail to dispatch any waiting outbound messages in the mail queue.

Similarly, you can insert the commands into ip-up to collect (using pop) any email waiting for you at your ISP.

6.20.1 Special routing

If you are linking two LANs, you will need to set up a specific route to the 'foreign' LANs. This is easily done using the `/etc/ppp/ip-up` script. The only difficulty arises if your machine handles multiple PPP links.

This is because the `/etc/ppp/ip-up` is executed for EVERY ppp connection that comes up, so you need to carefully execute the correct routing commands for the particular link that comes up.

Using the bash 'case' statement on an appropriate parameter that pppd passes into the script accomplishes this. For example, this is the `/etc/ppp/ip-up` script I use to handle our WAN links and the link to my home Ethernet (also handled on the same ppp server).

```
#!/bin/bash
#
# Script which handles the routing issues as necessary for pppd
# Only the link to Newman requires this handling.
#
# When the ppp link comes up, this script is called with
# the following parameters
```

```
#    $1   the interface name used by pppd (e.g. ppp3)
#    $2   the tty device name
#    $3   the tty device speed
#    $4   the local IP address for the interface
#    $5   the remote IP address
#    $6   the parameter specified by the 'ipparam' option to pppd
#
case "$5" in
# Handle the routing to the Newman Campus server
        202.12.126.1)
                /sbin/route add -net 202.12.126.0 gw 202.12.126.1
# and flush the mail queue to get their email there asap!
                /usr/sbin/sendmail -q &

                ;;
        139.130.177.2)
# Our Internet link
# When the link comes up, start the time server and synchronise
# to the world provided it is not already running
                if [ ! -f /var/lock/subsys/xntpd ]; then
                        /etc/rc.d/init.d/xntpd.init start &

                fi
# Start the news server (if not already running)
                if [ ! -f /var/lock/subsys/news ]; then
                        /etc/rc.d/init.d/news start &

                fi
                ;;
        203.18.8.104)
# Get the email down to my home machine as soon as the link comes up
# No routing is required as my home Ethernet is handled by IP
# masquerade and proxyarp routing.
                /usr/sbin/sendmail -q &

                ;;
        *)
esac
exit 0
```

As a result of bringing up the ppp link to our Newman campus and this script, we end up with the following routing table entries (this machine also is our general dial up PPP server AND handles our Internet link). I have interspersed comments in the output to help explain what each entry is) :-

```
[root@kepler /root]# route -n
Kernel routing table
Destination     Gateway     Genmask       Flags MSS  Window Use Iface
# the HOST route to our remote internet gateway
139.130.177.2   *       255.255.255.255 UH    1500  0       134 ppp4
# the HOST route to our Newman campus server
202.12.126.1    *       255.255.255.255 UH    1500  0        82 ppp5
# the HOST route to my home ethernet
203.18.8.104    *       255.255.255.255 UH    1500  0        74 ppp3
# two of our general dial up PPP lines
203.18.8.64     *       255.255.255.255 UH    552   0         0 ppp2
203.18.8.62     *       255.255.255.255 UH    552   0         1 ppp1
# the specific network route to the Newman campus LAN
202.12.126.0 202.12.126.1 255.255.255.0   UG  1500  0      0 ppp5
# the route to our local ethernet (super-netting two
# adjacent C classes)
203.18.8.0      *       255.255.254.0   U     1500  0      1683 eth0
# the route to the loop back device
127.0.0.0       *       255.0.0.0       U     3584  0       483 lo
# the default route to the Internet
default         139.130.177.2   *       UG    1500  0 3633 ppp4
```

6.20.2 Handling email

The previous section shows how to handle the outgoing mail - simply by
flushing the mail queue once the link is up.

If you are running a WAN link, you can arrange with the network
administrator of the remote LAN to do exactly the same thing. For
example, at the Newman Campus end of our WAN link, the
/etc/ppp/ip-up script looks like :

```
#!/bin/bash
#
# Script which handles the routing issues as necessary for pppd
# Only the link to Hedland requires this handling.
#
```

```
# When the ppp link comes up, this script is called with the
# following parameters
#     $1    the interface name used by pppd (e.g. ppp3)
#     $2    the tty device name
#     $3    the tty device speed
#     $4    the local IP address for the interface
#     $5    the remote IP address
#     $6    the parameter specified by the 'ipparam' option to pppd
#
case "$5" in
        203.18.8.4)
                /usr/sbin/sendmail -q
                ;;
        *)
esac
exit 0
```

If however you have only a dynamic IP PPP link to your ISP, you need to get your email from the account on your ISPs machine. This is usually done using the POP (Post Office Protocol). This process can be handled using the 'popclient' program - and the ip-up script can automate this process for you too!

Simply create a /etc/ppp/ip-up script that contains the appropriate invocation of popclient. For my laptop that runs Red Hat Linux (which I take on any travels), this is

```
popclient -3 -c -u hartr -p <password> kepler.hedland.edu.au |formail
-s procmail
```

You could use slurp or whatever to do the same for news, and so forth. Remember, the ip-up script is just a standard bash script and so can be used to automate ANY function that needs to be accomplished every time the appropriate PPP link comes up.

6.21   Shutting down the link

The existing /usr/sbin/ppp-off script should work just fine when run as user root. The only changes you may wish to make are for the script to wait for any outgoing email currently being processed by sendmail.

This is left as an exercise for the student!

In addition, you can create a script file that will be executed once the link has been terminated. This is stored in /etc/ppp/ip-down. It can be used to undo anything special that you did in the corresponding /etc/ppp/ip-up script.

6.22 Routing issues on a LAN

If you are connected to a LAN but still want to use PPP on your personal Linux machine , you need to address some issues of the routes packets need to take from your machine to reach your LAN (through your Ethernet interface) and also to the remote PPP server and beyond.

This section does NOT attempt to teach you about routing - it deals only with a simple, special case of (static) routing!

I strongly urge you to read the Linux Network Administrator Guide (NAG) if you are NOT familiar with routing. Also the O'Reilly book "TCP/IP Network Administration" covers this topic in a very understandable form.

The basic rule of static routing is that the DEFAULT route should be the one that points to the MOST number of network addresses. For other networks, enter specific routes to the routing table.

The ONLY situation I am going to cover here is where your Linux box is on a LAN that is not connected to the Internet - and you want to dial out to the Internet for personal use whilst still connected to the LAN.

First of all, make sure that your Ethernet route is set up to the specific network addresses available across your LAN - NOT set to the default route!

Check this by issuing a route command, you should see something like the following:-

```
[root@hwin /root]# route -n
Kernel routing table
Destination    Gateway    Genmask        Flags MSS    Window Use Iface
loopback       *          255.255.255.0  U     1936   0       50 lo
10.0.0.0       *          255.255.255.0  U     1436   0      565 eth0
```

If your Ethernet interface (eth0) is pointing at the default route, (the first column will show "default" in the eth0 line) you need to change your Ethernet initialization

scripts to make it point at the specific network numbers rather than the default
route (consult the Net2 HOWTO and NAG).

This will allow pppd to set up your default route as shown below:-

```
[root@hwin /root]# route -n
Kernel routing table

Destination  Gateway  Genmask         Flags MSS   Window Use Iface
10.144.153.51  *      255.255.255.255 UH    488   0      0 ppp0
127.0.0.0      *      255.255.255.0   U     1936  0      50 lo
10.1.0.0       *      255.255.255.0   U     1436  0      569 eth0
default               10.144.153.51   *     UG    488   0   3 ppp0
```

As you can see, we have a host route to the PPP server (10.144.153.51) via
ppp0 and also a default network route that uses the PPP server as its gateway.

If your set up needs to be more complex than this - read the routing documents
already mentioned and consult an expert at your site!

If your LAN already has routers on it, you will already have gateways established
to the wider networks available at your site. You should STILL point your default
route at the PPP interface - and make the other routes specific to the networks
they serve.

6.22.1   Note on Security

When you set up a Linux box on an existing LAN to link into the Internet, you are
potentially opening your entire LAN to the Internet - and the hackers that reside
there. Before you do this, I strongly urge you to consult your network administrator and site security policy. If your PPP connection to the Internet is used to
successfully attack your site, you will at the very least earn the intense anger of
your fellow users, network and system administrators. You may also find yourself
in very much more serious trouble!

Before you connect a LAN to the Internet, you should consider the security
implications of even a DYNAMIC connection - hence the earlier reference to the
O'Reilly "Building Internet Firewalls"!

6.23   Getting Help when totally stuck

If you can't get your PPP link to work, go back through this document and check everything - in conjunction with the output created by "chat-v..." and "pppd -d" in you system log.

Also consult the PPP documentation and FAQ plus the other documents mention herein!

If you are still stuck, try the comp.os.linux.misc and comp.os.linux.networking newsgroups are reasonably regularly scanned by people that can help you with PPP as is comp.protocols.ppp

You can try sending me personal email, but I do have a day job (and a life) and I do not guarantee to respond quickly (if at all) as this depends on my current work load and the state of my private life!

In particular - **DO NOT POST REAMS OF DEBUGGING OUTPUT TO THE NEWS GROUPS NOR SEND IT TO ME BY EMAIL** - the former wastes huge amounts of network bandwidth and the latter will be consigned to /dev/null (unless I have specifically requested it).

6.24   Common Problems once the link is working

One problem you will find is that many service providers will only support the connection software package that they distribute to new accounts. This is (typically) for Microsoft Windows :-(- and many service provider help desks seem to know nothing about Unix (or Linux). So, be prepared for limited assistance from them!

You could of course do the individual a favour and educate then about Linux (any ISP help desk person should be reasonably 'with it' in Internet terms and that means they should have a home Linux box - of course it does)!

6.24.1   I can't see beyond the PPP server I connect to

OK - your PPP connection is up and running and you can ping the PPP server by IP number (the second or "remote" IP number shown by ifcongig ppp0), but you can't reach anything beyond this.

First of all, try pinging the IP numbers you have specified in /etc/resolv.conf as name servers. If this works, you can see beyond your PPP server (unless this has the same IP number as the "remote" IP number of your connection). So now try pinging the full Internet name of your service provider - eg

```
ping my.provider.net.au
```

If this does NOT work, you have a problem with the name resolution. This is probably because of a typo in your /etc/resolv.conf file. Check this carefully against the information you acquired by ringing your service provider. If all looks OK, ring your service provider and check that you wrote down the IP numbers correctly.

If it STILL doesn't work (and your service provider confirms that his name servers are up and running), you have a problem somewhere else - and I suggest you check carefully through your Linux installation (looking particularly for file permissions).

If you STILL can't ping your service provider's IP name servers by IP number, either they are down (give them a voice call and check) or there is a routing problem at your service provider's end. Again, ring them and check this out.

One possibility is that the "remote end" is a Linux PPP server where the IP forwarding option has not been specified in the kernel!

A good general test is to try hooking in to your service provider using the software that most supply for (gulp) Microsoft Windows. If everything works from another operating system to exactly the same account, then the problem is with your Linux system and NOT your service provider.

6.24.2   I can send email, but not receive it

If you are using dynamic IP numbers, this is perfectly normal. See "Setting up Services" below.

6.24.3   Why can't people finger, WWW, gopher, talk etc to my machine?

Again, if you are using dynamic IP numbers, this is perfectly normal. See "Setting up Services" below.

6.25 Using Internet services with Dynamic IP numbers

If you are using dynamic IP number (and many service providers will only give you a dynamic IP number unless you pay significantly more for your connection), then you have to recognize the limitations this imposes.

First of all, outbound service requests will work just fine. That is you can send email using sendmail, ftp files from remote sites, finger users on other machines, browse the web etc.

In particular, you can answer email that you have brought down to your machine whilst you are off line. Mail will simply sit in your mail queue until you dial back into your ISP.

However, your machine is NOT connected to the Internet 24 hours a day, nor does it have the same IP number every time it is connected. So it is impossible for you to receive email directed to your machine, and very difficult to set up a web or ftp server that your friends can access! As far as the Internet is concerned your machine does not exist as a unique, permanently contactable machine as it does not have a unique IP number (remember - other machines will be using the IP number when they are allocated it on dial in).

If you set up a WWW (or any other server), it is totally unknown by any user on the Internet UNLESS they know that your machine is connected AND its actual (current) IP number. There are a number of ways they can get this info, ranging from you ringing them, sending them email to tell them or cunning use of ".plan" files on a shell account at your service provider (assuming that your provider allows shell access).

Now, for most users, this is not a problem - all that most people want is to send and receive email (using your account on your service provider) and make outbound connections to WWW, ftp and other servers on the Internet. If you MUST have inbound connections to your server, you should really get a static IP number. Alternatively you can explore the methods hinted at above...

6.25.1 Setting up email

Even for dynamic IP numbers, you can certainly configure sendmail on your machine to send out any email that you compose locally. Configuration of sendmail can be obscure and difficult - so this document does not attempt to tell you how to do this.

However, you should probably configure sendmail so that your Internet service provider is designated as your "smart relay" host (the `sendmail.cf` **DS** option). (For more sendmail configuration info, see the sendmail documents - and look at the m4 configurations that come with sendmail. There is almost certain to be one there that will meet your needs).

There are also excellent books on Sendmail (notably the 'bible' from O'Reilly and Associates), but these are almost certainly overkill for most users!

Once you have sendmail configured, you will probably want to have sendmail dispatch any messages that have been sitting in the outbound mail queue as soon as the PPP connection comes up. To do this, add the command

```
sendmail -q &
```

to your /etc/ppp/ip-up script.

Inbound email is a problem for dynamic IP numbers. The way to handle this is to:-

- configure your mail user agent so that all mail is sent out with a "reply to" header giving your email address at your Internet Service provider.
  If you can, you should also set your FROM address to be your email address at your ISP as well.

- use the popclient program to retrieve your email from your service provider.

You can automate this process at dial up time by putting the necessary commands in the **/etc/ppp/ip-up** script.

6.25.2 Setting Up a local Name server

Whilst you can quite happily use the domain name servers located at your ISP, you can also set up a local caching only (secondary) name server that is brought up by the ip-up script. The advantage of running a local (caching only) name server is that it will save you time (and bandwidth) if you frequently contact the same sites during a long on-line session.

DNS configuration for a caching only nameserver (that uses a "forwarders' line in the named.boot file pointing at your ISPs DNS) is relatively simple. The O'Reilly book (DNS and Bind) explains all you want to know about this.

There is also a DNS-HOWTO available.

One point of Nettiquette: ask permission of your ISP before you start using a secondary, caching only name server in your ISP's domain. Properly configured, your DNS will not cause any problems to your ISP at all, but if you get things wrong, it can cause problems...

6.26 Setting up a PPP server

As already mentioned, there are many ways to do this. What I present here is the way I do it (using a Cyclades multi-port serial card) and a rotary dial in set of telephone lines.

If you don't like the method I present here, please feel free to go your own way. I would however, be pleased to include additional methods in future versions of the HOWTO. So, please send me your comments and methods!

Please note, this section only concerns setting up Linux as a PPP server. I do not (ever) intend to include information on setting up special terminal servers and such.

Also, I have yet to experiment with shadow passwords (but will be doing so sometime). Information currently presented does NOT therefore include any bells and whistles that are required by the shadow suite.

6.26.1 Kernel compilation

All the earlier comments regarding kernel compilation and kernel versions versus pppd versions apply. This section assumes that you have read the earlier sections of this document!

For a PPP server, you **MUST** include IP forwarding in your kernel. You may also wish to include other capabilities (such as IP firewalls, accounting etc etc).

If you are using a multi-port serial card, then you must obviously include the necessary drivers in your kernel too!

6.26.2 Overview of the server system

We offer dial up PPP (and SLIP) accounts and shell accounts using the same username/password pair. This has the advantages (for us) that a user requires only one account and can use it for all types of connectivity.

As we are an educational organization, we do not charge our staff and students for access, and so do not have to worry about accounting and charging issues.

We operate a firewall between our site and the Internet, and this restricts some user access as the dial up lines are inside our (Internet) firewall (for fairly obvious reasons, details of our other internal firewalls are not presented here and are irrelevant in any case).

The process a user goes through to establish a PPP link to our site (once they have a valid account of course) is :-

- Dial into our rotary dialer (this is a single phone number that connects to a bank of modems - the first free modem is then used).

- Log in using a valid username and password pair.

- At the shell prompt, issue the command **ppp** to start PPP on the server.

- Start PPP on their PC (be it running Windows, DOS, Linux MAC OS or whatever - that is their problem).

The server uses individual **/etc/ppp/options.ttyXX** files for each dial in port that set the remote IP number for dynamic IP allocation. The server users proxyarp routing for the remote clients (set via the appropriate option to pppd). This obviates the need for routed or gated.

When the user hangs up at their end, pppd detects this and tells the modem to hang up, bringing down the PPP link at the same time.

6.26.3   Getting the software together

You will need the following software:-

- Linux, properly compiled to include the necessary options.

- The appropriate version of pppd for your kernel.

- A 'getty' program that intelligently handles modem communications.
  We use getty_ps2.0.7h, but mgetty is highly thought of. I understand that mgetty can detect a call that is using pap/chap (pap is the standard for Windows95) and invoke pppd automatically, but I have yet to explore this.

- An operational domain name server (DNS) that is accessible to your dial up
  users.
  You should really be running your own DNS if possible...

6.26.4 Setting up standard (shell access) dialup.

Before you can set up your PPP server, your Linux box must be capable of handling
standard dial up access.

This howto does NOT cover setting this up. Please see the documentation of the getty of your choice and serial HOWTO for information on this.

6.26.5 Setting up the PPP options files

You will need to set up the overall `/etc/ppp/options` with the common options
for all dial up ports. The options we use are:-

```
asyncmap 0
netmask 255.255.254.0
proxyarp
lock
crtscts
modem
```

Note - we do NOT use any (obvious) routing - and in particular there is no
defaultroute option. The reason for this is that all you (as a PPP server) are required
to do is to route packets **from** the ppp client out across your LAN/Internet and
route packets **to** the client from your LAN and beyond.

All that is necessary for this is a host route to the client machine and the use of
the 'proxyarp' option to pppd.

The 'proxyarp' option sets up (surprise) a proxy arp entry in the PPP server's
arp table that basically says 'send all packets destined for the PPP client to me'.
This is the easiest way to set up routing to a single PPP client - but you cannot use
this if you are routing between two LANs - you must add proper network routes
which can't use proxy arp.

You will almost certainly wish to provide dynamic IP number allocation to your dial up users. You can accomplish this by allocating an IP number to each dial up port. Now, create a `/etc/ppp/options.ttyXX` for each dial up port.

In this, simply put the local (server) IP number and the IP number that is to be used for that port. For example

```
kepler:slip01
```

In particular, note that you can use valid host names in this file (I find that I only remember the IP numbers of critical machines and devices on my networks - names are more meaningful)!

6.26.6   Setting pppd up to allow users to (successfully) run it

As starting a ppp link implies configuring a kernel device (a network interface) and manipulating the kernel routing tables, special privileges are required - in fact full root privileges.

Fortunately, pppd has been designed to be 'safe' to run set uid to root. So you will need to

```
chmod u+s /usr/sbin/pppd
```

When you list the file, it should then appear as

```
-rwsr-xr-x   1 root      root        74224 Apr 28 07:17 /usr/sbin/pppd
```

If you do not do this, users will be unable to set up their ppp link.

6.26.7   Setting up the global alias for pppd

In order to simplify things for our dial up PPP users, we create a global alias (in /etc/bashrc) so that one simple command will start ppp on the server once they are logged in.

This looks like

```
alias ppp="exec /usr/sbin/pppd -detach"
```

What this does is

- exec : this means replace the running program (in this case the shell) with the program that is run.

- pppd -detach : start up pppd and do NOT fork into the background. This ensures that when pppd exits there is no process hanging around.

When a user logs in like this, they will appear in the output of 'w' as

```
6:24pm  up 3 days,  7:00,  4 users,  load average: 0.05, 0.03, 0.00
User     tty        login@ idle   JCPU   PCPU  what
hartr    ttyC0      3:05am 9:14                 -
```

And that is it...I told you this was a simple, basic PPP server system!

6.27 Using PPP across a null modem (direct serial) connection

This is very simple - there is no modem in the way so things are much simpler.

First of all, choose one of the machines as a 'server', setting up a getty on the serial port so you can test that you do have connectivity using minicom to access the serial port on the 'client'.

Once you have this functioning, you can remove the getty UNLESS you want to make sure that the connection is validated using username/password pairs as for a dial up connection. As you have 'physical control' of both machines, I will presume that you do NOT want to do this.

Now, on the server, remove the getty and make sure that you have the serial ports on both machines configured correctly using 'setserial'.

All you need to do now is to start pppd on both systems. I will assume that the connection uses /dev/cua4 on both machines. So, on both machines execute the command:-

```
pppd -detach crtscts lock <local IP>:<remote IP> /dev/cua4 38400 &
```

This will bring up the link - but as yet you have no routing specified. You can test the link by pinging to and fro to each machine. If this works, bring down the link by killing one of the pppd processes.

The routing you need will of course depend on exactly what you are trying to do of course. generally, one of the machines will be connected to an Ethernet (and beyond) and so the routing required is exactly the same as for a PPP server and client.

So on the Ethernet equipped machine, the pppd command would be

```
pppd -detach crtscts lock proxyarp <local IP>:<remote IP> /dev/cua4
38400 &
```

and on the other machine

```
pppd -detach crtscts lock defaultroute <local IP>:<remote IP>
/dev/cua4 38400 &
```

If you are linking to networks (using a serial link!) or have more complex routing requirements, you can use /etc/ppp/ip-up in exactly the same way as mentioned earlier in this document. **Robert Hart**
Port Hedland, Western Australia
August 1996

Appendix A

Sources of Linux Information

This appendix contains information on various sources of Linux information, such as online documents, books, and more. Many of these documents are available either in printed form, or electronically from the Internet or BBS systems. Many Linux distributions also include much of this documentation in the distribution itself, so after you have installed Linux these files may be present on your system.

A.1 Online Documents

These documents should be available on any of the Linux FTP archive sites (see Appendix B for a list). If you do not have direct access to FTP, you may be able to locate these documents on other online services (such as CompuServe, local BBS's, and so on). If you have access to Internet mail, you can use the `ftpmail` service to receive these documents. See Appendix B for more information.

In particular, the following documents may be found on `sunsite.unc.edu` in the directory `/pub/Linux/docs`. Many sites mirror this directory; however, if you're unable to locate a mirror site near you, this is a good one to fall back on.

You can also access Linux files and documentation using `gopher`. Just point your `gopher` client to port 70 on `sunsite.unc.edu`, and follow the menus to the Linux archive. This is a good way to browse Linux documentation interactively.

The Linux Frequently Asked Questions List

> The Linux Frequently Asked Questions list, or "FAQ", is a list of
> common questions (and answers!) about Linux. This document
> is meant to provide a general source of information about Linux,
> common problems and solutions, and a list of other sources of in-
> formation. Every new Linux user should read this document. It is
> available in a number of formats, including plain ASCII, PostScript,
> and Lout typesetter format. The Linux FAQ is maintained by Ian
> Jackson, `ijackson@nyx.cs.du.edu`.

The Linux META-FAQ

> The META-FAQ is a collection of "metaquestions" about Linux;
> that is, sources of information about the Linux system, and other
> general topics. It is a good starting place for the Internet user wish-
> ing to find more information about the system. It is maintained
> by Michael K. Johnson, `johnsonm@sunsite.unc.edu`.

The Linux INFO-SHEET

> The Linux INFO-SHEET is a technical introduction to the Linux
> system. It gives an overview of the system's features and available
> software, and also provides a list of other sources of Linux informa-
> tion. The format and content is similar in nature to the META-
> FAQ; incidentally, it is also maintained by Michael K. Johnson.

The Linux Software Map

> The Linux Software Map is a list of many applications available for
> Linux, where to get them, who maintains them, and so forth. It
> is far from complete—to compile a complete list of Linux software
> would be nearly impossible. However, it does include many of the
> most popular Linux software packages. If you can't find a particular
> application to suit your needs, the LSM is a good place to start. It
> is maintained by Lars Wirzenius, `lars.wirzenius@helsinki.fi`.

The Linux HOWTO Index

> The Linux HOWTOs are a collection of "how to" documents, each
> describing in detail a certain aspect of the Linux system. They are
> maintained by Matt Welsh, `mdw@sunsite.unc.edu`. The HOWTO
> Index lists the HOWTO documents which are available (several of
> which are listed below).

The Linux Installation HOWTO

The Linux Installation HOWTO describes how to obtain and install a distribution of Linux, similar to the information presented in Chapter 2.

The Linux Distribution HOWTO

This document is a list of Linux distributions available via mail order and anonymous FTP. It also includes information on other Linux-related goodies and services. Appendix **??** contains a list of Linux vendors, many of which are listed in the *Distribution HOWTO*.

The Linux XFree86 HOWTO

This document describes how to install and configure the X Window System software for Linux. See the section "5.1" for more about the X Window System.

The Linux Mail, News, and UUCP HOWTOs

These three HOWTO documents describe configuration and setup of electronic mail, news, and UUCP communications on a Linux system. Because these three subjects are often intertwined, you may wish to read all three of these HOWTOs together.

The Linux Hardware HOWTO

This HOWTO contains an extensive list of hardware supported by Linux. While this list is far from complete, it should give you a general picture of which hardware devices should be supported by the system.

The Linux SCSI HOWTO

The Linux SCSI HOWTO is a complete guide to configuration and usage of SCSI devices under Linux, such as hard drives, tape drives and CD-ROM.

The Linux NET-2-HOWTO

The Linux NET-2-HOWTO describes installation, setup, and configuration of the "NET-2" TCP/IP software under Linux, including SLIP. If you want to use TCP/IP on your Linux system, this document is a must read.

The Linux Ethernet HOWTO

Closely related to the NET-2-HOWTO, the Ethernet HOWTO describes the various Ethernet devices supported by Linux, and explains how to configure each of them for use by the Linux TCP/IP software.

The Linux Printing HOWTO

This document describes how to configure printing software under Linux, such as `lpr`. Configuration of printers and printing software under UNIX can be very confusing at times; this document sheds some light on the subject.

Other online documents

If you browse the `docs` subdirectory of any Linux FTP site, you'll see many other documents which are not listed here: A slew of FAQ's, interesting tidbits, and other important information. This miscellany is difficult to categorize here; if you don't see what you're looking for on the list above, just take a look at one of the Linux archive sites listed in Appendix B.

A.2   Linux Documentation Project Manuals

The Linux Documentation Project is working on developing a set of manuals and other documentation for Linux, including man pages. These manuals are in various stages of development, and any help revising and updating them is greatly appreciated. If you have questions about the LDP, please contact Matt Welsh (`mdw@sunsite.unc.edu`).

These books are available via anonymous FTP from a number of Linux archive sites, including `sunsite.unc.edu` in the directory `/pub/Linux/docs/LDP`. A number of commercial distributors are selling printed copies of these books; in the future, you may be able to find the LDP manuals on the shelves of your local bookstore.

Linux Installation and Getting Started, by Matt Welsh

A new user's guide for Linux, covering everything the new user needs to know to get started. You happen to hold this book in your hands.

The Linux System Administrators' Guide, by Lars Wirzenius

This is a complete guide to running and configuring a Linux system. There are many issues relating to systems administration which are specific to Linux, such as needs for supporting a user community, filesystem maintenance, backups, and more. This guide covers them all.

The Linux Network Administrators' Guide, by Olaf Kirch

An extensive and complete guide to networking under Linux, including TCP/IP, UUCP, SLIP, and more. This book is a very good read; it contains a wealth of information on many subjects, clarifying the many confusing aspects of network configuration.

The Linux Kernel Hackers' Guide, by Michael Johnson

The gritty details of kernel hacking and development under Linux. Linux is unique in that the complete kernel source is available. This book opens the doors to developers who wish to add or modify features within the kernel. This guide also contains comprehensive coverage of kernel concepts and conventions used by Linux.

A.3 Books and Other Published Works

Linux Journal is a monthly magazine for and about the Linux community, written and produced by a number of Linux developers and enthusiasts. It is distributed worldwide, and is an excellent way to keep in touch with the dynamics of the Linux world, especially if you don't have access to USENET news.

At the time of this writing, subscriptions to *Linux Journal* are US$19/year in the United States, US$24 in Canada, and US$29 elsewhere. To subscribe, or for more information, write to Linux Journal, PO Box 85867, Seattle, WA, 98145-1867, USA, or call +1 206 527-3385. Their FAX number is +1 206 527-2806, and e-mail address is `linux@ssc.com`. You can also find a *Linux Journal* FAQ and sample articles via anonymous FTP on `sunsite.unc.edu` in `/pub/Linux/docs/linux-journal`.

As we have said, not many books have been published dealing with Linux specifically. However, if you are new to the world of UNIX, or want more information than is presented here, we suggest that you take a look at the following books which are available.

A.3.1 Using UNIX

Title: *Learning the UNIX Operating System*

Author: Grace Todino & John Strang
Publisher: O'Reilly and Associates, 1987
ISBN: 0-937175-16-1, $9.00

A good introductory book on learning the UNIX operating system. Most of the information should be applicable to Linux as well. I suggest reading this book if you're new to UNIX and really want to get started with using your new system.

Title: *Learning the* vi *Editor*
Author: Linda Lamb
Publisher: O'Reilly and Associates, 1990
ISBN: 0-937175-67-6, $21.95

This is a book about the vi editor, a powerful text editor found on every UNIX system in the world. It's often important to know and be able to use vi, because you won't always have access to a "real" editor such as Emacs.

A.3.2   Systems Administration

Title: *Essential System Administration*
Author: Æleen Frisch
Publisher: O'Reilly and Associates, 1991
ISBN: 0-937175-80-3, $29.95

From the O'Reilly and Associates Catalog, "Like any other multi-user system, UNIX requires some care and feeding. *Essential System Administration* tells you how. This book strips away the myth and confusion surrounding this important topic and provides a compact, manageable introduction to the tasks faced by anyone responsible for a UNIX system." I couldn't have said it better myself.

Title: *TCP/IP Network Administration*

Author:	Craig Hunt
Publisher:	O'Reilly and Associates, 1990
ISBN:	0-937175-82-X, $24.95

A complete guide to setting up and running a TCP/IP network. While this book is not Linux-specific, roughly 90% of it is applicable to Linux. Coupled with the Linux NET-2-HOWTO and *Linux Network Administrator's Guide*, this is a great book discussing the concepts and technical details of managing TCP/IP.

Title:	*Managing UUCP and Usenet*
Author:	Tim O'Reilly and Grace Todino
Publisher:	O'Reilly and Associates, 1991
ISBN:	0-937175-93-5, $24.95

This book covers how to install and configure UUCP networking software, including configuration for USENET news. If you're at all interested in using UUCP or accessing USENET news on your system, this book is a must-read.

A.3.3 The X Window System

Title:	*The X Window System: A User's Guide*
Author:	Niall Mansfield
Publisher:	Addison-Wesley
ISBN:	0-201-51341-2, ??

A complete tutorial and reference guide to using the X Window System. If you installed X windows on your Linux system, and want to know how to get the most out of it, you should read this book. Unlike some windowing systems, a lot of the power provided by X is not obvious at first sight.

A.3.4　Programming

Title:　　　　　*The C Programming Language*

Author:　　　　Brian Kernighan and Dennis Ritchie

Publisher:　　　Prentice-Hall, 1988

ISBN:　　　　　0-13-110362-8, $25.00

This book is a must-have for anyone wishing to do C programming on a UNIX system. (Or any system, for that matter.) While this book is not obstensibly UNIX-specific, it is quite applicable to programming C under UNIX.

Title:　　　　　*The Unix Programming Environment*

Author:　　　　Brian Kernighan and Bob Pike

Publisher:　　　Prentice-Hall, 1984

ISBN:　　　　　0-13-937681-X, ??

An overview to programming under the UNIX system. Covers all of the tools of the trade; a good read to get acquainted with the somewhat amorphous UNIX programming world.

Title:　　　　　*Advanced Programming in the UNIX Environment*

Author:　　　　W. Richard Stevens

Publisher:　　　Addison-Wesley

ISBN:　　　　　0-201-56317-7, $50.00

This mighty tome contains everything that you need to know to program UNIX at the system level—file I/O, process control, interprocess communication, signals, terminal I/O, the works. This book focuses on various UNIX standards, including POSIX.1, which Linux mostly adheres to.

A.3.5　Kernel Hacking

Title:　　　　　*The Design of the UNIX Operating System*

Author:	Maurice J. Bach
Publisher:	Prentice-Hall, 1986
ISBN:	0-13-201799-7, ??

This book covers the algorithms and internals of the UNIX kernel. It is not specific to any particular kernel, although it does lean towards System V-isms. This is the best place to start if you want to understand the inner tickings of the Linux system.

Title:	*The Magic Garden Explained*
Author:	Berny Goodheart and James Cox
Publisher:	Prentice-Hall, 1994
ISBN:	0-13-098138-9, ??

This book describes the System V R4 kernel in detail. Unlike Bach's book, which concentrates heavily on the algorithms which make the kernel tick, this book presents the SVR4 implementation on a more technical level. Although Linux and SVR4 are distant cousins, this book can give you much insight into the workings of an actual UNIX kernel implementation. This is also a very modern book on the UNIX kernel—published in 1994.

Appendix B

FTP Tutorial and Site List

FTP ("File Transfer Protocol") is the set of programs that are used for transferring files between systems on the Internet. Most UNIX, VMS, and MS-DOS systems on the Internet have a program called `ftp` which you use to transfer these files, and if you have Internet access, the best way to download the Linux software is by using `ftp`. This appendix covers basic `ftp` usage—of course, there are many more functions and uses of `ftp` than are given here.

At the end of this appendix there is a listing of FTP sites where Linux software can be found. Also, if you don't have direct Internet access but are able to exchange electronic mail with the Internet, information on using the `ftpmail` service is included below.

If you're using an MS-DOS, UNIX, or VMS system to download files from the Internet, then `ftp` is a command-driven program. However, there are other implementations of `ftp` out there, such as the Macintosh version (called `Fetch`) with a nice menu-driven interface, which is quite self-explanatory. Even if you're not using the command-driven version of `ftp`, the information given here should help.

`ftp` can be used to both upload (send) or download (receive) files from other Internet sites. In most situations, you're going to be downloading software. On the Internet there are a large number of publicly-available **FTP archive sites**, machines which allow anyone to `ftp` to them and download free software. One such archive site is `sunsite.unc.edu`, which has a lot of Sun Microsystems software, and acts as one of the main Linux sites. In addition, FTP archive sites **mirror** software to each other—that is, software uploaded to one site will be automatically copied

307

over to a number of other sites. So don't be surprised if you see the exact same files
on many different archive sites.

B.1   Starting `ftp`

Note that in the example "screens" printed below I'm only showing the most important information, and what you see may differ. Also, commands in *italics* represent
commands that you type; everything else is screen output.

To start `ftp` and connect to a site, simply use the command

```
ftp ⟨hostname⟩
```

where ⟨*hostname*⟩ is the name of the site you are connecting to. For example, to
connect to the mythical site `shoop.vpizza.com` we can use the command

```
ftp shoop.vpizza.com
```

B.2   Logging In

When `ftp` starts up we should see something like

```
Connected to shoop.vpizza.com.
220 Shoop.vpizza.com FTPD ready at 15 Dec 1992 08:20:42 EDT
Name (shoop.vpizza.com:mdw):
```

Here, `ftp` is asking us to give the username that we want to login as on
`shoop.vpizza.com`. The default here is `mdw`, which is my username on the system I'm using FTP from. Since I don't have an account on `shoop.vpizza.com` I
can't login as myself. Instead, to access publicly-available software on an FTP site
you login as `anonymous`, and give your Internet e-mail address (if you have one) as
the password. So, we would type

```
Name (shoop.vpizza.com:mdw):   anonymous
331-Guest login ok, send e-mail address as password.
Password:   mdw@sunsite.unc.edu
230- Welcome to shoop.vpizza.com.
230- Virtual Pizza Delivery[tm]:  Download pizza in 30 cycles or
```

```
less
230- or you get it FREE!
ftp>
```

Of course, you should give your e-mail address, instead of mine, and it won't echo to the screen as you're typing it (since it's technically a "password"). `ftp` should allow us to login and we'll be ready to download software.

B.3 Poking Around

Okay, we're in. `ftp>` is our prompt, and the `ftp` program is waiting for commands. There are a few basic commands you need to know about. First, the commands

> `ls` ⟨*file*⟩

and

> `dir` ⟨*file*⟩

both give file listings (where ⟨*file*⟩ is an optional argument specifying a particular filename to list). The difference is that `ls` usually gives a short listing and `dir` gives a longer listing (that is, with more information on the sizes of the files, dates of modification, and so on).

The command

> `cd` ⟨*directory*⟩

will move to the given directory (just like the `cd` command on UNIX or MS-DOS systems). You can use the command

> `cdup`

to change to the parent directory[1].

The command

> `help` ⟨*command*⟩

---

[1] The directory above the current one.

will give help on the given ftp ⟨command⟩ (such as ls or cd). If no command is specified, ftp will list all of the available commands.

If we type dir at this point we'll see an initial directory listing of where we are.

```
ftp> dir
200 PORT command successful.
150 Opening ASCII mode data connection for /bin/ls.
total 1337


dr-xr-xr-x  2 root       wheel       512 Aug 13 13:55 bin
drwxr-xr-x  2 root       wheel       512 Aug 13 13:58 dev
drwxr-xr-x  2 root       wheel       512 Jan 25 17:35 etc
drwxr-xr-x 19 root       wheel      1024 Jan 27 21:39 pub
drwxrwx-wx  4 root       ftp-admi   1024 Feb  6 22:10 uploads
drwxr-xr-x  3 root       wheel       512 Mar 11  1992 usr


226 Transfer complete.
921 bytes received in 0.24 seconds (3.7 Kbytes/s)
ftp>
```

Each of these entries is a directory, not an individual file which we can download (specified by the d in the first column of the listing). On most FTP archive sites, the publicly available software is under the directory /pub, so let's go there.

```
ftp> cd pub
ftp> dir
200 PORT command successful.
150 ASCII data connection for /bin/ls (128.84.181.1,4525) (0
bytes).
total 846


-rw-r--r--  1 root      staff        1433 Jul 12  1988 README
-r--r--r--  1 3807      staff       15586 May 13  1991 US-DOMAIN.TXT.2
-rw-r--r--  1 539       staff       52664 Feb 20  1991 altenergy.avail
-r--r--r--  1 65534     65534       56456 Dec 17  1990 ataxx.tar.Z
-rw-r--r--  1 root      other     2013041 Jul  3  1991 gesyps.tar.Z
-rw-r--r--  1 432       staff       41831 Jan 30  1989 gnexe.arc
-rw-rw-rw-  1 615       staff       50315 Apr 16  1992 linpack.tar.Z
-r--r--r--  1 root      wheel       12168 Dec 25  1990 localtime.o
```

```
-rw-r--r--   1 root      staff        7035 Aug 27  1986 manualslist.tblms
drwxr-xr-x   2 2195      staff         512 Mar 10 00:48 mdw
-rw-r--r--   1 root      staff        5593 Jul 19  1988 t.out.h

226 ASCII Transfer complete.
2443 bytes received in 0.35 seconds (6.8 Kbytes/s)
ftp>
```

Here we can see a number of (interesting?) files, one of which is called README, which we should download (most FTP sites have a README file in the /pub directory).

B.4   Downloading files

Before downloading files, there are a few things that you need to take care of.

- **Turn on hash mark printing.** *Hash marks* are printed to the screen as files are being transferred; they let you know how far along the transfer is, and that your connection hasn't hung up (so you don't sit for 20 minutes, thinking that you're still downloading a file). In general, a hash mark appears as a pound sign (#), and one is printed for every 1024 or 8192 bytes transferred, depending on your system.

  To turn on hash mark printing, give the command hash.

  ```
  ftp> hash
  Hash mark printing on (8192 bytes/hash mark).
  ftp>
  ```

- **Determine the type of file which you are downloading.** As far as FTP is concerned, files come in two flavors: *binary* and *text*. Most of the files which you'll be downloading are binary files: that is, programs, compressed files, archive files, and so on. However, many files (such as READMEs and so on) are text files.

  Why does the file type matter? Only because on some systems (such as MS-DOS systems), certain characters in a text file, such as carriage returns, need to be converted so that the file will be readable. While transferring in binary mode, no conversion is done—the file is simply transferred byte after byte.

  The commands bin and ascii set the transfer mode to binary and text, respectively. *When in doubt, always use binary mode to transfer files.* If you try to transfer a binary file in text mode, you'll corrupt the file and it will be unusable. (This is one of the most common mistakes made when using FTP.) However, you can use text mode for plain text files (whose filenames often end in .txt).

For our example, we're downloading the file README, which is most likely a text file, so we use the command

```
ftp> ascii
200 Type set to A.
ftp>
```

- **Set your local directory.** Your *local directory* is the directory on your system where you want the downloaded files to end up. Whereas the cd command changes the remote directory (on the remote machine which you're FTPing to), the lcd command changes the local directory.

    For example, to set the local directory to /home/db/mdw/tmp, use the command

```
ftp> lcd /home/db/mdw/tmp
Local directory now /home/db/mdw/tmp
ftp>
```

Now you're ready to actually download the file. The command

```
get ⟨remote-name⟩ ⟨local-name⟩
```

is used for this, where ⟨remote-name⟩ is the name of the file on the remote machine, and ⟨local-name⟩ is the name that you wish to give the file on your local machine. The ⟨local-name⟩ argument is optional; by default, the local filename is the same as the remote one. However, if for example you're downloading the file README, and you already have a README in your local directory, you'll want to give a different ⟨local-filename⟩ so that the first one isn't overwritten.

For our example, to download the file README, we simply use

```
ftp> get README
200 PORT command successful.
150 ASCII data connection for README (128.84.181.1,4527) (1433
bytes).
#
226 ASCII Transfer complete.
```

```
local:  README remote:  README
1493 bytes received in 0.03 seconds (49 Kbytes/s)
ftp>
```

B.5 Quitting FTP

To end your FTP session, simply use the command

    quit

The command

    close

can be used to close the connection with the current remote FTP site; the open command can then be used to start a session with another site (without quitting the FTP program altogether).

```
ftp> close
221 Goodbye.
ftp> quit
```

B.6 Using ftpmail

ftpmail is a service which allows you to obtain files from FTP archive sites via Internet electronic mail. If you don't have direct Internet access, but are able to send mail to the Internet (from a service such as CompuServe, for example), ftpmail is a good way to get files from FTP archive sites. Unfortunately, ftpmail can be slow, especially when sending large jobs. Before attempting to download large amounts of software using ftpmail, be sure that your mail spool will be able to handle the incoming traffic. Many systems keep quotas on incoming electronic mail, and may delete your account if your mail exceeds this quota. Just use common sense.

sunsite.unc.edu, one of the major Linux FTP archive sites, is home to an ftpmail server. To use this service, send electronic mail to

    ftpmail@sunsite.unc.edu

with a message body containing only the word:

```
help
```

This will send you back a list of `ftpmail` commands and a brief tutorial on using the system.

For example, to get a listing of Linux files found on `sunsite.unc.edu`, send mail to the above address containing the text

```
open sunsite.unc.edu
cd /pub/Linux
dir
quit
```

You may use the `ftpmail` service to connect to any FTP archive site; you are not limited to `sunsite.unc.edu`. The next section lists a number of Linux FTP archives.

B.7   Linux FTP Site List

Table B.1 is a listing of the most well-known FTP archive sites which carry the Linux software. Keep in mind that many other sites mirror these, and more than likely you'll run into Linux on a number of sites not on this list.

`tsx-11.mit.edu`, `sunsite.unc.edu`, and `nic.funet.fi` are the "home sites" for the Linux software, where most of the new software is uploaded. Most of the other sites on the list mirror some combination of these three. To reduce network traffic, choose a site that is geographically closest to you.

Site name	IP Address	Directory
ftp.cdrom.com	165.113.58.253	/pub/linux
tsx-11.mit.edu	18.172.1.2	/pub/linux
sunsite.unc.edu	152.2.22.81	/pub/Linux
nic.funet.fi	128.214.6.100	/pub/OS/Linux
ftp.mcc.ac.uk	130.88.200.7	/pub/linux
ftp.informatik.tu-muenchen.de	131.159.0.110	/pub/Linux
ftp.dfv.rwth-aachen.de	137.226.4.105	/pub/linux
ftp.informatik.rwth-aachen.de	137.226.112.172	/pub/Linux
ftp.ibp.fr	132.227.60.2	/pub/linux
ftp.uu.net	137.39.1.9	/pub/OS/linux
wuarchive.wustl.edu	128.252.135.4	/systems/linux
ftp.win.tue.nl	131.155.70.100	/pub/linux
ftp.ibr.cs.tu-bs.de	134.169.34.15	/pub/os/linux
ftp.denet.dk	129.142.6.74	/pub/OS/linux

Table B.1: Linux FTP Sites

Appendix C

Linux BBS List

Printed here is a list of bulletin board systems (BBS) which carry Linux software. Zane Healy (`healyzh@holonet.net`) maintains this list. If you know of or run a BBS which provides Linux software which isn't on this list, you should get in touch with him.

The Linux community is no longer an Internet-only society. In fact, it is now estimated that the majority of Linux users don't have Internet access. Therefore, it is especially important that BBSs continue to provide and support Linux to users worldwide.

C.1 United States

Citrus Grove Public Access, 916-381-5822. ZyXEL 16.8/14.4 Sacramento, CA. Internet: `citrus.sac.ca.us`
Higher Powered BBS, 408-737-7040. ? CA. RIME ->HIGHER
hip-hop, 408-773-0768. 19.2k Sunnyvale, CA. USENET access
hip-hop, 408-773-0768. 38.4k Sunnyvale, CA.
Unix Online, 707-765-4631. 9600 Petaluma, CA. USENET access
The Outer Rim, 805-252-6342. Santa Clarita, CA.
Programmer's Exchange, 818-444-3507. El Monte, CA. Fidonet
Programmer's Exchange, 818-579-9711. El Monte, CA.
Micro Oasis, 510-895-5985. 14.4k San Leandro, CA.
Test Engineering, 916-928-0504. Sacramento, CA.
Slut Club, 813-975-2603. USR/DS 16.8k HST/14.4K Tampa, FL. Fidonet

1:377/42

Lost City Atlantis, 904-727-9334. 14.4k Jacksonville, FL. FidoNet

Aquired Knowledge, 305-720-3669. 14.4k v.32bis Ft. Lauderdale, FL. Internet, UUCP

The Computer Mechanic, 813-544-9345. 14.4k v.32bis St. Petersburg, FL. Fidonet, Sailnet, MXBBSnet

AVSync, 404-320-6202. Atlanta, GA.

Information Overload, 404-471-1549. 19.2k ZyXEL Atlanta, GA. Fidonet 1:133/308

Atlanta Radio Club, 404-850-0546. 9600 Atlanta, GA.

Rebel BBS, 208-887-3937. 9600 Boise, ID.

Rocky Mountain HUB, 208-232-3405. 38.4k Pocatello, ID. Fionet, SLNet, CinemaNet

EchoMania, 618-233-1659. 14.4k HST Belleville, IL. Fidonet 1:2250/1, f'req LINUX

UNIX USER, 708-879-8633. 14.4k Batavia, IL. USENET, Internet mail

PBS BBS, 309-663-7675. 2400 Bloomington, IL.

Third World, 217-356-9512. 9600 v.32 IL.

Digital Underground, 812-941-9427. 14.4k v.32bis IN. USENET

The OA Southern Star, 504-885-5928. New Orleans, LA. Fidonet 1:396/1

Channel One, 617-354-8873. Boston, MA. RIME ->CHANNEL

VWIS Linux Support BBS, 508-793-1570. 9600 Worcester, MA.

WayStar BBS, 508-481-7147. 14.4k V.32bis USR/HST Marlborough, MA. Fidonet 1:333/14

WayStar BBS, 508-481-7293. 14.4k V.32bis USR/HST Marlborough, MA. Fidonet 1:333/15

WayStar BBS, 508-480-8371. 9600 V.32bis or 14.4k USR/HST Marlborough, MA. Fidonet 1:333/16

Programmer's Center, 301-596-1180. 9600 Columbia, MD. RIME

Brodmann's Place, 301-843-5732. 14.4k Waldorf, MD. RIME ->BRODMANN, Fidonet

Main Frame, 301-654-2554. 9600 Gaithersburg, MD. RIME ->MAINFRAME

1 Zero Cybernet BBS, 301-589-4064. MD.

WaterDeep BBS, 410-614-2190. 9600 v.32 Baltimore, MD.

Harbor Heights BBS, 207-663-0391. 14.4k Boothbay Harbor, ME.

Part-Time BBS, 612-544-5552. 14.4k v.32bis Plymouth, MN.

The Sole Survivor, 314-846-2702. 14.4k v.32bis St. Louis, MO. WWIVnet, WWIVlink, etc

MAC's Place, 919-891-1111. 16.8k, DS modem Dunn, NC. RIME ->MAC

Digital Designs, 919-423-4216. 14.4k, 2400 Hope Mills, NC.

Flite Line, 402-421-2434.   Lincoln, NE. RIME ->FLITE, DS modem

Legend, 402-438-2433.   Lincoln, NE. DS modem

MegaByte Mansion, 402-551-8681. 14.4 V,32bis Omaha, NE.

Mycroft QNX, 201-858-3429. 14.4k NJ.

Steve Leon's, 201-886-8041. 14.4k Cliffside Park, NJ.

Dwight-Englewood BBS, 201-569-3543. 9600 v.42 Englewood, NJ. USENET

The Mothership Cnection, 908-940-1012. 38.4k Franklin Park, NJ.

The Laboratory, 212-927-4980. 16.8k HST, 14.4k v.32bis NY. FidoNet 1:278/707

Valhalla, 516-321-6819.   14.4k HST v.32 Babylon, NY. Fidonet (1:107/255), UseNet (`die.linet.org`)

Intermittent Connection, 503-344-9838.   14.4k HST v.32bis Eugene, OR. 1:152/35

Horizon Systems, 216-899-1086. USR v.32 Westlake, OH.

Horizon Systems, 216-899-1293. 2400 Westlake, OH.

Centre Programmers Unit, 814-353-0566. 14.4k V.32bis/HST Bellefonte, PA.

Allentown Technical, 215-432-5699.   9600 v.32/v.42bis Allentown, PA. WWIVNet 2578

Tactical-Operations, 814-861-7637. 14.4k V32bis/V42bis State College, PA. Fidonet 1:129/226, `tac_ops.UUCP`

North Shore BBS, 713-251-9757.   Houston, TX.

The Annex, 512-575-1188. 9600 HST TX. Fidonet 1:3802/217

The Annex, 512-575-0667. 2400 TX. Fidonet 1:3802/216

Walt Fairs, 713-947-9866.   Houston, TX. FidoNet 1:106/18

CyberVille, 817-249-6261. 9600 TX. FidoNet 1:130/78

splat-ooh, 512-578-2720. 14.4k Victoria, TX.

splat-ooh, 512-578-5436. 14.4k Victoria, TX.

alaree, 512-575-5554. 14.4k Victoria, TX.

Ronin BBS, 214-938-2840. 14.4 HST/DS Waxahachie (Dallas), TX. RIME, Intelec, Smartnet, etc.

VTBBS, 703-231-7498.   Blacksburg, VA.

MBT, 703-953-0640.   Blacksburg, VA.

NOVA, 703-323-3321. 9600 Annandale, VA. Fidonet 1:109/305

Rem-Jem, 703-503-9410. 9600 Fairfax, VA.

Enlightend, 703-370-9528. 14.4k Alexandria, VA. Fidonet 1:109/615

My UnKnown BBS, 703-690-0669. 14.4k V.32bis VA. Fidonet 1:109/370

Georgia Peach BBS, 804-727-0399. 14.4k Newport News, VA.

Top Hat BBS, 206-244-9661. 14.4k WA. Fidonet 1:343/40

victrola.sea.wa.us, 206-838-7456. 19.2k Federal Way, WA. USENET

C.2   Outside of the United States

Galaktische Archive, 0043-2228303804.   16.8 ZYX Wien, Austria.   Fidonet 2:310/77 (19:00-7:00)

Linux-Support-Oz, +61-2-418-8750. v.32bis 14.4k Sydney, NSW, Austrailia. Internet/Usenet, E-Mail/News

500cc Formula 1 BBS, +61-2-550-4317. V.32bis Sydney, NSW, Australia.

Magic BBS, 403-569-2882. 14.4k HST/Telebit/MNP Calgary, AB, Canada. Internet/Usenet

Logical Solutions, 299-9900 through 9911. 2400 AB, Canada.

Logical Solutions, 299-9912, 299-9913. 14.4k Canada.

Logical Solutions, 299-9914 through 9917. 16.8k v.32bis Canada.

V.A.L.I.S., 403-478-1281. 14.4k v.32bis Edmonton, AB, Canada. USENET

The Windsor Download, (519)-973-9330. v32bis 14.4 ON, Canada.

r-node, 416-249-5366. 2400 Toronto, ON, Canada. USENET

Synapse, 819-246-2344. 819-561-5268 Gatineau, QC, Canada. RIME->SYNAPSE

Radio Free Nyongwa, 514-524-0829. v.32bis ZyXEL Montreal, QC, Canada. USENET, Fidonet

DataComm1, +49.531.132-16. 14.4 HST Braunschweig, NDS, Germany. Fido 2:240/550, LinuxNet

DataComm2, +49.531.132-17. 14.4 HST Braunschweig, NDS, Germany. Fido 2:240/551, LinuxNet

Linux Server /Braukmann, +49.441.592-963. 16.8 ZYX Oldenburg, NDS, Germany. Fido 2:241/2012, LinuxNet

MM's Spielebox, +49.5323.3515. 14.4 ZYX Clausthal-Zfd., NDS, Germany. Fido 2:241/3420

MM's Spielebox, +49.5323.3516. 16.8 ZYX Clausthal-Zfd., NDS, Germany. Fido 2:241/3421

MM's Spielebox, +49.5323.3540. 9600 Clausthal-Zfd., NDS, Germany. Fido 2:241/3422

Bit-Company / J. Bartz, +49.5323.2539. 16.8 ZYX MO Clausthal-Zfd., NDS, Germany. Fido 2:241/3430

Fractal Zone BBS /Maass, +49.721.863-066. 16.8 ZYX Karlsruhe, BW, Germany. Fido 2:241/7462

Hipposoft /M. Junius, +49.241.875-090. 14.4 HST Aachen, NRW, Germany. Fido 2:242/6, 4:30-7,8-23:30

UB-HOFF /A. Hoffmann, +49.203.584-155. 19.2 ZYX+ Duisburg, Germany. Fido 2:242/37

FORMEL-Box, +49.4191.2846. 16.8 ZYX Kaltenkirchen, SHL, Germany. Fido 2:242/329, LinuxNet (6:00-20:00)

BOX/2, +49.89.601-96-77. 16.8 ZYX Muenchen, BAY, Germany. Fido 2:246/147, info magic: LINUX (22-24,0:30-2,5-8)

Die Box Passau 2+1, +49.851.555-96. 14.4 V32b Passau, BAY, Germany. Fido 2:246/200 (8:00-3:30)

Die Box Passau Line 1, +49.851.753-789. 16.8 ZYX Passau, BAY, Germany. Fido 2:246/2000 (8:00-3:30)

Die Box Passau Line 3, +49.851.732-73. 14.4 HST Passau, BAY, Germany. Fido 2:246/202 (5:00-3:30)

Die Box Passau ISDN, +49.851.950-464. 38.4/64k V.110/X.75 Passau, BAY, Germany. Fido 2:246/201 (8:00-24:00,1:00-3:30)

Public Domain Kiste, +49.30.686-62-50. 16.8 ZYX BLN, Germany. Fido 2:2403/17

CS-Port / C. Schmidt, +49.30.491-34-18. 19.2 Z19 Berlin, BLN, Germany. Fido 2:2403/13

BigBrother / R. Gmelch, +49.30.335-63-28. 16.8 Z16 Berlin, BLN, Germany. Fido 2:2403/36.4 (16-23:00)

CRYSTAL BBS, +49.7152.240-86. 14.4 HST Leonberg, BW, Germany. Fido 2:2407/3, LinuxNet

Echoblaster BBS #1, +49.7142.213-92. HST/V32b Bietigheim, BW, Germany. Fido 2:2407/4, LinuxNet (7-19,23-01h

Echoblaster BBS #2, +49.7142.212-35. V32b Bietigheim, BW, Germany. Fido 2:2407/40, LinuxNet (20h-6h)

LinuxServer / P. Berger, +49.711.756-275. 16.8 HST Stuttgart, BW, Germany. Fido 2:2407/34, LinuxNet (8:3-17:5,19-2)

Rising Sun BBS, +49.7147.3845. 16.8 ZYX Sachsenheim, BW, Germany. Fido 2:2407/41, LinuxNet (5:30-2:30)

bakunin.north.de, +49.421.870-532. 14.4 D 2800 Bremen, HB, Germany. kraehe@bakunin.north.de

oytix.north.de, +49.421.396-57-62. ZYX HB, Germany. mike@oytix.north.de, login as gast

Fiffis Inn BBS, +49-89-5701353. 14.4-19.2 Munich, Germany. FidoNet 2:246/69,Internet,USENET,LinuxNet

The Field of Inverse Chaos, +358 0 506 1836. 14.4k v32bis/HST Helsinki, Finland. USENET; ichaos.nullnet.fi

Modula BBS, +33-1 4043 0124. HST 14.4 v.32bis Paris, France.

Modula BBS, +33-1 4530 1248. HST 14.4 V.32bis Paris, France.

STDIN BBS, +33-72375139. v.32bis Lyon, Laurent Cas, France. FidoNet 2:323/8

Le Lien, +33-72089879. HST 14.4/V32bis Lyon, Pascal Valette, France. FidoNet 2:323/5

Basil, +33-1-44670844. v.32bis Paris, Laurent Chemla, France.

Cafard Naum, +33-51701632. v.32bis Nantes, Yann Dupont, France.

DUBBS, +353-1-6789000. 19.2 ZyXEL Dublin, Ireland. Fidonet 2:263/167

Galway Online, +353-91-27454. 14.4k v32b Galway, Ireland. RIME, `@iol.ie`

Nemesis' Dungeon, +353-1-324755 or 326900. 14.4k v32bis Dublin, Ireland. Fidonet 2:263/150

nonsolosoftware, +39 51 6140772. v.32bis, v.42bis Italy. Fidonet 2:332/407

nonsolosoftware, +39 51 432904. ZyXEL 19.2k Italy. Fidonet 2:332/417

Advanced Systems, +64-9-379-3365. ZyXEL 16.8k Auckland, New Zealand. Singet, INTLnet, Fidonet

Thunderball Cave, 472567018. Norway. RIME ->CAVE

DownTown BBS Lelystad, +31-3200-48852. 14.4k Lelystad, Netherlands. Fido 2:512/155, UUCP

MUGNET Intl-Cistron BBS, +31-1720-42580. 38.4k Alphen a/d Rijn, Netherlands. UUCP

The Controversy, (65)560-6040. 14.4k V.32bis/HST Singapore. Fidonet 6:600/201

Pats System, +27-12-333-2049. 14.4k v.32bis/HST Pretoria, South Africa. Fidonet 5:71-1/36

Gunship BBS, +46-31-693306. 14.4k HST DS Gothenburg Sweden.

Baboon BBS, +41-62-511726. 19.2k Switzerland. Fido 2:301/580 and /581

The Purple Tentacle, +44-734-590990. HST/V32bis Reading, UK. Fidonet 2:252/305

A6 BBS, +44-582-460273. 14.4k Herts, UK. Fidonet 2:440/111

On the Beach, +444-273-600996. 14.4k/16.8k Brighton, UK. Fidonet 2:441/122

Appendix D

The GNU General Public License

Printed below is the GNU General Public License (the *GPL* or *copyleft*), under which Linux is licensed. It is reproduced here to clear up some of the confusion about Linux's copyright status—Linux is *not* shareware, and it is *not* in the public domain. The bulk of the Linux kernel is copyright ©1993 by Linus Torvalds, and other software and parts of the kernel are copyrighted by their authors. Thus, Linux *is* copyrighted, however, you may redistribute it under the terms of the GPL printed below.

D.1   Preamble

The licenses for most software are designed to take away your freedom to share and change it. By contrast, the GNU General Public License is intended to guarantee your freedom to share and change free software–to make sure the software is free for all its users. This General Public License applies to most of the Free Software

Foundation's software and to any other program whose authors commit to using it. (Some other Free Software Foundation software is covered by the GNU Library General Public License instead.) You can apply it to your programs, too.

When we speak of free software, we are referring to freedom, not price. Our General Public Licenses are designed to make sure that you have the freedom to distribute copies of free software (and charge for this service if you wish), that you receive source code or can get it if you want it, that you can change the software or use pieces of it in new free programs; and that you know you can do these things.

To protect your rights, we need to make restrictions that forbid anyone to deny you these rights or to ask you to surrender the rights. These restrictions translate to certain responsibilities for you if you distribute copies of the software, or if you modify it.

For example, if you distribute copies of such a program, whether gratis or for a fee, you must give the recipients all the rights that you have. You must make sure that they, too, receive or can get the source code. And you must show them these terms so they know their rights.

We protect your rights with two steps: (1) copyright the software, and (2) offer you this license which gives you legal permission to copy, distribute and/or modify the software.

Also, for each author's protection and ours, we want to make certain that everyone understands that there is no warranty for this free software. If the software is modified by someone else and passed on, we want its recipients to know that what they have is not the original, so that any problems introduced by others will not reflect on the original authors' reputations.

Finally, any free program is threatened constantly by software patents. We wish to avoid the danger that redistributors of a free program will individually obtain patent licenses, in effect making the program proprietary. To prevent this, we have made it clear that any patent must be licensed for everyone's free use or not licensed at all.

The precise terms and conditions for copying, distribution and modification follow.

D.2 Terms and Conditions for Copying, Distribution, and Modification

0. This License applies to any program or other work which contains a notice placed by the copyright holder saying it may be distributed under the terms of this General Public License. The "Program", below, refers to any such program or work, and a "work based on the Program" means either the Program or any derivative work under copyright law: that is to say, a work containing the Program or a portion of it, either verbatim or with modifications and/or translated into another language. (Hereinafter, translation is included without limitation in the term "modification".) Each licensee is addressed as "you".

   Activities other than copying, distribution and modification are not covered by this License; they are outside its scope. The act of running the Program is not restricted, and the output from the Program is covered only if its contents constitute a work based on the Program (independent of having been made by running the Program). Whether that is true depends on what the Program does.

1. You may copy and distribute verbatim copies of the Program's source code as you receive it, in any medium, provided that you conspicuously and appropriately publish on each copy an appropriate copyright notice and disclaimer of warranty; keep intact all the notices that refer to this License and to the absence of any warranty; and give any other recipients of the Program a copy of this License along with the Program.

   You may charge a fee for the physical act of transferring a copy, and you may at your option offer warranty protection in exchange for a fee.

2. You may modify your copy or copies of the Program or any portion of it, thus forming a work based on the Program, and copy and distribute such modifications or work under the terms of Section 1 above, provided that you also meet all of these conditions:

   a. You must cause the modified files to carry prominent notices stating that you changed the files and the date of any change.

   b. You must cause any work that you distribute or publish, that in whole or in part contains or is derived from the Program or any part thereof, to be licensed as a whole at no charge to all third parties under the terms of this License.

c. If the modified program normally reads commands interactively when run, you must cause it, when started running for such interactive use in the most ordinary way, to print or display an announcement including an appropriate copyright notice and a notice that there is no warranty (or else, saying that you provide a warranty) and that users may redistribute the program under these conditions, and telling the user how to view a copy of this License. (Exception: if the Program itself is interactive but does not normally print such an announcement, your work based on the Program is not required to print an announcement.)

These requirements apply to the modified work as a whole. If identifiable sections of that work are not derived from the Program, and can be reasonably considered independent and separate works in themselves, then this License, and its terms, do not apply to those sections when you distribute them as separate works. But when you distribute the same sections as part of a whole which is a work based on the Program, the distribution of the whole must be on the terms of this License, whose permissions for other licensees extend to the entire whole, and thus to each and every part regardless of who wrote it.

Thus, it is not the intent of this section to claim rights or contest your rights to work written entirely by you; rather, the intent is to exercise the right to control the distribution of derivative or collective works based on the Program.

In addition, mere aggregation of another work not based on the Program with the Program (or with a work based on the Program) on a volume of a storage or distribution medium does not bring the other work under the scope of this License.

3. You may copy and distribute the Program (or a work based on it, under Section 2) in object code or executable form under the terms of Sections 1 and 2 above provided that you also do one of the following:

a. Accompany it with the complete corresponding machine-readable source code, which must be distributed under the terms of Sections 1 and 2 above on a medium customarily used for software interchange; or,

b. Accompany it with a written offer, valid for at least three years, to give any third party, for a charge no more than your cost of physically performing source distribution, a complete machine-readable copy of the corresponding source code, to be distributed under the terms of Sections 1 and 2 above on a medium customarily used for software interchange; or,

    c. Accompany it with the information you received as to the offer to distribute corresponding source code. (This alternative is allowed only for noncommercial distribution and only if you received the program in object code or executable form with such an offer, in accord with Subsection b above.)

The source code for a work means the preferred form of the work for making modifications to it. For an executable work, complete source code means all the source code for all modules it contains, plus any associated interface definition files, plus the scripts used to control compilation and installation of the executable. However, as a special exception, the source code distributed need not include anything that is normally distributed (in either source or binary form) with the major components (compiler, kernel, and so on) of the operating system on which the executable runs, unless that component itself accompanies the executable.

If distribution of executable or object code is made by offering access to copy from a designated place, then offering equivalent access to copy the source code from the same place counts as distribution of the source code, even though third parties are not compelled to copy the source along with the object code.

4. You may not copy, modify, sublicense, or distribute the Program except as expressly provided under this License. Any attempt otherwise to copy, modify, sublicense or distribute the Program is void, and will automatically terminate your rights under this License. However, parties who have received copies, or rights, from you under this License will not have their licenses terminated so long as such parties remain in full compliance.

5. You are not required to accept this License, since you have not signed it. However, nothing else grants you permission to modify or distribute the Program or its derivative works. These actions are prohibited by law if you do not accept this License. Therefore, by modifying or distributing the Program (or any work based on the Program), you indicate your acceptance of this License to do so, and all its terms and conditions for copying, distributing or modifying the Program or works based on it.

6. Each time you redistribute the Program (or any work based on the Program), the recipient automatically receives a license from the original licensor to copy, distribute or modify the Program subject to these terms and conditions. You may not impose any further restrictions on the recipients' exercise of the rights granted herein. You are not responsible for enforcing compliance by third parties to this License.

7. If, as a consequence of a court judgment or allegation of patent infringement or for any other reason (not limited to patent issues), conditions are imposed on you (whether by court order, agreement or otherwise) that contradict the conditions of this License, they do not excuse you from the conditions of this License. If you cannot distribute so as to satisfy simultaneously your obligations under this License and any other pertinent obligations, then as a consequence you may not distribute the Program at all. For example, if a patent license would not permit royalty-free redistribution of the Program by all those who receive copies directly or indirectly through you, then the only way you could satisfy both it and this License would be to refrain entirely from distribution of the Program.

   If any portion of this section is held invalid or unenforceable under any particular circumstance, the balance of the section is intended to apply and the section as a whole is intended to apply in other circumstances.

   It is not the purpose of this section to induce you to infringe any patents or other property right claims or to contest validity of any such claims; this section has the sole purpose of protecting the integrity of the free software distribution system, which is implemented by public license practices. Many people have made generous contributions to the wide range of software distributed through that system in reliance on consistent application of that system; it is up to the author/donor to decide if he or she is willing to distribute software through any other system and a licensee cannot impose that choice.

   This section is intended to make thoroughly clear what is believed to be a consequence of the rest of this License.

8. If the distribution and/or use of the Program is restricted in certain countries either by patents or by copyrighted interfaces, the original copyright holder who places the Program under this License may add an explicit geographical distribution limitation excluding those countries, so that distribution is permitted only in or among countries not thus excluded. In such case, this License incorporates the limitation as if written in the body of this License.

9. The Free Software Foundation may publish revised and/or new versions of the General Public License from time to time. Such new versions will be similar in spirit to the present version, but may differ in detail to address new problems or concerns.

   Each version is given a distinguishing version number. If the Program specifies a version number of this License which applies to it and "any later version", you have the option of following the terms and conditions either of that version or of any later version published by the Free Software Foundation. If the Program does not specify a version number of this License, you may choose any version ever published by the Free Software Foundation.

10. If you wish to incorporate parts of the Program into other free programs whose distribution conditions are different, write to the author to ask for permission. For software which is copyrighted by the Free Software Foundation, write to the Free Software Foundation; we sometimes make exceptions for this. Our decision will be guided by the two goals of preserving the free status of all derivatives of our free software and of promoting the sharing and reuse of software generally.

NO WARRANTY

11. BECAUSE THE PROGRAM IS LICENSED FREE OF CHARGE, THERE IS NO WARRANTY FOR THE PROGRAM, TO THE EXTENT PERMITTED BY APPLICABLE LAW. EXCEPT WHEN OTHERWISE STATED IN WRITING THE COPYRIGHT HOLDERS AND/OR OTHER PARTIES PROVIDE THE PROGRAM "AS IS" WITHOUT WARRANTY OF ANY KIND, EITHER EXPRESSED OR IMPLIED, INCLUDING, BUT NOT LIMITED TO, THE IMPLIED WARRANTIES OF MERCHANTABILITY AND FITNESS FOR A PARTICULAR PURPOSE. THE ENTIRE RISK AS TO THE QUALITY AND PERFORMANCE OF THE PROGRAM IS WITH YOU. SHOULD THE PROGRAM PROVE DEFECTIVE, YOU ASSUME THE COST OF ALL NECESSARY SERVICING, REPAIR OR CORRECTION.

12. IN NO EVENT UNLESS REQUIRED BY APPLICABLE LAW OR AGREED TO IN WRITING WILL ANY COPYRIGHT HOLDER, OR ANY OTHER PARTY WHO MAY MODIFY AND/OR REDISTRIBUTE THE PROGRAM AS PERMITTED ABOVE, BE LIABLE TO YOU FOR DAMAGES, INCLUDING ANY GENERAL, SPECIAL, INCIDENTAL OR CONSEQUENTIAL DAMAGES ARISING OUT OF THE USE OR INABILITY TO USE THE PROGRAM (INCLUDING BUT NOT LIMITED TO LOSS OF DATA OR DATA BEING RENDERED INACCURATE OR LOSSES SUSTAINED BY YOU OR THIRD PARTIES OR A FAILURE OF THE PROGRAM TO OPERATE WITH ANY OTHER PROGRAMS), EVEN IF SUCH HOLDER OR OTHER PARTY HAS BEEN ADVISED OF THE POSSIBILITY OF SUCH DAMAGES.

END OF TERMS AND CONDITIONS

D.3 Appendix: How to Apply These Terms to Your New Programs

If you develop a new program, and you want it to be of the greatest possible use to the public, the best way to achieve this is to make it free software which everyone can redistribute and change under these terms.

To do so, attach the following notices to the program. It is safest to attach them to the start of each source file to most effectively convey the exclusion of warranty; and each file should have at least the "copyright" line and a pointer to where the full notice is found.

> ⟨one line to give the program's name and a brief idea of what it does.⟩
> Copyright ©19yy ⟨name of author⟩
>
> This program is free software; you can redistribute it and/or modify it under the terms of the GNU General Public License as published by the Free Software Foundation; either version 2 of the License, or (at your option) any later version.
>
> This program is distributed in the hope that it will be useful, but WITHOUT ANY WARRANTY; without even the implied warranty of MERCHANTABILITY or FITNESS FOR A PARTICULAR PURPOSE. See the GNU General Public License for more details.
>
> You should have received a copy of the GNU General Public License along with this program; if not, write to the Free Software Foundation, Inc., 675 Mass Ave, Cambridge, MA 02139, USA.

Also add information on how to contact you by electronic and paper mail.

If the program is interactive, make it output a short notice like this when it starts in an interactive mode:

```
Gnomovision version 69, Copyright (C) 19yy name of author
Gnomovision comes with ABSOLUTELY NO WARRANTY; for details type
'show w'.  This is free software, and you are welcome to
redistribute it under certain conditions; type 'show c' for
details.
```

The hypothetical commands 'show w' and 'show c' should show the appropriate parts of the General Public License. Of course, the commands you use may be called something other than 'show w' and 'show c'; they could even be mouse-clicks or menu items–whatever suits your program.

You should also get your employer (if you work as a programmer) or your school, if any, to sign a "copyright disclaimer" for the program, if necessary. Here is a sample; alter the names:

> Yoyodyne, Inc., hereby disclaims all copyright interest in the program 'Gnomovision' (which makes passes at compilers) written by James Hacker.
>
> ⟨signature of Ty Coon⟩, 1 April 1989
> Ty Coon, President of Vice

This General Public License does not permit incorporating your program into proprietary programs. If your program is a subroutine library, you may consider it more useful to permit linking proprietary applications with the library. If this is what you want to do, use the GNU Library General Public License instead of this License.

Index

*, 94
- to begin command options, 87
.bash_profile, 121
.bashrc, 121
.profile, 121
.tcshrc, 121
/
    in pathnames, 79
    root directory name, 80
/Image, 126
/bin/bash, 93
/bin/csh, 93
/bin/sh, 93
/bin/tcsh, 93
/dev/console, 90
/dev/cua, 90
/dev/hd, 90
/dev/lp, 90
/dev/null, 90
/dev/pty, 90
/dev/tty, 90
/dev/ttyS, 90
/etc, 90
/etc/Image, 126
csh.login, 121
/etc/fstab, 140
/etc/getty, 143
/etc/group
    format of, 131
/etc/host.conf, 173
/etc/hosts, 172

/etc/init, 143
/etc/inittab, 143
/etc/networks, 172
/etc/passwd, 129
/etc/profile, 121
/etc/rc, 144
/etc/rc.local, 144
/etc/resolve.conf, 173
/etc/zImage, 126
/home, 91
/lib, 91
/proc, 91
    mounting of, 141
/sbin, 91
/tmp, 91
/usr, 91
/usr/X11R6/lib/X11/XF86Config,
    153
/usr/X386, 91
/usr/etc, 91
/urs/g++-include, 92
/usr/include, 92
/usr/lib, 92
/usr/local, 92
/usr/man, 92
/usr/src, 92
/var, 92
/var/adm, 92
/var spool, 92
/vmlinux, 126
/zImage, 126

<, 98
>, 97
?, 95
~
  to refer to home directory, 81
386BSD, 23

account
  creating, 76
addgroup, 131
adding users, 128
  with adduser, 130
  with useradd, 130
adduser, 130
afio, 135
alpha, 18
archiving files, 132–134
argument
  command
    defined, 78

backflops, 135
background process, 105
backgrounding jobs, 107
backups, 134–135
  incremental, 135
  multi-volume, 135
  to floppy disk, 135
bash, 93
BBS list, 199–203
BBS software, 13
  FidoNet, 13
beta, 18
bg, 108
/bin, 89
books, 185–188
boot floppy, 61, 145
  creating, 126
boot scripts, 143
booting, 49, 125–127

from maintenance floppy, 145
problems, 63–65, 71
with LILO, 126–127
booting Linux
  with boot floppy, 126
booting non-Linux systems, 126
Bourne again shell, 93
Bourne shell, 7, 93
broadcast address
  defined, 168
bugs, 18

C News, 180
C Shell (csh), 7, 93
cat, 89
  to view file contents, 86
cd, 82–83, 87
chfn, 131
chmod, 102
chsh, 131
client
  news
    defined, 180
Coherent, 24
command
  argument
    defined, 78
  defined, 78
command not found error message, 78
commands
  – to begin options, 87
  grouping with shell scripts, 117
  summary of basic, 87–89
commercial support, 32
compress, 133
compressing files, 132–134
configuration scripts
  for TCP/IP, 169

console
    defined, 77
    device name for, 90
    virtual, 77
copy files, 85
copying Linux, 15–17, 23, 204–210
copyright, 15–17, 204–210
core dumps, 6
cp, 85, 88
csh, 7
current working directory
    defined, 81

databases, 14
debugging
    core dumps, 6
delete
    directory, 86
    files, 86
deleting users, 130
deluser, 130
/dev, 90
/dev/sd, 90
/dev/sr, 90
/dev/st, 90
development
    alpha, 18
    beta, 18
    conventions, 18
device driver, 90
devices
    /dev/console, 90
    /dev/cua, 90
    /dev/hd, 90
    /dev/lp, 90
    /dev/null, 90
    /dev/pty, 90
    /dev/sd, 90
    /dev/sr, 90

/dev/st, 90
/dev/tty, 90
/dev/ttyS, 90
accessing, 90
console, 90
fd, 90
floppy disk, 90
hard drives, 90
null, 90
parallel ports, 90
pseudo-terminals, 90
SCSI, 90
serial ports, 90
virtual consoles, 90
dip, 174
    chat script for, 177–179
    connecting to SLIP server with,
        177–179
    dynamic IP address with, 176
    static IP address with, 175
directory
    . to refer to, 82
    /etc, 90
    /home, 91
    /lib, 91
    /proc, 91
    /sbin, 91
    /tmp, 91
    /usr, 91
    /usr/X386, 91
    /usr/bin, 91
    /usr/etc, 91
    /urs/g++-include, 92
    /usr/include, 92
    /usr/lib, 92
    /usr/local, 92
    /usr/man, 92
    /usr/src, 92
    /var, 92

`/var/adm`, 92
`/var spool`, 92
`/bin`, 89
creating, 84
current working
    defined, 81
defined, 79
delete, 86
`/dev`, 90
home
    ~ to refer to, 81
    defined, 80
listing contents of, 83–84
nesting, 79
parent, 79
    .. to refer to, 82
permisions
    execute, 100
    read, 100
    write, 100
permissions
    changing, 102
    dependencies of, 101
root
    defined, 80
structure, 80
    moving around in with `cd`, 82
tree, 80
working
    defined, 81
disabling users, 130
disasters
    recovery from, 145–147
        with maintenance floppy, 145
distributions, 18, 35–44
    Internet, getting from the, 36
    list, 189–191
    mail order, 37
    online sources, 37

documentation, 182–188
    books, 30, 185–188
    Frequently Asked Questions, 182
    HOWTO documents, 183
    info files, 8
    Linux Documentation Project, 30, 184–185
    Linux Software Map, 15
    online, 29, 182–184
        FAQ, 29
        HOWTO documents, 29
    `texinfo`, 8
Doom, 15

e-mail, 179–180
    mailer
        defined, 179
    transport
        defined, 179
`e2fsck`, 142, 146
`echo`, 89
editor
    defined, 110
editors, 6
`efsck`, 142
`elm`, 179
Emacs, 6, 110
emergencies
    recovery from, 145–147
        with maintenance floppy, 145
end-of-text signal, 96
environment
    customizing, 117–121
    variables
        `PATH`, 120
EOT (end of text) signal, 96
error messages
    error messages
        `command not found`, 78

ethernet, 12
  supported cards, 167
executable
  defined, 83
executables, 5
exit, 78
export, 119

FAQ, 29
fdisk, 48, 53–56
  under MS-DOS, 48
features
  kernel, 4–6
  system, 4–6
fg, 108
FidoNet, 13
file
  copy, 85
  delete, 86
  executable
    defined, 83
  move, 85
filename
  defined, 79
filenames
  wildcard characters in, 94–96
files
  appeding to, 99
  archiving, 132–134
  backing up, 134–135
  compressing, 132–134
  defined, 79
  device, 90
  hidden
    not matched by wildcards, 95
  inode numbers of, 103
  links, 103–104
  listing, 83–84

listing permissions of with ls,
    100
  MS-DOS, 165
  owership of by group, 100
  owership of by user, 100
  permisions
    execute, 100
    read, 100
    write, 100
  permissions
    changing, 102
    defined, 100
    dependencies of, 101
    group, 131
    interpreting, 100
  permissions of, 100–102
  recovering, 147
  viewing contents of, 86
filesystem
  exploring, 89–93
filesystems, 5, 45, 46, 140–142
  /etc/fstab, 140
  checking, 141
  creating, 57
  fixing corrupted, 146
  mounting, 140–141
  on floppy disk, 135
  root, 46
  unmounting, 142
    unmounting with shutdown or
        halt, 141
filter
  defined, 98
find
  for incremental backups, 135
FIPS, 47
floating-point math, 5
floppy disk
  boot/root, 145

device names for, 90

maintenance, 145

unmounting, 136

floppy disks

as backup medium, 135

file systems on, 135

foreground process, 105

free software, 15

Free Software Foundation, 15, 204

Frequently Asked Questions, 182

fsck, 142, 146

FTP

anonymous, 36

archive site list, 198

using, 192–198

ftpmail, 197

fullname

setting with chfn, 131

functionality, 19

games, 15

Doom, 15

gateway address

defined, 169

gcc

upgrading, 139

gdb, 10

General Public License, 15–17, 204–
210

getting help, 28

getty, 143

GNU, 6

General Public License, 15–17,
204–210

gprof, 10

grep, 89

groff, 7

group ID

defined, 129

groupadd, 131

groups, 100, 131

adding, 131

deleting, 131

groups, 131

gzip, 133

hacker, 17

halt, 128

hard drive

problems, 67

hard drives

device names for, 90

hardware

problems, 65–69

conflicts, 65–67

hard drive, 67–68

SCSI, 68–69

hardware support, 24–28

CD-ROM, 27

controller, 25

CPU, 25

drive space, 26

ethernet cards, 28, 167

hard drive, 25

memory, 25

mice, 27

modems, 28

monitor, 26

motherboard, 25

printers, 27

SCSI, 26, 27

tape drives, 27

video card, 26, 149

help

getting, 32–34

online, 86

home directory

˜ to refer to, 81

defined, 80, 129
hostname
    `hostname`, 144
    defined, 76
    setting, 144, 173
`hostname`, 173
HOWTO documents, 29, 183
HURD, 23

`ifconfig`, 170
`inetd`, 171
Ingres, 14
`init`, 143
initialization files
    for shells, 121
initialization scripts
    for shells, 121
`inittab`, 143
INN, 180
inode number
    defined, 103
input
    redirecting, 98
installation, 35–74
    boot floppy, 61
    booting Linux, 49
    LILO, 61
    `mke2fs`, 57
    `mkswap`, 56–57
    other procedures, 62
    overview, 44–45
    preparation, 44–49
    problems, 63–74
        booting, 63–65, 71
        errors, 69
        file permissions, 73
        hardware, 65–69
        LILO, 72
        logging in, 73

        media errors, 69
        postinstallation, 71–74
        repartitioning, 45, 47–49
Internet, 12, 36
    mailing lists, 32
IP address
    defined, 168
IRQ, 66

job
    background, 105, 107, 108
        kill, 107
    defined, 105
    forground, 105
    interupt, 106
    inturpting, 106
    kill, 106
    restarting, 108
    stopping, 108
    suspended, 106
job control, 4, 105–110
`jobs`, 107

kernel
    compiling, 137
    compiling compressed image, 138
    features, 4–6
    sources for, 137
    upgrading, 137
kernel image
    compressed, 126
    file name of, 126
`kill`, 107

LaTeX, 7
libraries, 10
    fixing corrupted, 147
    shared, 5
    upgrading, 138
LILO, 61, 126–127

as boot loader, 126
    installing, 127
    problems booting, 63
    problems installing, 72
    selecting default operating sys-
        tem for, 127
links, 103–104
    display number of, 103
    hard, 103
    symbolic, 104
Linux, 1–210
    and cost, 23
    bugs, 18
    commercial support, 32
    copying, 23
    copyright, 15–17, 204–210
    development, 18
    distributions, 18
    getting, 36
    history, 2
    installing, 35–74
    philosophy, 17–20
    pronunciation, 1
    sources of information, 28
    stability, 23
    system features, 4–6
Linux Documentation Project, 30,
    184–185
Linux Journal, 185
Linux Software Map, 15, 183
Linux-Activists mailing list, 32
listing directory contents, 83–84
logging in, 76
    problems, 73
logging out
    with exit command, 78
login, 76
login name
    defined, 75

login shell
    defined, 121, 129
    setting with chsh, 131
ls, 83–84, 87
    listing file permissions with, 100

mail order, 37
mailer
    for e-mail, 179
mailers, 12
mailing lists, 32
    Linux-Activists, 32
mailx, 179
maintenance floppy, 145
man, 86, 88
manual pages, 86
master boot record, 45
Mbase, 14
METAFONT, 9
Microsoft Windows, 14
    emulator, 166
Minix, 3, 24
mkdir, 84, 88
mke2fs, 57
    for floppy disk, 135
mkswap, 56–57, 142
money, 23
more, 86, 88
Motif, 11
mount, 140
    mounting floppy disk with, 135
    to mount MS-DOS partition, 165
mount point
    defined, 135
move files, 85
MS-DOS, 21
    accessing files from, 14, 165
    emulator, 14, 166

mounting partion under Linux, 165

repartitioning, 48

running programs from Linux, 166

using Mtools to access files, 166

multitasking, 4

defined, 75

multiuser

defined, 75

mv, 85, 88

named, 172

nameserver address

defined, 169

NET-2, 166

support for serial line Internet protocol (SLIP), 166

NetBSD, 23

netstat, 174

network address

defined, 168

network mask

defined, 168

networking, 5, 12–13

and X Windows, 12

ethernet cards, supported, 28, 167

FTP, 12

NET-2, 166

news, 12, 180–181

NFS, 12, 171

NNTP, 12

PPP, 174

SLIP, 12, 166

TCP/IP, 166–179

UUCP, 13, 179

news, 180–181

client

defined, 180

news readers

defined, 180

rn, 180

rn, 180

server

C News, 180

defined, 180

INN, 180

UUCP, 179

news readers, 12

defined, 180

NFS, 171

null file, 90

operating sytems

booting non-Linux, 126, 127

OS/2, 22

output

redirecting, 97

parallel port

device name for, 90

parent directory, 79

.. to refer to, 82

partition table, 45

partitions, 45, 46

fdisk, 48, 53–56

Linux, 51–52

size, 47

passwd, 79, 130

password

changing with passwd, 79

defined, 75

fixing root, 146

password file

format of, 129

pathname

absolute, 81

defined, 79

full, 81
relative, 81
permissions
changing, 102
defined, 100
dependencies of, 101
execute, 100
for shell scripts, 118
group, 131
interpreting, 100
of files, 100–102
problems, 73
read, 100
write, 100
pipelining
defined, 99
pipes
creating, 99
using, 98–99
POSIX.1, 4
Postgres, 14
PPP, 5, 174
process
background, 105
kill, 107
defined, 105
forground, 105
ID
defined, 105
interupt, 106
interupting, 106
kill, 106
ps to list, 105
programming, 10
core dumps, 6
languages, 10
libraries, 10
UNIX, 10
utilities, 10

protected mode, 5
ps, 105
pseudo-terminals, 90

RAWRITE.EXE, 36
rc, 144
files
defined, 169
for TCP/IP, 170
rc.inet, 170
rc.inet1, 170
sample, 170
rc.inet2, 170, 171
sample, 171
rc.local, 144
rc.net, 170
rdev, 126
reading
suggested, 185–188
redirection
non-destructive, 99
standard input, 97
standard output, 97
repartitioning, 47–49
concepts, 45
fdisk, 48
under MS-DOS, 48
FIPS, 47
rm, 86, 88
rmdir, 86, 88
rn, 180
root
fixing password for, 146
root account, 122–123
eithical issues, 123
privleges of, 123
using different prompt for, 123
root device
setting name of with rdev, 126

root directory
    defined, 80
root filesystem, 46
route, 170
    entry in /etc/networks required
        for, 172
routed, 171

scientific software, 15
SCSI
    problems, 68–69
SCSI devices
    names for, 90
security, 124
sendmail, 179
serial line Internet protocol, 166, 174–
    179
serial ports
    device names for, 90
setenv, 119
Seyon, 13
shareware, 16
shell script, 6
    defined, 117
shell scripts
    comments in, 118
    defined, 93
    initializtion, 121
    permissions for, 118
    variables in, 118
shell variables
    exporting to environment, 119
shells, 6, 93
    Bourne again shell, 93
    Bourne shell, 93
    C shell, 93
    defined, 77
    initializtion files, 121
    job control provided by, 105

prompt, 77
variables
    defined, 118
wildcard characters for, 94–96
wildcard expansion, 94
shutdown command, 62, 128
shutting down, 128
Slackware
    getting, 37–44
    installing, 58–61
slattach, 174
SLIP, 5, 12, 166, 174–179
    connecting to servier with dip,
        177
    device names for, 175
    dynamic IP address with dip,
        176
    static IP address with dip, 175
    static IP address with slattach,
        176
Smail, 179
software, 6–15
    bash, 7
    installing, 136–139
    tcsh, 7
    upgrading, 136–139
    where to find releases, 139
sound support, 15
sources of information, 182–188
stability, 23
standard input, 96–100
    redirecting, 98
standard output, 96–100
    redirecting, 97
standards, 4
startup scripts, 143
slattach
    static IP addresses with, 176
stdin, 96

stdout, 96
superblock
    defined, 146
    fixing corrupted, 146
swap file, 46, 142–143
    deleting, 143
swap partition
    in `/etc/fstab`, 141
swap space, 5, 46
    creating, 56–57
    creating temporary, 143
`swapoff`, 143
`swapon`, 141, 143
`syslogd`, 171
system administration
    adding users, 128
    booting Linux, 125–127
    duties, 125
    security issues, 124
    shutting down, 128
system security, 124
system-defined accounts
    `root`, 122

Tanenbaum, Andy, 3
`tar`, 132
TCP/IP, 5, 12–13, 166–179
    `/etc/host.conf`, 173
    `/etc/hosts`, 172
    `/etc/networks`, 172
    `/etc/resolve.conf`, 173
    broadcast address, 168
    configuration scripts for, 169
    configuring, 167, 168
    debugging, 173
    displaying routing tables, 174
    gateway address, 169
    hardware requirements for, 167
    `ifconfig`, 170

    `inetd`, 171
    IP address, 168
    `named`, 172
    nameserver address, 169
    NET-2 implementation of, 166
    network address, 168
    network mask, 168
    over serial line, 174–179
    point-to-point connection, 174
    PPP, 174
    `rc.inet`, 170
    `rc.inet1`, 170
      sample, 170
    `rc.inet2`, 170
      sample, 171
    `rc.net`, 170
    `route`, 170
    `routed`, 171
    SLIP, 174–179
      device names for, 175
      dynamic IP address with `dip`,
        176
      static IP address with `dip`, 175
      static   IP   address   with
        `slattach`, 176
    `syslogd`, 171
    troubleshooting, 173
Tcsh, 93
`tcsh`, 93
telecommunications, 13
`term`, 13
TEX, 7
`texinfo`, 8
text editor
    comparing, 110
    defined, 110
text editors, 6
text processing, 7–9
`tin`, 180

Torvalds, Linus, 3, 18
transport
    for e-mail, 179
trouble
    running into, 63–74

UID
    defined, 129
umount, 142
    unmounting floppy disks with,
        136
UNIX
    basic concepts, 75–81
    commercial, 17, 20, 22–24
    directory structure, 80
    for the PC, 22–24
    free implementations, 23
    manual pages for, 86
    multitasking
        defined, 75
    popularity, 2
    wizards, 1
unmounting filesystems, 141, 142
upgrading, 20
USENET, 180–181
    Linux-related newsgroups, 30
    posting tips, 33
user account
    creating, 76
user ID
    defined, 129
useradd, 130
userdel, 130
username
    defined, 129
users
    adding, 128
        adding with adduser, 130
        adding with useradd, 130

changing fullname for, 131
changing login shell for, 131
deleting, 130
disabling, 130
full name of, 129
group ID of, 129
home directory of, 129
in groups, 100
list groups for, 131
login shell of, 129
password of, 129
setting attributes for, 130
setting guidelines for, 125
setting password for, 130
system security and, 124
user ID of, 129
username of, 129
UUCP, 13, 179

variables
    environment, 119
    in shell scripts, 118
    shell, 118
vendor
    list, 189–191
vi, 6, 110–116
    changing text, 113–114
    command mode, 110
    deleting text, 112–113
    edit mode, 110
    including files, 116
    inserting text, 111–112
    last line mode, 110
    moving cursor, 114
    quitting, 115
    saving changes, 115
    shell commands from, 116
    starting, 111
    switching files, 115